A FENCE AROUND THE CUCKOO

Other books

Novels

The Harp in the South
Poor Man's Orange
Missus
The Witch's Thorn
A Power of Roses
Dear Hearts and Gentle People
The Frost and the Fire
Serpent's Delight
Swords and Crowns and Rings

Children's Books

The Muddle-Headed Wombat Series
Callie's Castle
When the Wind Changed
Playing Beatie Bow
Things in Corners
James
My Sister Sif
Roger Bandy

A FENCE
AROUND THE CUCKOO

RUTH PARK

VIKING

Viking
Penguin Books Australia Ltd
487 Maroondah Highway, PO Box 257
Ringwood, Victoria, 3134, Australia
Penguin Books Ltd
Harmondsworth, Middlesex, England
Viking Penguin, A Division of Penguin Books USA Inc.
375 Hudson Street, New York, New York 10014, USA
Penguin Books Canada Limited
10 Alcorn Avenue, Toronto, Ontario, Canada M4V 1E4
Penguin Books (N.Z.) Ltd
182-190 Wairau Road, Auckland 10, New Zealand

First published by Viking Australia, 1992
1 3 5 7 9 10 8 6 4 2
Copyright © Kemalde Pty Ltd, 1992

Typeset in Perpetua 14/15 by Midland Typesetters Pty Ltd, Maryborough, Victoria
Made and printed in Australia by Australian Print Group

CIP
Park, Ruth.
A fence around the cuckoo.

ISBN 0 670 84679 1.

1. Park, Ruth—Biography—Youth. 2. Women novelists,
Australian—20th century—Biography. 3. Novelists, Australian
—20th century—Biography. 4. New Zealand—Social conditions
—20th century. I. Title.

A823.3

For my sister

I would like to thank The Literary Trustees of Walter de la Mare and The Society of Authors for their kind permission to include an extract from *All That's Past*.

The Three Wise Men of Gotham loved the springtime
so greatly they could not bear to see it vanish. So they built
a fence around the cuckoo.

PART ONE

· 1 ·

What I am doing, I think, is walking softly behind this child as she creeps down a hallway. Her aunts are in the kitchen, the only warm room in the house, and she is going to eavesdrop.

She doesn't know me, and I doubt whether I know her. One thing I do understand, she is very frightened. If I could put my hand on her bony little shoulder, I would feel her trembling.

It is a winter's night. The frost that will sparkle in the late starlight is already in the air. The dripping tap in the bathroom drips no more; a sword of ice depends into the bath. But this child trembles because she fears her mother is going to die. No one tells her anything. No one has explained so that she can comprehend.

In the confusion and chaos of the past few days she has been the least of their worries. The critically ill woman, the frail, whimpering baby, the doctor coming and going, the aunts arriving by train in the middle of the night. Grandma . . . Did Grandma come? Or was that later? Then her mother going off to the train on a stretcher on the back of a truck, for there is no ambulance in that foundering country town.

The train is to take her mother to a big hospital in a town called Hamilton, wherever that is. Because – because why? Who has time for the child, big-eyed, creeping around, asking questions?

'Be a good girl and eat your breakfast, there's a pet.'

'Can you get yourself ready for school?'

'Don't you worry your head about it, darling. You'll be late if you don't run off now.'

The little girl in her nightgown sidles down the hall. She can hear her aunts conversing quietly; she must listen, for how else will she find out anything? Through the crack she sees the two pretty young women sitting side by side before the stove, their stockinged feet on the cake tray in the oven. Wendela, the older one, is brushing her hair. She has never had it cut; it is black and perfectly straight like Chinese hair.

I listen too. The nightmares of a lifetime have kept the words in my mind, even the voices of those two girls – the plaintive voice of Rosina, the faint Swedish lilt in the other's.

'If it comes to the worst, Win.'

'Oh, shut up, Rose!'

'But we have to talk about it. What I want to say, if it comes to . . . you know . . . I'll take the baby. But I don't think I could manage the big one.'

Aunt Wendela takes her feet out of the oven and thumps them down on the hearth.

'She'll never be without a home as long as I have breath in my body!'

The child flees back to her bed. It takes a while before she understands that she, seven years of age, is the big one. She understands, too, that her young mother, whom she ardently loves, may not come home again.

In the dreams I try to comfort the little girl, to tell her the story has a happy ending. But there is a wall of glass between us. The child is lost in an inexpressible grief which marks her for ever. Not knowing how to live with it, she retreats into near-silence, an obedient, compliant silence. When she does speak, it is with a stammer.

'Are you all right, ducks?'

'Yes, thank you, Auntie. Yes, thank you, Grandma.'

In later years my Auntie Wendela said, 'You were such a good, sensible child, no trouble at all during that awful time. But then, I suppose you were so busy with your own little affairs you didn't notice much.'

· 2 ·

As with a dog, a child has a burning heart when it comes to those it loves. I had this kind of closeness with my mother and father. This may have been in part because I had a singular childhood. Between the ages of three and six I spent much of my life like a bear cub or possum, alone in the forest. It was rain forest, pathless, dense. Its solemn light, as faintly green as a glow-worm's, still inhabits my mind. It must have made luminous New Zealand, the lovely islands, less than two centuries ago, when forest covered the land. It was the light, I fancy, which illumined much of the earth, before mankind, that fractious, fidgety species, began to change it.

How did I become a possum?

My father Mera was a bridge builder and road maker, one of the first to drive roads through the formidable territory of North Auckland and the King Country. Most of that landscape stood on end. My mother and I accompanied him. She was a delicate, slender city girl, and the camping life must have been hard. Still, she sometimes said that those were the happiest years of her life.

The working gangs, many of them Maori, lived in camps downstream, and we three in some secluded clearing further up the creek. My mother and I rarely saw the men. They were shy, anyway, and would not have wanted to see us.

'But we'd hear them singing in the evening,' she said. 'Harmonising naturally the way they do. And sometimes one of them played a mouth organ, or a comb wrapped in paper. Their singing made me sad. I don't know why. The bush never frightened me or made me lonely. But I worried because you didn't have other children to play with.'

In fact, I never thought about other children. I scarcely knew they existed, for that country, apart from a few starveling farms hacked out of the bush, was unpopulated.

Our tent was always pitched beside a creek, one of many pell-mell streams you could jump over, bustling along over stones and gravel, the water so celestially clear you might mark its passage only by a bubble or a blink of sunlight. The tent was as comfortable as my father, a practised bushman, could make it, with a collapsible wooden floor and a kerosene cooker. It was no sooner erected than the wekas found it, cocky flightless birds that waddled into camp and stole everything they could lay their beaks on.

The moment I was set free from breakfast, my intractably curly hair untangled, my mother said, 'Off you go' and I flew into the bush. Sometimes it was secretive, twilit with rain, and I became a small hidden creature . . . not an animal, as New Zealand lacks native animals . . . but an indeterminate being, the shadow of something I knew not what. But mostly there was gauzy, capricious light sifting from an unseen sky, illuminating what it wished, sometimes me, sometimes a toadstool, or the satiny eye of a lizard on wet bark.

'Weren't you afraid I'd get lost?' I asked my mother.

'No. You were permitted to go into the bush only four times what you could count. That was about twenty steps when you were very young.' She laughed. 'I never saw anyone learn to count so fast, you were so anxious to explore.'

'But still I might have lost myself in that thick bush.'

'All you had to do was to follow the creek downstream, and you'd come out right beside the tent.'

As well, I suppose, my mother kept an eye on me; adults become invisible to a child involved in a game that requires concentration, and mine always did. So that was my particular and quiet kingdom, for big old trees are not talkative. As with many rain-forest species, these were centuries old, many with massy flanges like flying buttresses, and their heads far away in the sky. The forest gave an impression of immense depth, a windless place often profoundly wet, as though the water table had welled up to meet the rain. In summer it exhaled sweet odours of acid sap, earth, stone and leaf litter. My father showed me how to part the litter and see there in the moist warmth the children of the tree, seedlings half as long as my finger, two tiny green leaves lifted like praying hands.

I cannot emphasise sufficiently the importance of my early life as a forest creature. The mindset it gave me has dominated my physical and spiritual being. The unitive eye with which all children are born was never taken away from me by the frauds of civilisation; I always did know that one is all and all is one. It came as the greatest surprise to me in later life to find that many primitive races know this, and that some religious philosophies are profoundly aware of it, though their implementation may be lost in shameful bureaucracy. I have always seen that the bittern and the python are of the same stuff, and are of equal value to the planet . . . that 'entire and perfect chrysolite'.

· 3 ·

Mera was my path to this awareness. Together we examined stick insects pretending to be dry twigs, and once saw one of these quaint phasmids shoot out a fusillade of eggs, like peas from a peashooter.

We searched for, and found, an obscure burrow in a sandy bank where a native bee, small and dowdy, dwelled with her eggs or larvae.

'They don't live in hives like honey bees,' said Mera. 'They're private.'

Once a serpentine stoat oozed silently through the ferns, carrying a rabbit kitten. Unalarmed, it dropped the kitten and grimaced like a devil. A paragon of neatness, it had small button ears, wide-apart eyes, and a close, yellowish coat. No doubt, as Mera explained, it was a murderous, imported pest, but I admired it greatly.

We found a vegetable caterpillar, the only one I have seen. First there was an unremarkable plant shoot poking through the litter. Amazingly, it grew out of the head of a large grub, once alive, perfect in all its obese folds, pedal ridges and mouth parts, like some marvellous artefact fashioned from wood.

'I could snap it like a carrot,' said Mera. 'It's one of Nature's mysteries,' he added.

Like so many bush boys he was a brilliant observer and often intelligent theorist about his own environment. But he knew little science. He had never heard that the sub-terranean grass grub is sometimes invaded by a lethal fungus which converts its flesh into solid material.

For years, on and off, the enigma of the caterpillar worried me. Could *anything* turn into wood? Could I? My imagination provided me with the possibility of rigid toes that snapped like carrots, wooden legs that weighed a ton. Any bump on the head – and with my kind of life I had plenty – instantly became an embryo sprout, pushing and pecking at the inside of my scalp. A roar or two of horror would have brought parental reassurance, but I did all my roaring silently, a great folly regrettably continued throughout life.

My father and I yearned for a magnifying glass, a magical object he often described to me. He said that if you looked through it you could see the feathers on a bee's leg. But such a treasure remained a dream. My father also taught me a great deal of Maori; as well as Maori history, not the kind recorded in European books, but that which he had learned from the old men sitting in the sand around a campfire on the beaches of Raglan, Kawhia or Aotea; the real history, not a word changed for forty generations.

I also learned Maori ways of catching eels on a bob of teased flax, and trout by tickling them along the belly as they dreamed.

But the main thing was the stories. My father was an entrancing storyteller. His head was crammed with the savage hero tales of his ancestral land. It was a time for kerosene lamplight, moreporks hoo-hooing in the dark, the tent fly crackling with frost, and myself, this possum child, agog at the stories I would play out in the rain forest next day. The names that abraded my mind were harsh as rock – Cameron, Glencoe, Culloden, Lochiel.

I had to be every character: William Wallace, executed on Tower Hill; the black-hooded executioner with his fan-shaped axe, wicked King Edward strutting triumphantly; Wallace's brave daughter climbing up Traitor's Gate to take away her father's head. My mother said my dialogue could be heard for half a mile.

These solitary games, played by a child with few other frames of reference, developed in me a furiously visual imagination.

Many years later, in Holyrood Castle in Edinburgh, as I stood in the room where the musician Rizzio was murdered at the feet of the pregnant Queen of Scots, I marvelled at the accuracy of my childish reconstruction of the deed. My father had described the physical scene to me; he had, of course, visited the Queen's chamber. Here was the little door behind the arras where the assassins sidled in, there the Queen's couch. Here the stabbed man fell. I knew it well.

My father also had this kind of imagination. He was able to make me see, feel with, love and hate people dead for centuries. He was a storyteller, which is all I have ever wanted to be.

· 4 ·

In the depths of winter, when driving roads through wild wet country became impracticable, the men were paid off for a few weeks and, like circus people, our family retired to a nearby town. This was frequently Te Kuiti, probably because Mera's eldest brother lived there. My Uncle Jim was so much older than my father that, as a boy, he had actually been encamped on the side of Mount Tarawera when the volcano blew itself to pieces in 1886. A gentle, dignified man, he was a gifted inventor. Innumerable useful inventions came from his workshop, and he did not patent one of them. The Parks, as will be seen, were bad businessmen.

Te Kuiti, the largest town in the King Country, had a population of two thousand, mostly needy. Ah, the King Country, the Rohe Potae, the brim of the hat, as the dispossessed Maoris scornfully called it!

The creation of this extraordinary enclave, a native territory completely enclosed, living by its own laws, in the middle of a country ruthlessly confiscated by foreigners, was the last shot in the locker of the often well-meaning British Establishment. The King Country was not, as many colonists believed, a reservation to keep the disaffected Maoris in; neither was it, as many Maoris hoped, a principality to which the 'booted ones' would be denied access forever. It was a desperate attempt by both races to end the land wars, which, given the resolute character of the Maori, were likely to go on for ever.

Most of the fine farming and grazing land had already gone, one way and another, so the Maoris were given for their own this vast tract of primeval wilderness. It covered, by the first survey, something like seven thousand square miles – eighteen thousand square kilometres. My father saw it as a youngster, long afterwards; by then the King Country had been opened to white settlement for fifteen years. From the upland where he stood he saw the forest plunging over the endless hills like a great green tide.

'There wasn't a break in it,' he said. 'It was like a sheep's fleece. And there was no telling what it covered.'

What it covered was a domain of wilful rivers, precipitous hills and breakneck gorges. It had a climate both cold and wet. In some places the annual rainfall was two and a half metres and often more.

'Mud, mud, mud!' groaned my mother. The old people of Te Kuiti competed against each other with mud stories.

'Remember the time a bullock team and jinker sank in the main street?'

'The parson went in up to his dog collar just outside his own back door.'

'Pity he didn't stay there.'

The tribes who took refuge in the Rohe Potae elected a king, a paramount chief, but not all Maoris favoured that. Being a race which cherished ferocious tribal feuds, they continued to fight each other, as well as the pakeha, both military and settler, until an amnesty was declared in 1883. The King Country lasted as an enclave just over twenty years.

Under the name of Tokangamutu, Te Kuiti had been a historic stronghold of the powerful Ngati-Maniapoto tribe. When I knew it, it was a mid to late Victorian village, a town of corrugated-iron roofs: little grey-painted verandahs; granny bonnets, larkspur and cosmos in the gardens. Its genesis had been an encampment of railway workers on the Main Trunk Line.

For a while, it was the chief seat of the Maori King. This tradition of electing some chiefly person as king has persisted for well over a century. At present the Maori people have a queen.

Like all areas given over mainly to dairying, Te Kuiti was hit hard by fall after fall overseas in butterfat prices. Still, as with other slumps, the Government confidently predicted that prosperity was just around the corner. Every month appeared new indications that they were fools.

My father had done much contract work for the Waitomo County Council, and now he was offered more. So many so-called roads in the countryside were almost impassable cattle tracks. On one fearful bush road out near Ongarue a hand-lettered sign was nailed to a tree: 'Speed Limit, Fifteen Miles a Month.'

I suppose that Mera, seeing the Depression advancing like a flood, felt that work for the Council would consolidate the family finances. My mother put up a spirited fight. She wanted to return to the city. Also she could not bear the thought of living in Te Kuiti. Disliking it on earlier, briefer visits, she now took a scunner to the town that lasted till her dying day. But it was a time when a man's work dictated his family's whereabouts.

For me the town was paradise. Who was I to notice empty shops, unpainted houses, most without sewerage or town water? If there was mud, I was pleased. I liked mud. The light of other days shows me a marvellous place for a child, ditches full of frogs; hills and caves; limestone that often turned up fossil scallops and limpets and something long with whiskers; paddocks and tree-houses; hedgehogs, and dogs without number.

In Te Kuiti, which a ring of ferny hills held as in the hollow of a half-closed hand, water was lord of all. Through the deepest declivities hastened the Mangaokewa River; the townland was, I think, its hereditary water meadows. During floods it dumped deltas of volcanic silt on surrounding paddocks. Its own banks it strewed with garlands of pumice like frozen foam. Then we children tore out to collect a store of handy-sized pieces for our mothers to clean the pots with.

The river was fed by many creeks. Ours was a leaky land, the water fountaining up in chilly springs and freshets and oozing into swamps where mud eels and wild duck lived. All over that countryside, ponds and lagoons looked up with blue eyes.

Aside from plentiful surface water, the town had a secret cellar, a mysterious subterranean world that existed unseen below the sunny meadows and hills. No doubt the Mangaokewa had intimate contact with this dark domain, but to us it was a marvel and a worry. If I put my ear to the ground I heard the loud labials of streams and, far away, the sonorous growl of rapids. There was a waterfall under the school paddock, where the farmers' children grazed their horses during school hours. And occasionally the ground fell in, creating an oubliette of raw earth out of which rose frightening plinks and gurgles and squishing sighs. These pits were called tomo, an abstruse word used sometimes of caves, such as the celebrated Waitomo Caves. But the race from whose language it comes had no doors, so tomo could well mean entrance or exit or both.

The Council promptly dealt with these cracks in the underworld. Soon someone rumbled up with a dray and dumped down a few loads of shingle. Left to themselves, the shallow tomo rapidly filled with repeated small landslides.

I did not care for tomo, my imagination supplying grisly answers not to the question of what might fall in, but what was likely to crawl out. However, like most of the children, I relished the mild earth tremors Te Kuiti experienced so frequently.

Windows that imploded, chimneys that stepped off the roof into space, these were the most dramatic events. The tremors were little more than a twitch of the planet's pelt. But well I recall our pretty pleasure when the inkwells leaped spouting from the desks, the blackboard fell down, and our dear Australian nuns called upon Jesus, Mary and Joseph.

As a young child I always knew when an earthquake was on the way. I became unaccountably itchy and uneasy, and my ears felt as though they were filled with treacle. Undoubtedly this oppression was caused by mysterious changes in atmospheric pressure, the same changes that, too subtle to be called a wind, will often bend down a long hillside of tall grass in an undulating motion, two or three seconds before the shock hits the spot where you stand.

Te Kuiti was the place for me. But there were people who upset me, many of them, whom I could not bring myself to confront because I didn't know how. The adults and children with untreated harelips or crossed eyes; the many returned soldiers, lurching along on one leg, or with an empty coat sleeve pinned to a shoulder. Some of these had dreadfully scarred faces, all the more dreadful because they belonged to men not much older than thirty. Others were so mummified, so parched and yellow, they were like dead men walking. They had been gassed. These were not around for very long.

The war was still very real. Even for such a small town there were many names on the Memorial down by the river, and often flowers, or the sprigs of green leaves left by the Maori bereaved.

Britain had rejected Maori volunteers for two wars, the Sudanese and the Boer. It was only after Indian troops had been admitted into the Imperial Army, and France had conscripted Algerians, that the Polynesian warriors, later described as fiercer and more audacious than the Gurkhas, were permitted to fight for the old enemy, England. The first went into action at Gallipoli; later they fought in France. The Maori Pioneer Battalion, which also included some Cook Islanders and Niuéans, comprised 2227 soldiers. Of the 1671 Maoris, 336 were killed and 734 wounded, many from our local tribe, the Maniapoto.

Amongst the Anzac Day crowd around the Memorial, I once saw a barefooted, shawled old woman stand and raise the tangi – the mourning cry. It echoed solitarily up and down the river, and well it might, for the pakeha people, dressed in their best, gloved, hatted, each with a sprig of rosemary on his or her breast, stood with their heads bowed, their hearts full of pain, but not a word out of their mouths.

Their silence was not what would today be called racism. It was shyness. In New Zealand you bore loss with bravery and reserve. You did not shout your grief and deprivation to the skies. A dignified self-effacement was regarded as a primary virtue; it was a tradition inherited from the settlers from the British Isles.

A memorable example of this quiet reserve occurred in 1940 when the First Echelon of the 2nd NZEF marched down Queen Street, Auckland, before their embarkation for Egypt. There were crowds on both sides of that long, important street, almost silent crowds. I recall a patter of clapping, a stifled murmur as someone recognised a friend under the stiff, awkward khaki. The heavy rhythm of marching feet, creak of leather, a faint grunt of concerted breathing, that was all. A young girl subject to sudden and imprudent indignations, I began to cheer. A woman next to me said sharply, 'Behave yourself!'

I would have retorted angrily had I not seen tears in her eyes.

She whispered, 'Don't you know what's going to happen to many of them? There's nothing to cheer about.'

No, there was nothing to cheer about. But still I was more at home in the vociferous hullabaloos I later experienced in similar situations in Australia.

Going home from the Anzac Day service that day the Maori mother assaulted the skies with her grief, Mera taught me the 1st Maori Battalion's song:

He roa te wa ki Tipirere
He tino mamao . . . .

When I finally got to London and walked through Piccadilly, I remembered the quaint and unsuitable song, and greeted that historic dog's breakfast of a circus as those Maori soldiers had done. E noho Pikatiri! But nothing surprises Londoners.

Yes, the war was still a painful, raw memory in Te Kuiti. The ultimate pejorative was Hun.

Anything could be a Hun – a peevish cow, a blowfly in the meatsafe, the stove that wouldn't light. It was also a cover word for all foreigners – the flaxenhaired Bergmans, the handsome Christiansens, Slavichs and Radichs beyond tally. The more expensive of the Chinese fruiterers achieved notoriety as Ah Hun.

I don't recall anyone ever being nasty to these miscalled outlanders. Pity was involved. They weren't real New Zealanders, who were, by and large, proudly descended from English, Scots and Irish, with a heavy emphasis on the Scots. Still, many of the foreigners were pleasant, industrious, decent people. In this case they were merely 'a bit of a Hun'.

My mother kept her own foreignness close to her chest. She told no one that her mother was Irish, and certainly not that her father was a Swede who never untangled his w's and v's. But she was unmistakably northern European in appearance and manner, with fair hair in a classic knot, a soft rosy face and dark blue eyes. She was slim and tall, always elegantly dressed. Compared with her, other people's mothers became in my eyes progressively dowdier and dumpier. I used to wake in the night and be glad I had her for a mother.

· 5 ·

Near the river, in King Street, my parents presently found a house to rent, and I began attending school. I knew about school; my mother had often explained it to me, but it was a genuine culture shock. I was dumbfounded at the sight of children playing together, something I had never imagined. My mother hadn't thought to tell me they did that.

Though my years as a possum have been of inestimable value to me as a writer, they were poor preparation for being a normal child. Other children sensed at once that I was not.

'She's got ginger hair!'

'She's real tall!'

'She talks funny.'

'Where do you come from? What's your name? Eh? *That* isn't a name!'

I was shoved from one to the other and then pushed over. They had never heard my name before. They themselves were called Kathleen, Phyllis, Mavis, Vera, Jimmy, Jack and Trevor. The Maori children had more splendid names, but they hadn't pushed. Indeed they never did.

It was completely beyond me why I had been attacked and my knees made to bleed. Someone dragged off my schoolbag and tipped out the contents. I sat there gaping at these violent strangers like a visitor alien to earth.

After a while a nun, tall as a tree, clad in singular garments, hurried up, rescued my schoolbag and took me by the hand.

Long before, my parents had taught me how to read and write. Had there been any books in my life I would have been a fluent reader. As things were I had read only newspapers, public signs and the interesting information on golden syrup tins and packets of Amber Tips tea.

I was sat down amongst a lot of weeping children shorter than I, and given a slate and slate pencil, the like of which I had never seen. When I made up stories at home I wrote with chalk on the back of a door, where editorial corrections could easily be effected.

The Sister showed us all how to write, or draw, a

pothook. I studied this peculiar symbol for a long time. What did it mean? What was it for? Suppressed screams of confusion and alarm felt like a fistful of tacks in my chest.

'Do try, dear,' said the Sister. 'Try to write a pothook.'

So I wrote POTHOOK in my large round hand. It seemed I was out of jeopardy for the moment, but no, I got a sharp slap across the fingers.

'Ah, here's a little new girl who likes to show off,' said Sister. Showing off was a cardinal sin in New Zealand society; anyone with a big head had it deflated smartly. I was taken up to the desk in front of the class and cautioned against conceit. I couldn't understand any of it. The poor nun probably thought that although I could write POTHOOK like an expert, I was in some way backward.

I felt so inexplicably different from the other children that at one stage I had a theory that I might be Chinese. It never occurred to me to find out if I looked like one. I suppose I chose the most foreign or unusual race in our community. Today, a similarly 'different' child might believe itself an alien. However, all was made clear in the end, and my school days, in spite of my being a battered child for most of the time, were happy. My parents did not batter me, though my mother used the strap rather often. The Sisters certainly did not. My black eyes, bloody noses, scratched face and yanked hair came from other children. Maybe children were more barbarous then, or perhaps it was traditional to settle all scraps with fists or feet. Certainly every new boy had to fight all other boys in his class.

Roha Tawhai began school on the same day as I. Paralysed by shyness, she pulled up her cardigan over her head and face and wouldn't come out. The Sister didn't bother her. She knew Roha believed she was invisible.

After school her brother Harry took us both home. Of

course we did not walk with him. For a big boy in Standard 1 to walk with two little girls would have been a calamitous loss of prestige. We walked a few paces behind and were glad to do so.

The Tawhais were my friends ever after.

<h1 style="text-align:center">· 6 ·</h1>

The school, St Joseph's, consisted of two large rooms and a corridor. Oh, how happy I was when, aged seven, I 'went up' into Standard 3, and the Corridor. It was presided over by Sister Hilarion, a slender brown-eyed Victorian girl who'd lived on the shores of Bass Strait and once had a pet koala that choked on a banana.

The school was small and austere. It had been built and staffed solely through the efforts of the parish priest, who had badgered bishops and the distant Provincial of the Sisters of St Joseph, an Australian order that specialised in teaching poor and isolated children.

The Provincial was Sister Mary Laurencia. Through her, years later, I was brought into contact with the young Australian writer D'Arcy Niland, whom I was to marry.

That parish priest, Father Deough, was a legend in the King Country. At first his name had worried Te Kuiti. Hun? Coupled with his accent, could there be any doubt? His first sermon was awaited with alarm. The sensible man explained at once that his surname was a historic West of Ireland name, and was pronounced as follows. The explanation caused even more consternation amongst the faithful.

'Did he really say Duck?'

'To my way of thinking it was Duck with a sort of choke in it. Or a little class of a cough, maybe.'

'Oh, Lord, Mrs Kennedy, I can't say it, and I never will.'

In spite of the fact that he was called Father Duck thenceforth, he soon put himself in his proper position, which was in charge. Tough as a gorse root, capable and resourceful, he was renowned for giving curry to his parishioners. For this he was more admired than feared.

He had a voice like a bull, and when he sang Benediction it was a disaster. It was said that he never refused a night sick call, and in earlier times when there were few motor vehicles and fewer roads, he had ridden over those pitch-black crossgrained hills on a surefooted pony, carrying the Sacrament and the holy oils under his streaming slicker.

He called my father Parkes. Never altered it, although he knew he was wrong; my father, who felt awkward about addressing him as Father, called him nothing. They some-times went on fishing expeditions to Kawhia on the coast, fished all day and played stud poker all night, Father Duck being on a permanent winning streak which he attributed more to a villainous childhood than to the Lord. My father thought him a grand class of a man.

Father Duck, like so many Irish priests of that time, could fight like a broken windmill and did not hesitate to pull a man off his horse and use his fists if honour and good sense so required. He did one great thing, long before my time, though the whole of Te Kuiti happily remem-bered it. He called out the grocer Dominic Bannagh.

Bannagh was a gombeen man if ever I saw one, with a mean little squinched-up mug that would have done better on a Pekingese, eyes that watered and winked, and one of those sugar-plum voices that the southern Irish come up with, sweet, breathy and cozening. A customer would allow this voice to trickle into her ear, and then all at once she'd look up and see Dominic's thumb pressing down hard on the scales. He gave short measure with the flour and the chicken feed, and a quarter pound of cheese always looked too slim for its weight when you got it home.

He had a silent, sadfaced wife and six or seven silent sadfaced kids. They led hidden lives, going nowhere except to Mass. His children never played with anyone; they were always busy delivering groceries or scrubbing out the shop. It was said that Dominic led family Rosary every evening, before they got their daily hidings.

His eldest daughter, sixteen or so, became pregnant by a boy who took the train to Auckland the moment he heard of it. Dominic threw her out, in the middle of the night, with nothing but the nightgown she was wearing. Not knowing what to do, she went to Father Duck, and she slept, if indeed she slept, with the presbytery housekeeper that night.

The next morning Father Duck rode down to the township, and at a busy hour, ten o'clock or so, he stood outside the grocery shop and in his lion's voice roared, 'Come you out here, Dominic!'

Out came Dominic, obsequious and smiling, shaking in his little boots. Father Duck gave him the length and breadth of his tongue. They said you could hear him half a mile away. He ordered the father to take the girl back and care for her in her trouble, or there wouldn't be a whole bone left in his body.

'I will, Father,' said Dominic, 'oh, you may be sure I will.'

His revenge was that he made Nora serve in the shop, until the very day she had the child. The poor humble girl was shamed as far as he could do it.

Hard as it may be for people of today to understand the desperate situation of such an unwed mother, the fact was that what had happened to her was a social and economic catastrophe. If her family could not or would not assist her, there was nowhere for her to go. The State provided no support either for the girl or her child. If she starved or killed herself, that would be a warning to other girls. Even by charitable organisations, and their resources were limited as always, she was treated as if she were there to be punished.

The social disgrace brought upon the family was real and so severe that many families adopted the puritanical attitude of Dominic Bannagh. Nothing to do with me! Don't think I countenance this kind of thing! She brought it on herself! And out the poor girl went, her child to be forcibly adopted or put in an orphanage, and her own life changed irrevocably.

One of the worst things Nora Bannagh had to suffer was the dreadful unwritten licence given to the louts of the village to harass her. She had fallen, she had 'given in' once, so now they could chance their arm. Trapped behind the counter, shrinking amongst the bags of oats and pollard, the tins of honey, her long apron sticking out over her guilty stomach, she faced little bands of them, cackling and pushing each other, waiting for the boldest to make an obscene remark.

My mother was in Bannagh's once when this happened. She said old Bannagh stood there with a grin, showing his little brown teeth.

'Not a word did he say,' she said.

My mother's temper was like that of her sisters, up in the air with a fizz like an exploding bottle of soda, and down again just as quickly. Whoosh!

An open sack of potatoes stood at her feet.

'I only threw three or four,' she protested later to my father, who was rolling around in a laughing fit. 'But the first one got the ringleader fair in the nose. It just spouted blood, all over his Tom Mix shirt. He was as mad as a hornet. I got another hound in the back of the head as they ran, but the potato splathered. Trust old Bannagh to have rotten spuds in stock.'

'And what did you say to Bannagh?' asked my father.

'I gave him a look that could kill, and said good afternoon, Mr Maggot, and then I *swept* out.'

I could imagine how she did it, too, in her well-cut grey 'costume' with the black braid coiling down the jacket revers, her elegant European head held high. With this costume she always wore gunmetal court shoes with small silver buckles and waisted Louis heels. Those shoes were queenly. They had first belonged to her sister Wendela, but nobody knew that.

My mother was a shy woman, never putting herself forward in company. But she did not begin to tremble until she was home making herself a cup of tea.

Of course these things happened when I was small, when our family first visited Te Kuiti. The grey suit and the shoes did not belong to those times at all, but to the present. Still, somehow, that was always how I saw my mother, fair face flushed with outrage, letting those mindless brutes have it hot and strong with the potatoes.

This story has a happy ending. When Nora's little boy was four or so, another sadfaced silent child, she married a decent young fellow who adopted Stevie. The three of them left Te Kuiti for ever. I don't know what happened to old Dominic, but whatever it was, it would be better than what the Park family wished for him.

· 7 ·

Unlike many Convent-educated writers I have no vengeful or derisory stories about nuns. True, I met one or two who were atrocious human beings. As an adult I can see that they would have been ruffians in lay life as well. They were faulty creatures who could not resist torturing the helpless. One of my friends had a long, bad experience in an Italian POW camp. Almost fatally ill with dysentery, his great regret was not for his freedom or his life, but that he would not live long enough to murder Sister Medusa. Every tender little boy who passed through her white wicked hands bore ever after little silvery scars behind his ears, which she had twisted mercilessly.

But Medusa was an exception. In childhood I loved most of the Sisters, and three or four have been models for me throughout life. Sisters Serenus, Hilarion, Laurencia, and above all Bertille of St Benedict's College in Auckland, to you my gratitude and affection for ever.

Their brown shadows are always with me, so that I close doors gently, sit with my feet together, tend to be formal rather than otherwise, and believe that meanness and discourtesy are the mark of the ill-bred. I also remember that a spoonful of honey catches more flies than a pint of vinegar, and that life gives back to us what we give to it.

Now, as a woman, I wonder how the nuns lived at all. The Depression crept into its lowest years. The times were heartbreaking. My father, whose work as a contractor and bridge builder took him into the remote rural districts, the backblocks, said that everywhere were deserted farms, crumbling and rotting. Creeks choked by weeds overflowed and became bogs; culverts fell in and ruined the clay and pumice roads. Dairy paddocks and even kitchen gardens reverted to scrub and fern, and on the hills the old enemies, ragwort and blackberry, marched down into the damp gullies.

At dusk in sandy areas, you could see the countryside hopping with rabbits. Around springs and creeks they clustered like flies about spilled jam. Without dogs to harry them, and farmers to trap them, they proliferated beyond all counting. Maori families, whose land had been sold off, literally lived on them. Rapeti and paukena, that was their diet – their attempts at the English words, as rabbit and pumpkin were unknown before European settlement, and so had no words of their own.

'It's them banks!' said people, commiserating with dazed families who had walked off their land, maybe their grandfather's land. 'Them rotten banks!'

In truth, it *was* to a large degree 'them banks'. Of the six trading banks in New Zealand at that time, five were owned by overseas interests. They had a pawnbroker mentality – if you can't afford to redeem your property, we'll take it. This imbecilic policy resulted in thousands of closed, boarded-up shops and small factories falling down where they stood. Who could afford to buy them? The workers thus thrown out of jobs remained workless.

The *King Country Chronicle* was overloaded with auction notices. The goods that were sold! A child's rusty scooter, dog kennels, battered saucepans, chipped crockery, blankets, a child's cot. Once I saw a bag of used socks sold for a shilling. Mera and I often went to auctions in the hope of picking up cheaply a roll of wire netting, a slash hook, a grindstone. Once he bought a carpenter's toolkit. Spotting the previous owner disconsolately lurking on the edge of the crowd, he returned it to him. This was not uncommon, for everyone knew that a tradesman deprived of his tools was a man deprived of future hope of work. Not everyone did as Mera did. Many, as always in times of crisis, grabbed what they could.

Later I was to use this incident in my novel *Swords and Crowns and Rings*.

Abandoned farms remained abandoned, some until the outbreak of the second World War. Good milking cows were driven to the abattoir. Our house was on the main droving track, and day by day we saw mobs of dusty sheep cramming the road, kept in order by busybody little dogs. They were *en route* to the boiling-down works.

Not everybody survived these desperate times. One day my father met a madman on a bridge near Otorohanga. He was a big man carrying an axe. He said: I've just killed my missus. She said I was mad. Do you think I'm mad? My father said: Well, there's one way to tell for sure. If your tongue's turned black, you're mad. Show me your tongue. So the madman stuck out his tongue. My father said: Red as a strawberry. You're all right, boy. The madman was so relieved he cried. He gave Mera his axe because he felt so tired, and the two of them walked back over the bridge into Otorohanga and into the hospital.

I used that incident in another novel, which was set in Australia but where similar things happened in the Depression.

The first swaggie to trudge past was an event. Besides his swag he carried a blackened billy can and a frying pan made of the cut-off bottom of a kerosene tin. Then such wanderers became common, looking for work, ready to do anything to keep alive.

'I wonder, madam, if I might mow your lawn, chop some firewood for a cup of tea?'

Many of these men spoke like educated men. Professors!

'You'll do no such thing. Sit down there and rest your feet and I'll stir up a meal in no time.'

The spirit of colonial hospitality was still strong. It was shameful to send a traveller on his way without a full belly and something in his swag for the morrow. Later on, when townspeople themselves were living on the smell of an oilrag, it might have been different. But we had left for the city by then.

· 8 ·

When I was at St Joseph's, poverty and apprehension already lay over our town like a cloud come down too far. The Sisters must have survived with difficulty.

My father Mera dug the Convent garden, and put in carrots, cabbages and silver beet. Mr Tawhai, father of my friends Roha and Harry, regularly brought down a flax kit of potatoes. Other fathers mended the leaky roof and the fallen-over fence, or left a brace of pheasant or wild duck, drawn and plucked, wrapped in a clean teatowel, on the back step. But I think most of the time the Sisters lived as frugally as birds, far more frugally than their vow of poverty demanded.

In 1979 the Sisters of St Joseph were withdrawn from that school, which was surely a very different one from the non-funded unheated little building I knew. Many of the Joeys, as we called them, were Australian women who suffered greatly in the deathly winters when frost lying in shaded places did not melt for days on end. I remember their black mittens, and fingers swollen with chilblains.

They knew times were harder still for many of their pupils, especially farmers' children from the backblocks, double-banking on a barebacked horse. Sometimes they rode three to the horse, the little one in the middle. Their hands were often covered with bleeding warts, for these children were up at four in the morning with heaven knows how many cows to milk before they left for school. Most ate their breakfast, bread and cocky's joy – golden syrup – on the horse's back. The Sisters sent some of them down to the Convent for hot cocoa at playtime, and we sturdier children had our noses snapped off if we remarked on it. When the farm children fell asleep, their heads on their workbooks, the nuns often let them sleep, putting an old coat or cardigan over their bony backs.

These children were not miserable waifs. They were just ordinary kids living in hard times. Let out of school, they laughed and scampered, kicked the sodden old football, screeched and pecked at each other like birds. As with the wind, they had no concern with either the past or future. The only mopey ones were the young Bannaghs, lurking together at playtime like a row of sparrows, forbidden to play. But now and then one of them, sparkling-eyed, took a punt at the ball if it rolled his way.

The children felt about things the way Mr Tawhai did. Mr Tawhai was of aristocratic lineage, yet he was a roadman, working for the Council filling potholes. His was the beautiful hazelnut colour of the Arawa tribe. My mother said, 'What a handsome young fellow that is!'

To me Mr Tawhai, aside from being the father of my best friend, was just a voice.

I didn't know about faces. They were merely something that finished off the front of the head. Just as well, for if I had looked in Mr Tawhai's dark eyes I might have seen the proud humiliation that I have later recognised in the eyes of people who have had their country stolen, filched, or conned away from them.

Mr Tawhai never fully conquered English, but he was a dab hand with Latin. He sang in the choir, and to hear him rolling out *Tantum Ergo Sacramentum* in his sumptuous Maori voice was to half-drown in a tide of sensuous joy.

Once when he had cut his foot badly with a scythe, my father picked him up in one of his trucks and brought him to our place for my mother to give emergency treatment. The bloody bones of his instep were visible, and he himself had turned the ashy grey of a frightened or injured brown man.

'It must hurt very much, Mr Tawhai,' she said.

'It all on outside,' he replied stoically.

This was the way with the farm children. Indeed it was the way with all of us young ones. Whatever hardship came our way was all on the outside. Inside we knew, without doubt, that Life was aware of us and somehow had us in its care.

Thus the Joeys began my education, and years later it was they, too, who persuaded my mother, determined for no reason to keep at home her young scholarship child, smart, industrious and crazy to get an education, to send me to secondary school.

'We can't afford books!' said my mother defensively.

'We'll find them,' replied Sister Bertille, principal of St Benedict's in Auckland.

'She hasn't any shoes!'

'Oh, St Joseph will get her a pair. He's a practical old saint.'

They were beggars and traders, shameless in their determination to help the needy. St Joseph did get me a pair of shoes. I never knew who had originally worn them, but her feet were not my feet, and the shoes gave me a bump on my heel which I have to this day.

For never explained reasons of her own, my mother had not had me baptised. Just the same I was reared as a Catholic, and the Sisters who, like me, did not know I was a heathen, did their conscientious duty by me. I admired them so much I would have turned myself into a sincere Jain or Moslem if such had been their wish. Mostly because of a superior memory, I was always top of the catechism class. Christian Doctrine, it was called. But at the same time, I simply did not like many of the characters in the Greatest Story ever told.

God the Father appalled me. He was, as far as I could see, a tumultuous, hairy tyrant forever commanding people to do hard or even impossible things, and vengefully smiting them with boils or burning them up if they couldn't. I was shocked that he was willing to have his own little boy murdered for a reason incomprehensible to me. The person described to me by the Sisters was nothing more or less than a Hun.

Jesus was all right. He liked children, lambs, going out on boats, having picnics. Nevertheless, the picture of the Sacred Heart offended me terribly. Standing around showing his insides like that! What was his mother doing, letting him be so rude?

I didn't care for insides, or umbles as my father called them. My own interior was completely empty, clean, dusted and varnished. If my mother's visitors, in homely chat, mentioned maladjustments to their own bowels or kidneys, I turned faint and had to go outside and seek comfort with the dog, whose inside also was devoid of all furnishings.

My inability to like any of the monumental figures of Christian Doctrine worried me, as no one else seemed to mind them. I knew that if I asked Sister she would say, 'Sit down, you silly girl!', the inevitable answer to any unorthodox query. My mother would find my doubt just one more thing that made me unlike a nice ordinary child.

My best friend was horrified, crying that I'd go to hell for sure. This spurred me to consult Father Duck in Confession. It took me a long time to psych myself into a suitable frame of mind, during which time my relationship with God the Father became no mellower, so that I was forever inspecting my legs for boils or mysterious charrings. I was also apprehensive of Father Duck, his black, black garments, his large blundering boots and the hair in his ears.

However, in Confession I managed to gasp out my problem. The result was terrible. I thought I'd killed him. Grunts, snorts, and the words 'Hun' and 'umbles' choked out as if he were having a fit. I ran aghast from the confessional, his belated absolution hitting me between the shoulders like a stone.

For days afterwards I lived in abject fear, imagining Father's burly form wedged in the tiny confessional box. Stiff and starched, I said to myself, this being what I thought the Sisters said about the dead, in their case mostly martyrs or the squashed rat the Convent cat had left in the church.

Not knowing how to express my panic I became silent and grumpy.

'Sickening for something,' said my mother. My chest was examined for pink spots, my tongue was inspected.

'She's all right,' said my father reassuringly. 'Her nose is as cold as ice. I'll tell you what,' he went on. 'She needs a little treat. Let's go to the pictures on Saturday night. Buster Keaton might be on.'

Mera was a great believer in a treat for fixing anything wrong with me, or indeed anyone else. It is a remedy I have found singularly successful in life. But my mother worried away, not listening.

'Constipation,' she diagnosed. At the dread word my

heart shrivelled into something the size of a walnut. I was going to be questioned.

My mother, when she wished to know something her child intended to keep private, was a skilled and merciless tracker. She was the hound of heaven, and the only way to distract her was to have the chimney catch fire.

How can I emphasise enough the importance of bowels in those days? Their arcane processes were the bodily phenomenon honoured, observed, and hideously hassled above all others, just as the heart and circulatory system are today. Patent medicines proliferated. People exchanged hints about paraffin oil, Kruschen salts, senna pods and enemas. Doctors advocated a good clean-out.

Children suffered most. Some had slivers of Sunlight soap pushed up their bottoms, a therapeutic sodomy. My mother swore by castor oil. It was given to me in orange juice on the top of which it floated in a viscid greenish layer. I wanted to throw up before I drank it, or after, or both. But my mother had a will of iron, and I didn't.

Still, so simple was I that it was years before I discovered that lies were the only alternative to castor oil.

· 9 ·

Lies were also the only alternative to my mother's discovery of my occasional visits to the Pa with Roha and other Maori children. During the inquest on my late return from school, my excuses were artistically simple.

Sister kept me in.

I had to run a message for Father.

Roha had a sore foot so I walked slowly with her.

It was not that my mother disliked or mistrusted the Maori people. It was just that the Pa was no place for a little girl like me. I might catch something. I might see something I didn't like. This I did.

He was a revered rangatira, old as Pharaoh and in poorer condition, laid out in state on a bier. I didn't like him at all: he was enough to put you off dying. The Sisters told us that the angels came and got you, but that was obviously not so for everyone. The dead chief awaited the arrival of kinsfolk and friends by buggy and slow train. In earlier days the mourners had sometimes waited three weeks.

Old ladies waving green boughs wailed melodiously around the dead man, interrupting themselves to call cheerfully, 'E hine! E ko!' to me and Roha.

Though white people called the impressive structure the Pa, it wasn't one. A pa is a fortified village, stockaded and defended by cunning trenches and stake-lined pits. This building was a meeting house, a carved house both famous and precious. It dominated the hills.

Its name was Tokanga-nui-a-noho. It was, and is, amongst the most magnificent carved houses in the land.

Terrible images of ancestors and demiurges glared down on Te Kuiti with glittering blue shell eyes. They poked out their tongues, too, a gesture I thought fully justified, seeing that this had been their hereditary kingdom until less than a century before.

Te Kooti Rikirangi, the charismatic guerrilla, had it built as a gift for the hospitable Waikato and Ngati-Maniapoto people of the King Country, who offered him refuge in that place where the pakeha policeman could not follow. Te Kooti was one of those extraordinary men, part prophet, part healer, great patriot, who rise so often from oppressed races. In his time he was regarded as a brigand and outlaw; now that history can be examined disinterestedly, it is plain he was tricked into exile without a trial, and that his predatory bands of 'rebels' who harried settlers and the British Army up and down the North Island regarded themselves correctly as partisans. In 1883 Te Kooti's warriors understood at last that the white man was never going to pack up and go home. The Government declared an amnesty and pardoned Te Kooti. In some psychic manner this doused his fire, and though he lived on peacefully, a revered man, he was a heap of dead ashes.

Roha was one of those hungry kids, a bottomless pit. She always made straight for the hangi, the earth ovens, where food was being prepared for the guests. Although Maori women were already domestically using camp ovens, saucepans, and various cooking vessels contrived from the ubiquitous kerosene tin, at important gatherings at the Pa they presided over hangi.

They were large, dignified women in long black skirts, white blouses and brilliant scarves. Many wore earbobs of greenstone or shark's teeth with narrow red or green ribbons attached; all had luxuriant hair flowing down to their waists. In my childhood many Maori women had hair straight as water, but as I grew older I saw this less and less.

Several Maniapoto families showed the mysterious urekehu strain. They had fairer skin which freckled and hair with bronze or coppery tints. Roha and Harry Tawhai had this hair. Sometimes the sun tweaked sudden glints from their curly manes and the tips of their eyelashes.

Traditionally, the urekehu were an ancient pale-skinned race that occupied the Pacific islands before the Polynesian immigrants swept down from the north. Driven by those fierce warriors into the mountains and misty haunted places, they became 'the fairies', half believed in, rarely seen, and eventually extinct. Yet the Maoris who settled New Zealand had infrequent contact with these children of the sky, as they were called, and even love affairs. The

Maori knew, surprisingly for an always brown-eyed race, that there are green, blue and grey eyes, and were not horrified at the physical appearance of Europeans, as many other brown-eyed races have been.

Roha was related, either by family or tribe, to nearly every person at the Pa. She hovered around the hangi where the boss lady was her mother's aunt Huruti. The old lady, tattooed formally on chin and lower lip, gave her a hug. Fearing I might feel left out, she gave me one, too. The Maori women were always affectionate to us pakeha children unless we were cheeky or patronising.

'What's in there, Auntie Huruti?' asked Roha eagerly, sniffing the air like a starved puppy.

'Potato, kumara, pummikin, mutton bird, mussel, eel, smoke fish, pig head . . .'

The hangi is a steam oven, a Stone Age invention which cooks any amount of food deliciously and wholesomely. Alas, the number of hangi I have attended which, created by Europeans, blaspheme against the honest cuisine of the Maori. Serving fish defiled by wet mud, or a mess of vegetables freely dusted with sand, they say, 'Of course, that's all part of the genuine hangi.' No, it isn't and wasn't and any slave who presented an oldtime chief with such abomination, would have found himself joining the kumara and taro in the next oven.

I did not linger with Roha because I was a little embarrassed around Auntie Huruti. She had a reputation, that old lady, as a healer and native herbalist, especially with toothache. Bad teeth were the rule, though not for me. I had teeth like a hound dog. Children often had swollen faces, gumboils, whimpered tearfully in school. How Huruti knew about toothache I do not know, as the oldtime Maori had resplendent teeth. Perhaps they had them knocked out or broken in war, and so had discovered which sap, what resin, took away the pain.

Timorously, even a little scared, I went to her with my freckles. I didn't mind freckles myself but I was fed up with being twitted about them. Auntie Huruti lived on what we called Tawhai land but which was really Maniapoto land, in the keeping of Mr Tawhai's Maniapoto wife. The old lady lived up a sheltered gully with a spring and a quince tree. Her house was a true Maori whare, built of squared-off treefern trunks and thatched with nikau fronds. It had a chimney made of sods and an interior atmosphere thick with the woeful fumes of torori, the black native pigtail tobacco.

Three of my friends kindly waited for me behind the house's tall flax windbreak.

She received me hospitably; advised at once.

'You put wi on them, hine,' she said.

'Wee what?' I inquired in my Scots incomprehension.

Perhaps she thought I was being smart or mocking, because she lost her temper, yelling, 'You too pirurri cheeky. Go on, go away. Piti off!'

When one of my lurking friends told me what she had meant, I was scandalised. But I suppose urine would bleach freckles as well as any other acid.

Sometimes I crept into the carved house. No one had forbidden me to do so, but I had an uneasy feeling that the people didn't like it. On overcast days the interior was gloomy; it seemed to me like a vast hollowed-out tree, dark and fibrous. Now and then a random blue spark from the eye of monster or hero pierced my own eye. I never looked these fantastic three-fingered forms in the face. They were from an archaic world which my ancestors had never imagined, and we had nothing to do with each other. I have a fancy that small fires smouldered in stony pits. Sometimes people slept beside them. Once, I saw a skeletal old man wrapped in a blanket, spitting blood into half a dried gourd.

Mostly I listened to the storytelling on the marae, where attentive crowds squatted to hear the honoured elders and oral historians. I had enough Maori to follow the speech of those majestic old men, tall and broad still, some with only one cheek tattooed, or the indigo scroll of a fern frond on a nostril.

I understand now that the storytelling, especially at funerals, was not only a confirmation of tribal history, but a cathartic for the people. They laughed, wept and sometimes broke into song. As they spoke or recited, the elders stalked ceremoniously up and down the marae, occasionally halting to thump a long staff on the ground. A dramatic pause was needed, and each storyteller waited just long enough to make the crowd shift and shudder. Sometimes these listeners raised the elegaic cry of 'Aue!' Written, the word looks nothing, but to hear those sonorous voices intone it, each vowel given its pure Italianate value, was to hear something far from the common translation of 'Alas!' This was a cry of longing and unbearable regret, but for what I did not know. It stirred my heart so painfully that after I was ten or so, I did not go to the Pa again.

· 10 ·

From my earliest days I was a kind of a writer.

I wrote constantly, on butcher's paper and the back of the kitchen door. I didn't know it was writing, I called it 'putting things down'. Very quickly I learned that wanting to write stories or poetry was unacceptable amongst my peers. Comments ranged from a good-humoured 'You're mad!' to a jeering 'Suppose you think you're smart!' I learned to keep my mouth shut.

When two or three of my offerings were published in the *New Zealand Herald*'s children's page, I was teased tirelessly. Even beloved Sister Hilarion asked doubtfully, 'Are you sure your mother didn't help you just a little, dear?'

I was truly shocked to learn that this wonderful person didn't know that there is no satisfaction in publishing something that is not all one's own work. Experience soon taught me never to write about anything that mattered to me – the Maoris, animals, the unemployed men, the empty boarded-up houses that frightened me. The subsequent trampling of my inner sensibilities would have destroyed me. Soon everything I wrote came only from imagination. This brought more gibes of 'You're barmy!' but was safe.

In later years, when I read how 'boys of the town' had pelted the young Hans Christian Andersen with horse manure because he tried to write plays, I realised that probably all young writers – especially in those times – attracted teasing. It was the yellow sparrow syndrome. If one of your fellows differs from you, peck him.

The *Herald*'s children's page was edited by Miss Elsie K. Morton, one of the country's rare women journalists. I revered her as if she were George Eliot. She also wrote a column for the Saturday supplement, my major reading material, and I admired it so much I learned some of her text by heart. I worshipped that lady; she was the literary light of my life.

But if only there had been books, any books at all to expand my horizons, increase my vocabulary, pervade my soul! For years I thought this and mourned. But now I think that whatever little gift I inherited probably needed for its development the circumstances into which I was born – a solitary childhood; an introspective, often numinous landscape; people very close to their ancestral roots and showing it on their faces and in their idiom and manner of thought. But at the time I yearned for, died for books.

There *were* two books in our house – *In Darkest Africa* and the doctor's book. I was allowed to read neither, the first because of bloodthirsty pictures which would give me nightmares, and the second because of recondite information which might do the same thing. No one I knew had any books. It was thought that reading poked your eyes out and kept you from doing wholesome things. The school library was eight books behind a glass door. Out of these Sister read selections on Friday afternoons. Poems by detestable poets: *On Linden when the sun was low, All bloodless lay the untrodden snow. Sir Ralph the Rover tore his hair and paced the deck in his despair. Grace Darling, who pulled away through the dashing spray.* There was also *Fabiola*, a drear though revered tome written by a Cardinal. It concerned itself with Christian persecution in the olden days.

'Read out the bloody bits, go on, Sister!'

'Sit down at once, Donald. There aren't any bloody bits.'

'How did martyrs get scoffed by lions then?'

There followed a vigorous discussion on what had happened when the dogs ate Don's guinea pigs. But no bloody bits were ever read out.

Probably I was not the only child berserk for books. One lucky classmate was given a *Pears' Dictionary* for his birthday. He adored it, read it all the time under the desk. Sensibly, he would never lend it to me, even for a furious read at lunchtime, but he was good enough to retell what was in it.

Somehow I was aware that the world was full of enchanting books. It was just that I didn't have access to them. I turned instead to the study of people around me. No one was safe, from Mr Tawhai to my youngest, most frivolous aunt. I observed, I eavesdropped. Most of the time I was invisible, as children are to adult groups. Like all children, I had learned the secrets of cryptic behaviour, melting into the background like an insect, and storing away everything – words, expressions, stories – though comprehending very little.

Mera may have suspected. I sometimes noticed him gazing at me thoughtfully. But my darling aunts chattered and giggled on, forgetting the child absorbed in her jam tart and custard, a child with periscope eyes and ears and total recall. When, at ninety-two years of age my mother was leaving this world, she uttered some words which, all in a flash, made sense of what I had heard her and her sisters murmuring when I was seven. Not important, no, but all those years those enigmatic whispers had remained in my memory.

· 11 ·

Probably because my early life had been so unorthodox, I much preferred animals to humans. Like the gosling whose first glance falls on the goose girl, so that it becomes imprinted and for ever after believes her its mother, so I would willingly have been a dog or tree. My positive belief was that animals and plants are the real people, and the sooner the other kind get off the planet the better for all concerned.

My attitude has not changed. I am at one with Mera, my father, who closed his memoirs with these words: 'I have had a great life. I have known some good people and many wonderful dogs.'

Whatever I was under my human guise, civilised life brought me unexpected afflictions.

I used to believe my mother did not know a heart ticked under the box-pleated serge 'gym' of her child. All my howls at the horror of the world were met with a severe face that bewildered and frightened me.

'You're a big girl now. You can't do anything about these things. Just don't do them yourself.'

So little by little I learned not to tell her of the many agonies of my life, the runover dog, the way the big boys would stick a straw into a frog's anus and blow it up until it burst, the drunken Maori I saw under the bridge, crawling amongst the bushes, blind and crazy from drinking methylated spirits.

When I was older I understood that she was trying, in her young way, to teach me to detach myself from the unavoidable terrors of life. She too had a passionate temperament and felt all things both good and bad profoundly.

But I went on kicking and punching the big boys, getting kicked and punched back. Occasionally Harry Tawhai appeared and they stopped. He was by now a tall massive boy with the imperturbable golden features of his father and a commanding personality.

'Cut it out, you jokers.'

If they'd thrown some possession of mine, shoe, hat, blazer, high up into the big pine tree where I could not climb, Harry often dislodged the object with stones. He had an eye like a hawk and an arm like a first-class bowler. Otherwise he climbed up and retrieved it, courteously handing it to me without a word.

My feelings about Roha's older brother were complex and obscure. He was so far outside my little world that I could not say I liked him, any more than one would like a mountain or rainstorm. He was a sign and symbol of something, and I was not old enough to know what. All I knew was that the very sight of him brought disquiet.

Too bashful to say thank you properly, I would mutter at him and go away quickly, my chest tightening and my ears buzzing. Sometimes I had to blow my nose, as though tears were running down inside. As with most children, my subconscious feelings translated themselves into physical symptoms.

Like several of my clan I have had, all my life, half a handful of second sight. Sometimes, thank God, it goes away for years and all of a sudden returns, so that for months I am plagued with dreams or waking certainties of future dangers or blisses. The sad fact is, that whether the coming event is good or bad, one does not want to know about it.

Whence this disturbing faculty comes, I cannot guess. My Irish grandmother, who never knew her own mother, a poor girl called Elisabeth McBride who bled to death at her daughter's birth, said that Elisabeth had had the clear sight, and had been afraid to marry because of it. My other grandmother, Mary Ann Park, born in Hobart Town, Tasmania, but also Irish, always knew when my father, her favourite child, was coming home. This was attested to by many. Her boys worked away from home for six or eight months at a time; their life in the bush was irregular, governed by weather, and their homecoming unpredictable. Of course they never wrote letters; where would they have posted them in that wild country?

Yet there she would be, Mary Ann Park, leaping out of bed at dawn with no reason in the world for it, lighting the fire, singing her head off because Mel was coming home that day. She aired his town clothes, cooked his favourite dishes, and sure enough in he would walk.

When he was old, very ill with a worn-out heart, I used to make the trip from Australia to New Zealand as often as funds allowed. He was very dear to me.

One time he said to me, 'Funny . . . I dreamed about Mother last night. I haven't dreamed about her for so many years. She was ironing my stiff white shirt, the one I used to go dancing in. So I guess I mightn't be seeing you again.'

'But I'll let you know,' he added with a smile. So he did.

How the heart aches when one recalls these things. It's a specific ache, I find, constricting the chest, moving upwards and grasping the throat in an iron grip. What fool said that one ever forgets love and grief, dear voices and faces?

But what I felt about Harry Tawhai was incomprehensible to me when I was young. Why should I be upset for this big strong boy who was of no significance except that he was Roha's brother? I avoided him as much as possible and went on interfering in dogfights, screeching at children busily hammering baby birds to pulp with stones. I was always covered with scabs and bruises.

'What did you do this time, for goodness sake?'

'Fell over.'

My father understood very well, but had no answer to the enigma of cruelty.

'It's awful, but it's there.'

He didn't teach me how to fight dirty, which would have been useful, but a little later on, when a child or two in the district had been interfered with, as it was described, he taught me how to knee, kick or butt a man in the groin.

'That'll give the cow something to think about.'

'Why, Dad?'

'Never you mind.'

For quite a long time I had been aware that my father was a person. He must have been forty-four or so. For those days he had married late, in his mid-thirties. Before that he had been engaged to a girl called Josephine. She had Maori blood and was dark and beautiful.

She contracted tuberculosis, then an almost incurable disease which was regarded as endemic amongst half-castes, though why I do not know. During the years she suffered in a sanitarium, my father was faithful to her.

I never heard him mention this lost love. It was one of the aunts, who had married the poor girl's brother, who whispered it to me, a romantic story which I must never repeat. But I know Josephine was well-educated and musical with a rope of lustrous hair, which the doctors ordered cut off because it drew on her strength.

'That was the last straw, and so she died.'

I often shed a few tears about lost Josephine's hair. But it never entered my head that she might have been my mother.

Was my father with her when she died? Was he grief-stricken, or after so many years had love become just a mournful memory? I do not know. I do not know when or where he met my mother. Both hid their early difficulties, passions, sorrows and blisses from us children. They kept their young days to themselves, that generation.

My father was one of a bravura pioneering family, with so many sons that in their town seven-a-side football was played, with the Parks forming one team and a miscellany of Ryans, McKays, Thompsons and Manawaiti the other. I liked absolutely everything about him, his height, his breadth, his clear Scots skin with a lick of crimson across the high cheekbones, his soft voice that was rich with the idiom of an elder New Zealand, and beyond that his Scots and Irish forebears.

He said pattren, westren, lantren, and called a female dog a slut. He explained to me that the earth was just a queer old sundial, and after I'd had my hair 'bustered' and slicked down with bay rum, he said that I looked like a wet ferret. A lazy employee he described as lying back at his ease like a bishop, and a tattooed Maori as a talking Turkey carpet.

When I confessed that we had accidentally set fire to Grandma, all he said was, 'Did she burn well?'

The Maoris called him Mera, their attempt at his name Melville.

He was my best friend for much of my life, and I think he was the reason why I have had such great good luck with men.

When I was six and seven Mera danced with me, every night after he'd come home from work. 'Three O'Clock in the Morning', 'Meet Me Tonight in Dreamland' and 'The Sheik of Araby' – these tunes he whistled or sang. I rode on his boots, as he whirled out into the hall or reversed into the kitchen, where he pretended to be immovably stuck between the sink and a tall cupboard known as the press.

His redhaired child, her arms around his hips and her face pressed into his middle, breathed with joy the cherished odour of her father, tobacco, shaving soap, petrol, timber sap, and perhaps a stinging whiff of gunpowder from the cartridge case in his pocket.

My father, like all bush boys, had been a powerful dancer, thinking nothing of riding twenty kilometres to a bush 'hop', his starched white shirt and dancing pumps rolled in a slicker across the saddle. Then home down the moonlit track at dawn, for forty winks before he faced another day of the heavy labour that was his lifelong lot. It cost a shilling to get into a dance hall, and that entitled a boy and his partner to supper, which was provided by the older ladies, who each 'brought a plate' as well as chaperoning the young people.

Like most countrymen of his time, my father took hard work for granted. He did not question that men were strong, enterprising. They accepted difficult situations and were proud that they were capable of handling them. Mera felt that a man ought to be equal to anything, responsibilities as well as privileges, and he did his best to be so. But all this was quite unconscious, for he was a natural man.

Mera was also naturally a good father, and I believe that all of the seven-a-side football team were the same. This was probably because their father also was a strong, humorous, loving man, a Paisley Scotsman. I remember him clearly, though I was only three years old when I last saw him. John Park his name was, Hellfire Jack to his intimates, because he settled most disputes with his fists. When he was dying, it was suggested that a minister or priest be brought to intercede for him. His blue eyes sparked.

'What for?' he demanded. 'God and me have never fallen out.'

He'd had a strenuous, adventurous life, that old John. There was something courtly and gentlemanly about him, and indeed he had come from a respected family. They were wealthy woollen-mill owners, descendants of the African explorer Dr Mungo Park, friend of Sir Walter Scott and protégé of Sir Joseph Banks. In 1863, John came to New Zealand in a violent and unexpected way.

He had quarrelled with his stepfather, run away and joined the Royal Navy. At eighteen years of age he was a seaman on the *HMS Orpheus* when she struck a shoal as she entered the Manukau Harbour, Auckland's western port. Only sixty-nine survived from a complement of 258. These are the official figures for what is considered the worst maritime disaster on New Zealand's often fatal coasts.

But at least two other boys came ashore, my grandfather and another youngster named Jack Avery. John said they swam. A descendant of Jack Avery who wrote to me said they were picked up by Maori fishermen. This sounds more likely, for although the warship had struck on a calm bright morning, very soon a fearful squall blew up, and the seas were mountainous. Also they came ashore at Waiuku, which is at the end of a long reach, adding unnecessary distance to an already exhausting swim.

They decided not to report their survival, and took to the bush, following the Waikato River. There were one or two solitary settlers, undoubtedly living in dread of a Maori tomahawk in the wishbone, for the country was afire with guerrilla attacks and ambushes. The *Orpheus* had been sent out to help quell such trouble.

What did the two castaways think of the forest, as thickset as moss, as unlike the open woodlands of Europe as it could possibly be? What did they eat? We know. Raw potatoes from Maori plantings, berries that they believed would not be poisonous because they looked like Cape gooseberries. As ravenous as wolves, they reached Rangiriri, a little river port where they worked for old clothing to replace their uniforms. As was common, settlers were sympathetic towards deserters and runaways, as in Australia they were protective of most bushrangers.

My grandfather settled at Ngaruawahia, at the confluence of the slow peaty Waipa and the clear green Waikato. A magnificent Maori pa, chief fortress of the dispossessed Waikato tribes, had once stood there, but in 1863 there was only a small white hamlet clustered about a military post. John Park became what was called a soldier settler.

Look at their adventure how you will, he and Jack Avery were deserters from the Navy, which notoriously has a long arm. To the end of his life old John was nervous that he might be tracked down, taken back to England and possibly hanged.

The extensive clan he left behind him in New Zealand

know that Park was not his name. It was his mother's maiden name. He had been born Ingram. What name he used when he enlisted on the *Orpheus* we do not know. It was neither of these.

John Park was one of those vigorous, sharp-witted, bossy Scotsmen who so dominate British colonial history. In no time he qualified for three engineer's certificates, civil, mining and marine. I have before me the gold pocket watch with which he rewarded himself. He never became prosperous. This may have been because while he and his large family were young, he and other settlers were repeatedly stripped to the bone by successive slumps, the tragic consequences of the Home Country's witless colonial policies.

On the other hand it might have been because he was a bad businessman. When I was adolescent I got as mad as a wet bee when I heard my father and any visiting brother say cheerfully, 'Of course all the Parks are bad business-men.' It was one of those statements which must not be challenged by God or child, like 'all the Parks have blue eyes'. It sounded to me as if they were proud of this inadequacy, as though it were endearing, or at the very least quaint.

As for myself, I believed business management, like any other technical skill, could be learned.

But old Grandpa, poor businessman or not, was loved and respected by his family. He was the very ideal of a pioneer, indomitable, enduring and full of laughter. He used to carry little pink musk lollies around in his breast pocket and every time I smell musk today, I am reminded vividly of that old man, who believed that a man's word was his bond and his honour. An impoverished life, which was often his lot, meant nothing to him. But an impov-erished heart – that was something he never knew.

· 12 ·

Now and then the maternal aunts descended upon Te Kuiti, usually in pairs. I use the word descended because their visits were exactly like that – a shower of gold or twinkling beads. It was a blissful time for me and many of my classmates as well, because I spent playtime and lunchtime minutely describing what they did, said and wore, right down to the jazz garters with the little golden bells on them.

My mother was one of six sisters. There was also a brother, but he was born so long after the rest of them that he was known as Poor Jack and hardly considered to be a family member. The girls were exquisite, giggly, capricious creatures with good hearts, terrible tempers, and a soap opera approach to life. Fortunately this took the form of fights, larks and laughter rather than anything tragic or melancholy.

They were the children of the redhaired Irish Mary Ann McBride, who emigrated at seventeen, and a Scandinavian seaman who'd run away from home in Stockholm because he'd had six sisters who bullied him. Just the same he named his six daughters after them.

'It just shows you can't escape Fate,' said Rosina, the second youngest, who tended to be a bit mystic and read Marie Corelli.

They treated their husbands – and they had quite a number – simply abominably, and were adored in return.

The eldest sister Almida had married well and settled

down, so she never came to Te Kuiti to cheer up poor Christina. The youngest sister had run away from home and vanished from sight. She was never spoken of, and that's all I knew, except that my father said that Willy was the prettiest thing you ever saw outside of a rose bush.

These fancy-feathered birds from the city always caused a sensation when they appeared in Te Kuiti. They carried Japanese sunshades made of oiled paper, wore satin helmet hats down to their lovely eyebrows, and skirts shorter than life. Their bead necklaces reached to their knees, forever catching on things and breaking.

'Oh, rats!'

Their stockings were glittering art. Silk, and their shoes such fashionable shapes that they spent their old age hobbling about and moaning, 'Oh, God!'

These shoes were often made of satin, which they dyed and re-dyed. Unfortunately the dyes were never fast, so that if they were caught in the rain, the aunts went around with heliotrope or powder blue feet for a week.

They also carried drawstring Dolly-bags, with tassels of beads dangling from the bottom. The beads constantly slid off and tinkled to the floor, where the dog ate them and gave himself fearful diarrhoea.

Once one of the aunts appeared in an eau-de-Nil coat, baggy at the shoulders and excessively tight at the knees. It was trimmed lavishly on collar and cuffs with long shiny black hair called monkey-fur.

'Now Rosie,' said my father sternly. 'You had no call to kill the sheepdog.'

'Oh, you! Mean article. Isn't he a mean article? Now I'll never be able to wear it again!'

Perfume wafted behind them, Caprice and Cashmere Bouquet, Rimmel's Parma Violette. They used Coty face powder and Pompeian Bloom, which was rouge, and Tangee lipstick. They let me try them all. They also corrupted me by teaching me the Charleston. They said fascinating baffling things like 'big boy' and 'whoopee!' When I said it, my mother threatened, 'I'll whoopee you!' but didn't, so I really never knew what it meant.

The sisters were so involved with one another that they scarcely found the external world a necessary thing. Probably their mother, that ruthless Irishwoman, had with a few scalding words stopped their running to her with their dramas and romantic affairs. She had enough troubles of her own, what with Karl Johann her husband and the little trembling delicate son, Poor Jack.

Most of the time they were as thick as thieves, wearing each other's clothes, much preferring each other's company to that of other people, even husbands'. Even while this was going on, a ritual squabble pattern was in progress. If Theresa and Wendela were not speaking to Almida, and Rosina dared to speak to Almida, then Rosina was sent to Coventry as well. A few days later the order would be reversed and no one would be speaking to Theresa. My mother, being a castaway in the King Country, was never involved in this ceremony, and indeed remained aloof from it all her life.

The trouble was that, in spite of their Scandinavian beauty, they were Irish to the crooked bone, and never let friendship stand in the way of a witty remark which more often than not took the skin off you. They were affectionate, generous and lawless. They could knock a laugh out of almost anything. I loved them dearly and still do.

They always brought me presents, tall wax dolls whose eyelids melted if I left them in the sun, sticking their blue crystal eyes for ever shut. In their poverty-stricken childhood they'd had no toys at all – their father used to make them dolls out of wooden clothespegs – so they were compensating for this, in a way, by giving them to me.

I didn't like to tell them I didn't care for dolls.

'A book would be much, much cheaper, Auntie!'

'Oh, fiddlesticks, you don't want a silly old book!'

But I did, I did.

Nevertheless their visits were rapturous, full of fun and impetuous adventures, their departures at the railway station crammed with hugs and tears, and impulsive presents – here, Cis, you have this, it suits you better than me. I don't think my mother could have lasted without those visits from her sisters.

· 13 ·

Oh, my poor mother, how she hated the King Country. When she spoke of it in times to come, she referred bitterly to her twelve wasted years. In fact we lived there less than seven years. Her loathing of it, her refusal to go even quarter-way to meet her life there, had caused a temporal distortion, the kind of thing that happens if you are in pain or otherwise wretched.

Even when I was very young I knew she was wretched, because of an awful gift all her family had. They had many, but this was the worst. When they were unhappy or agitated, even though they kept their feelings to them-selves, everyone else caught it. In some way they electrified the air about them and everyone shared the voltage. Grandma's was the severest case. She did not keep her feelings to herself, *and* she electrified the air.

My mother hated Te Kuiti so much that she refused to make friends, possibly on the grounds that such would be giving in to her situation. She sealed herself tightly into a little box of a life that wasn't good enough for her free and questing spirit. On our rare visits to the local picture palace she would drag me out before the end, stumbling up the aisle in the dark so that she wouldn't meet anyone she knew and be forced to speak to them.

Because in those days the comedy came at the end of the programme, in this way I missed all of Laurel and Hardy.

My mother's predicament was the same as that of multitudes of other women, then and today. When I came to understand it, at the age of twelve or thirteen, I did not realise the problem was universal. Thinking it was my mother's private tragedy, I pitied her with all my heart and often secretly wept for her. From the little she had confided, I knew that she had expected to share a new life with this admirable man, but found instead she was to be added to the one he already had.

'I might have been a wheelbarrow,' she said. 'Something useful.'

'And the awful thing is,' she once added desolately, 'your father is such a good man.'

Undoubtedly her situation was better than that of many other women. She had a truly loving husband, even though, like Freud, he couldn't imagine what women wanted and wouldn't believe them when they told him. But still the thousand small and demeaning accommodations of marriage must have been too much for her. She hadn't wanted to get married; she hadn't wanted to settle in the King Country, which she found rustic, meanminded, an abomination of rain and mud. She was homesick for her mother and sisters.

'Never forget,' she said to me many times, 'that in marriage a woman and her children are paupers. Always make sure that you are independent. Somehow. Independent.'

Hers was an ardent, speculative, and romantic temperament. She loved to read, but at the library, small and sparse, you could borrow books only if you were a ratepayer. She loved music, but where was it? It was true that the town had a hearty Salvation Army band, and on sacred days such as New Year's Day and Anzac Day pipers would appear from nowhere and set up a groan and a screaming on the Domain. But it isn't every music lover whose sensibilities are satisfied by bagpipes going off like a rooster at dawn.

I remember her rubbing glycerine and sugar into her hands, lamenting, 'I used to be able to work with silk. Now they're not even good enough for tussore.'

She was a fine, meticulous dressmaker, or had been. Now she was expected to find contentment in cooking on a fuel stove, scrubbing bare floors, and the backbreaking labour of the wash-house. Every time I smell that unmistakable stink of stale dirty suds, soap turned to grey jelly, or an unrinsed, closed-up washing machine, I remember our wash-house.

There was a copper poked into a corner so that you almost had to lie on your stomach to light it, and a pair of sodden wooden tubs. No matter how much those tubs were scrubbed and dried, wet splinters got under her fingernails and festered. A constant ailment of housewives in those times was an insufferable thing called a whitlow, an infection all around the nail.

'Good morning, Mrs Williams, and how is your whitlow?'

'Thank the good Lord, the nail fell off last night. I'll get a bit of relief now. But there's one coming up on my thumb . . . '

Whitlows came along with the wedding ring. Housework was hands-on, there were no rubber gloves, and the harshest of detergents.

'A girl's hands last about three months,' said my mother.

Aside from whitlows, the most painful affliction, hands constantly immersed in water, often hot soda water, developed chaps, cracks and dermatitis. This was one reason why gloves were always worn when one 'went out', to hide ruined hands.

When I had a cough my mother rubbed my chest with camphorated oil. It was like being rubbed with stiff brown paper, rasping and painful. I complained once, and saw tears spring into her eyes, but she said nothing.

Like a picture magically appearing on a dark polaroid film I see Monday morning, the piles of heavy white sheets, tablecloths, towels, my singlets and pants and school blouses, Mera's best shirts. Everything white. All had to be soaked, boiled, rinsed, blued, and some starched, before they were lugged out to the clothes line, weighing a tonne. Then the coloureds were done, treated gently in case they 'ran'. Salt was put in the final rinsing water to fix the unreliable post-war dyes. Socks, stockings. Ladies' bloomers were put on the line folded over to disguise their brazen shape.

When the washing was dry it was all lugged in again, the tablecloths and sheets shaken and cornered between my mother and myself, other items damped down for ironing, and almost all ironed in the end.

We all had a bath on washing day, the copper boiled up again while its firebox was in the mood, and the hot water carried in kerosene tin buckets to the bathroom. My mother washed her beautiful long ash-blonde hair then, too, rinsing it in the liquor of boiled camomile flowers to keep the fairness; sometimes I was allowed to brush it.

We children never spoke amongst ourselves of what happened in the home. It was an unwritten rule. So I really didn't know if other mothers and fathers argued, and if so, what the fights were about. Mine, who deeply loved each other, I believe, always argued about the same thing. My mother wanted to work.

'Not outside the home, Mel, no, no,' she would plead. 'I'll always be here to keep things nice. You won't even *know*, Mel.'

My mother's ingenuity and skill with the sewing machine could have made our day-to-day life much easier, as well as given her personal satisfaction.

'But, Mel, I'm a *good* dressmaker. If I have an accomplishment why can't you let me help out a little?'

No, he wouldn't. I don't suppose he thought about it for two minutes. She was shut out forever from the exercise of her craft by the obstinacy of a man good, honest and tenderhearted. But he had never queried the validity of tradition. Men were men and women were women; the question needed no consideration.

'I'd be so much happier, Mel.'

'I won't be kept by a woman,' was what he said, furious at last, a flush rising on his face.

'For goodness sake! Who's going to keep you?'

She explained that usurping his valued position as bread-winner was the last thing in her mind; she just wanted to contribute, to put coverings on the bare floors so that winter wouldn't be so arctic. Not to scrinch and pinch. That did it. Her words meant that he wasn't earning enough, and it was a deadly insult to a dedicated bread-winner, even though true.

'I work like a bloomin' bullock!' he flashed. 'Anyway, you're always well dressed. Like something off the lid of a chocolate box you are.'

He wouldn't have meant that the money which might have bought some linoleum to cover the kitchen floor had gone instead on her back. He was the last man in the world to make a snide remark. But she took it that way, reminding him furiously that the garments she and I wore had once been her sisters', unpicked and remade. At six years old I was a devil of an unpicker. My little fingers, my eagle's eyesight were just the thing for unpicking tucks, braid, beading – all the fashionable trifles of that time. My mother and I went on unpicking for years, for somehow her sisters were always better off than she was, a circumstance that must have wounded her sensitive soul.

The pieces of an unpicked garment were pressed under a damp cloth, and then my mother set to work to solve the puzzle. How could a new pattern of a blouse or a child's dress be made to fit these jigsaw pieces?

My mother's sewing machine – known in the household as The Singer – must have been a great consolation to her. It was a treadle machine, set in a wrought-iron pedestal so romantically ornamented with flowers and leaves of metal that I once managed to get myself shamefully suspended by a nostril from a tiny gilded vine trendril. Because I so often went to sleep while the machine hummed in the next room, I thought it was called a Singer because it sang. My mother's Singer was second-hand when Wendela bought it; she sold it to Rosina, who sold it to my mother. Probably it still works as well as ever.

Because of that Singer I was the best-dressed child in Te Kuiti. I had no new shoes for years, but I was well-dressed. This anomaly was repeated when I attended secondary school, a time when my wardrobe was graced by a Patou and a Schiaparelli, but I had to wear the Sisters' cast-off black bloomers.

There was a certain Depression look amongst schoolchildren, the unmistakable look of hand-me-downs, always too big or too long. We took it for granted that no one ever had *new* new clothes, unless an auntie or grandma made us something for Christmas.

There seemed to be no embarrassment or self-consciousness about wearing secondhand clothing. Perhaps there was even a kind of inverted snobbery, as there was during the second World War, when we tended to draw other people's attention to the patches on our elbows and the darns on our skirts, as though we were purposefully helping the War Effort. In fact, we had run out of clothing coupons.

Most of my cousins were boys, so I had to wear Helga's old shoes. Helga was my Auntie Wendela's daughter, four or five years older than I. Her father was a Norwegian, and Helga looked like a child Greta Garbo, with sea-blue eyes and a wild rose flush. When I eventually visited Norway, I saw beautiful Helga everywhere. I saw her feet too.

When I inherited her shoes they had to be stuffed with tissue paper, cotton-wool, cut-up old socks. But still they fell off, spilling their squalid contents. I abhorred Helga's shoes, and wished I could go barefoot in summer like everyone else. There was a widespread belief that going barefoot kept a child from catching infantile paralysis. Later called polio, it was a dreaded and usually fatal disease.

Alas, my mother never won the fight to be herself, to use her valuable talent to relieve the economic burden. No doubt she pleaded, wept, cajoled and was angry, but Mera was adamant. For better or worse, for richer or poorer, they had made the marriage commitment. He was the breadwinner; she stayed home and cared for house and children.

How humiliated to death he must have been when, only a few years later, my mother and I went out cleaning people's houses, just so we could pay the rent. She was paid five shillings for doing the washing and some ironing; I cleaned the house from top to bottom, scrubbing and polishing, for half a crown. Sometimes I even polished the silver and cleaned the windows for that sum. Of course, I didn't get to keep the half crown; it joined the family finances.

It must have been gall to him. Dressmaking was after all so much more ladylike than scrubbing other people's dirty sheets and towels. These menial jobs were never mentioned in our house. We just paid the seven and six to the landlord and were glad we could do so. But I, with my intense rapport with my father, knew his unbearable shame.

Years after the dressmaking controversy I asked my mother why there'd never been any money, why Helga's shoes and bare floors? She was still resentful in a small residual way, and said, 'Your father did work like a slave. Never a man worked harder. But all he earned, or nearly all, went into paying off the trucks. The Bank. He'd got a loan, you see, and I'm sure there was something he didn't understand about it.' She sighed. 'All the Parks . . . '

'Are bad businessmen,' I suggested.

She longed and longed for a home of her own, even if it had to be in dreaded Te Kuiti.

'A bungalow,' she said. 'With gas to cook with instead of that sooty old stove. I'll end up with black hair, that's what, with all the smuts. But most of all I'd like a little shop selling pretty clothes for children. I'd make them and you could sell them, and write stories in between.'

She did not say these things when Mera could hear them. She understood him better than he did her.

During my mother's unsettled years he was bewildered, as I saw him bewildered later when she put to him some sensible and foresighted proposition. How could this be an idea worth consideration when his pretty, fragile young wife had thought of it first?

He probably hadn't an idea in the world why she was frustrated, why she so often cried. Once when I won a story competition in the *Herald*'s children's page, instead of being thrilled, she unexpectedly began to sob.

'You'll never get a chance in life, never! You're a poor man's child.'

This preyed on my mind for a long time. As I understood it, being a poor man's child meant that I would in some inexplicable way be blocked from learning how to be a proper writer when I grew up. For all I knew there was a law against it. I had seen incomprehensible things happen to other children and knew they were totally without power. But of course my mother was thinking of education or opportunity for this child of hers who had a little gift of imagination and a devotion to words. What prospects could that child have in a nothing town like Te Kuiti, in a time of ruin?

But it was because my parents were who they were, because they were poor, that I became a writer. The first fact meant everything to me and the second nothing at all.

· 14 ·

Can it have been so cold that winter my mother became ill? Maybe my memory has turned Te Kuiti into the land of the Frost Giants. Where water ran off roofs it froze into semi-translucent spikes and bristles and eventually chandeliers. Every puddle was solid; grassplants wore two or three pearls in their centres. I cannot have imagined the frost itself, blindingly white as far as the eye could see, with sometimes a dark path through the blanched fields where a rabbit had bolted. The birds were fluffed up, huddled and paralysed. Often the sun had to shine for half an hour before they could fly, and many I found dead, with their twiggy feet up.

Always I went out in the early mornings to help my father get the huge old solid-tyred Republic lorry started. She was his first truck, and was built like a battle-ship. Though unable to drive, he had bought her a hundred miles away, hopped into the cab, which was immensely high and resembled a sentry-box, and drove away to Te Kuiti. The harrowing adventures they shared on the road created an enduring bond. I, too, had a peculiar affection for this vast vehicle, regarding her as a kind of elephant. I cut little pieces from her tyres for erasers and inherited her discarded ball bearings, the prized 'steelies' of the marbles aficionados. One steelie to twenty-four ordinary clay stinkers was what I charged, and a fair price it was.

The Republic featured in my school as well as my domestic life, for whenever she snarled up the Awakino Hill – many paddocks and streets away – the classroom windows rattled and St Anthony fell off the wall. But no matter how Sister complained, I felt proud and safe. Mera was in the Republic and all was right with the world.

She was also historic, being the first vehicle to enter Kawhia, an isolated, largely Maori settlement on the West Coast, hitherto accessible only by ship or bridle track. The Republic groaned in over a road Mera and his crew had hacked from the bush, and stuck in the sand a kilometre from town.

'The entire tribe came out with ropes and chains and dragged us into the village,' Mera recalled. 'Crikey, the war cries! There were old women and kids and dogs piled up on top of our gear, on the running-board, everywhere. They thought the chief should ride on the bonnet and hoisted him up before I could mention it was pretty near red hot. He let out a skelloch the like of which I never want to hear again.'

Though she could pull or carry enormous loads, the Republic was a Hun to start on frosty mornings. Kettle after kettle of boiling water in the radiator, myself in the lofty cab manipulating what I must guess was the choke, and my father cranking and sweating and dodging back-fires. Sometimes it took an hour to get the old brute ticking over.

Those days my mother stayed in bed longer, for she had just had a little baby. It was a great surprise to me. Such innocence is impossible to comprehend today, but it was so. The knowledge of sex and birth was kept strictly from us.

Some of us had seen calves and foals born, but we did not connect this messy and alarming process with human beings. Human beings were special; they were created in the image of God and differed in all their ways from other creatures. Everyone said so, and, I presume, did not doubt this dangerous doctrine for a moment.

There was, however, a certain sweet delicacy in the tradition of guarding the young, and especially the female young, against what was considered crudity. And this lasted for a long, long time. Ten or twelve years later, when I worked as an assistant proofreader on the *Auckland Star*, and galleys from its subsidiary the *Farmer's Weekly* had to be read, any article on mating, lambing, uterine ailments and the like was given for checking to proofreaders with male assistants. I recall our head proofreader, pushed into a corner with no one else available, asking me if I minded reading an article 'with a rude word in it'. The word turned out to be 'faeces'.

So my mother's baby, as I thought of this new little child, was a complete surprise to me.

However, for weeks before my sister's arrival, my

mother had dropped hints about my soon getting an exciting present. Regrettably the baby's birth coincided with the family's acquiring a puppy, and I took that to be the exciting present and was most grateful.

'We'll go and give Mum her breakfast,' said Mera 'while the engine warms up.'

He had lit the fire very early. The porridge was cooked, and the kitchen warm as toast. I thought it might be nice if my mother and the baby came in there and lay on the couch, so I ran into the bedroom to ask her.

She was sitting up, her long plait over her shoulder, her cheeks scarlet. She was plucking at the red flowered quilt that covered the bed, saying agitatedly, 'Just look at that, blood everywhere!'

She was quite delirious. She looked into the little cot beside the bed and said, 'Oh, my goodness! Someone's left their baby here!'

Poor young woman, she almost died from a kidney infection which she must have had for weeks, though the doctor had not spotted it. All her illness and pain she had put down to the burden of pregnancy and patiently endured.

She was jolted off to Hamilton Public Hospital on a stretcher in the guard's van, my father with her, and aunts coming from everywhere to look after me and the fragile little baby. My mother's kidney was removed. Atrocious surgery it must have been, judging by the scars. She was in hospital many weeks.

What I experienced during this critical time was pure, inconsolable grief. I did not recognise this until, as an adult, I suffered it again. That my mother did not die made no difference. Her return to me did not erase what I had already endured, and which made ineradicable changes in my character.

My father's hair turned grey, and his sight was affected,

so that all at once he could not see newsprint. With me, because I was only seven, nothing showed.

During my mother's absence her sisters rostered themselves to take care of us children. Grandma came for a while and did the washing and cooking. Poor Jack accompanied her. I liked the long thin boy, timid and melancholy, very dependent upon his elderly mother. He was the only person I have ever known who burned his nose with his own cigarette. Poor Jack! I loved my Grandma too, but life was so confused and chaotic with all the helpers falling over one another that she had time to say only one sentence to me. I suppose I was slow doing something she had told me to do, for she suddenly fizzed over and shouted, 'You're so lazy that if you was a dog you'd lean your head against a wall to bark!'

· 15 ·

The arrival of my sister was not of great significance in my life, beyond the coincidence of the event with the fearful trauma of my mother's illness. I gazed benevolently at this charming little creature with its black feather eyebrows and complexion like a certain pink china egg-cup which our mother used in darning the family socks. My attitude was that of a large dog amiably checking over a puppy.

For months, years possibly, after that brutal surgery, my mother was ill and feeble, dragging herself around, thin as a reed. But I think she was much happier. Her new little daughter comforted and delighted her. Though I do not doubt her love and care, I believe I had always been a puzzle and an irritation to her. The new little girl was dependent and biddable, different in every way. Perhaps my mother knew intuitively that this child would be her greatest friend throughout her long life.

I was far more involved with our puppy, a handsome fox terrier who swiftly grew into a true warrior like most of his now unfashionable breed. A dog with no fear and no spatial comprehension, he engaged an Alsatian in battle with the same appetite as he would a strange tomcat. In public, Flash Jack embarrassed me constantly by his officious air. He inspected everything and everyone and disapproved of most. He had, as well, a deep distrust of my ability to take care of myself and once, when I fell in the Mangaokewa, he almost drowned me saving my life.

Being a good swimmer, I was in no danger, but as I rose to the surface, a small black and white body hurtled from a four-metre bank, and with a reassuring shrill yip, landed on my shoulders. To have one's life saved by a large, noble dog might be a memorable experience. What a small dog does is to grab one by the back of the collar and paddle for the shore, his four sharp little paws striking downwards and excoriating one's back. It was terrible. When blood started to tinge the water, and I screamed for him to let go, all that happened was that he yipped with his mouth full of dress. A comforting yip it was, easily translatable as 'Never fear, Flash Jack is here.'

The Mangaokewa has a fast current. Away downstream we went, myself now under water, now on top, Flash Jack holding fast. Somehow we reached the bank. Spewing water, I fell on my face, while Flash Jack bustled about, giving my ears a reviving licking, and sending out ululations for human help. I almost died of mortification.

I was distraught with anxiety about the destruction of

my school uniform. I thought I'd be scolded severely about it.

'I just slipped in, Mum. It wasn't my fault. Can't it be mended?'

'If ever there was such a fathead of a child! Who cares about the old dress? Look at your poor back! Oh, Mel, she might have drowned!'

My mother's tears were sweet to me. I did so many things she didn't like, or that worried her to death. I gazed on her wet cheeks and thanked God, or someone, for the Mangaokewa's muddy banks.

My back was anointed with Zambuk and swathed in torn-up old sheeting. I was dosed with Phosferine for my nerves. I enjoyed every moment of the fuss. So did Flash Jack who was dried, given a bone, and fulsomely praised as hero and loyal friend. Which was only the truth.

It was scarcely to be expected that during a strenuous life with such a dog, hauling him out of fights, washing him after he had rolled in cow manure, and preventing him from murdering other people's hens and ducks, I should spare much thought for a little baby. The baby was there, and it was a nice baby, and none of my business, was my conclusion.

However, for a long time after my mother was returned to me, I continued to show my gratitude to whatever orders our days. During her near-fatal illness I had done some damned silly things, promising God many acts of bravery if only he would spare her life. These I faithfully performed, walking slowly across the Jersey bull's paddock; climbing down a tree headfirst; giving cheek to the scrutable gentlemen in the Chinese laundry who, because of their identifying noises had been named by my Aunt Wendela Ah Spit and Ah Choke. It was well known that they always chased cheeky kids with hatchets. However,

Ahs Spit and Choke merely stared at me as though I were mad.

In spite of these ritual offerings, I still could not come to terms with the idea of God as a being who could be bribed by anything at all, let alone by a person's creeping down a tree frontways and falling on her head.

How different was the Maori concept of the Supreme Deity, Io the Parentless, never prayed to, never propitiated in any way, simply there and acknowledged. He was honoured by stately names, the Hidden One, the Lord of the Dark Face. Like the lowlier people of the ancient Maori, I never dared speak of, never thought of, this power and presence. He lived in the back of my head, and I was glad he was there.

Long before, however, Roha had confided that certain rocks, trees and springs had their own indwelling divinities. I was not at all surprised. Being a pagan child, I was profoundly religious.

Just inside the lower fence of the Tawhai land stood an enormous volcanic rock which had been tapu, or sacred, for ever. Regularly Auntie Huruti placed offerings before it – a freshwater mussel shell, green twigs, or a kingfisher feather. Other unknown people did the same thing, including myself, nipping through the fence when no one was in sight.

It was a benevolent rock, bigger than a house, elephant grey and pocked with gas holes. It was left over from the days when the Pacific boiled and the volcanoes thundered. My prayers were always the same. Don't let Mum get sick again. Don't let Flash Jack chase sheep and get shot. Please send me some books. My offerings were different from the old lady's – a pearl button, a holy picture Sister had given me for getting my arithmetic right. Once, a Mintie. I was almost caught that time. I heard Huruti thumping down the gully path, and fled into the bushes.

'Keraiki!' she exclaimed, happily eating the Mintie. Luckily I had never confused the offered object with the intention, and watched approvingly.

Either by the will of the genius of the rock or some other, all three of my prayers were granted.

· 16 ·

I was so happy and grateful to have my mother back home again that I sailed through life like a bird. The times were terrible, terrible, but not for me. Every day we said prayers at school for the unemployed, a term now synonymous with poor or starving people. The Government had not come up with any palliative scheme for such an emergency as New Zealand was now suffering.

'They're running around like a chook with its head off,' Mera said, and so they were. Not until 1931 was any relief work scheme instituted, and even then there was no assistance for unemployed women.

Where there had once been eight or nine swaggies knocking at the back door in a month there were now twenty. My mother, the kindest of women towards the needy, was often in tears as she said to some dusty, exhausted man, 'All I can give you is some bread and butter and a cup of tea.'

Often what these men most wanted was a place to wash and shave. My mother kept a big enamel dish and soap and towel on the back verandah where the man could be private. There was a little mirror there too. They all carried razors; it was the last personal possession a man relinquished. My mother also bullied her sisters into giving her their husbands' old shirts and underclothes. These she patched and mended – made decent, as she said. For these poor wanderers were decent men, failed tradesmen, bankrupt shopkeepers and clerks, and needed to keep their self-respect.

Sometimes they left little presents, clothes-pegs whittled from wood, a scarf ring carved from a lamb's leg bone. My mother received these offerings with the sweetest grace. She could do this as readily as she could think up the most bloodthirsty fate for the then Prime Minister of the failing Coalition Government.

Mr Tawhai, 'let go' by the Waitomo Council, took on the job of driving Mera's International truck, with his son Harry as his offsider. Harry had illegally left school two years before. He had large capable hands, and soon learned to drive the lorry as well as his father. Nevertheless my father didn't like the big lad being taken away from school so early.

'He's only fifteen, Rangi,' he expostulated. 'Why don't you apprentice him to a trade? Jock might take him on at the motor workshop.'

Mr Tawhai smiled. 'You say so, friend? Would you give work to a Maori mechanic? Or would you wait for a white man?'

Sometimes in the summer evenings the three of them would sit on our verandah and talk, mostly of the old days, the days gone for ever. The Tawhai family traditionally remembered the names of stars. Their grandfather had known three hundred names but no pakeha had bothered to collect them. I wish I remembered more of Rangi Tawhai's conversation; I know that the heliacal rising of the Pleiades announced the Maori New Year, but at Te Kuiti I never saw the Pleiades because of the hills. Years afterwards, when I lived on broad plains, I saw that heliacal rising, a handful of sparks on the horizon, until the sun blew them out. Mr Tawhai called them Te Matariki.

I suppose I stared at Harry, not only because he was the only boy I could watch in the process of growing up, but because my cloudy feelings about him still disturbed me. My father didn't like it. Probably he thought I had reached the age when I could get soppy about any boy.

'Just cut it out, that's all. It'll make the kid feel real awkward.'

'Why, Dad?'

'Now, don't be Uncle Willy. You're old enough to know why.'

I thought that one over. People stared at me a lot, as in those times they did stare at the then rare auburn or red hair. But although I hated that, they didn't stare at me as much as they did at one of my classmates who had two thumbs on one hand. Suddenly I realised what my father meant, and was outraged.

It was the first time my father and I had fallen out. We scowled at each other, horrified equally by the situation. He was a reserved and modest man, and although he felt it his duty to forestall any girlish silliness on my part, he was shocked that I understood him.

As for myself, I felt I had had a blow on the head. All at once I had an inkling of what it was about Roha's brother that had always made me sorrowful. That was the word – not foreboding, or uneasiness. I really hadn't known sorrow, except when my mother was ill; I didn't know it has many aspects, some incomprehensible to the human mind.

What I felt now was pure impersonal mourning, not just for Harry but for many other young men. He was a symbol of them, and somehow I had always known

· 71 ·

it. Uncountable thousands of boys his age were going to die.

How? Why? It flashed across my mind that there was going to be another worldwide epidemic, like the Spanish Flu that had ravaged humanity after the Great War. I had heard a great deal about it.

But there was nothing I could say to my father.

'Come on, now,' he said. 'Get your bottom lip up off the ground, and go and make us all a cup of tea.'

Thoughtless people think it must be exciting, wonderful, to be one of those who, perhaps only rarely, find the integument between material phenomena and the other, uncharted kind, thinner than it should be. But it isn't. I don't believe humankind is programmed to cope with this vulnerability. Perhaps once it was, at the dawn of man's life, but not now.

After that I dreamed of Harry now and then, fragmentary dreams, sometimes as one of his own warrior ancestors in a flax kilt, his smooth brown face precisely inscribed with the blue markings of his lineage; other times he was on a bare hillside. There were trees whose leaves the wind blew green one way and silver the other, and Harry was throwing stones, as he used to throw them to rescue my child's belongings from the tall pine trees around the school. Sometimes there were other things that awoke me in a horror of dry sobs, and a feeling that I had been somewhere I'd never heard of.

And then there were months, years even, when I did not even think of him.

There was no reason why I should, after all.

· 17 ·

Passing into Standard Five, I fell into the rigorous hands of the best teacher I ever met in my life, Sister Serenus. She took my writing aspirations by the scruff, wrung them out, and set me straight. She read all that I had had published, slapping the clippings down on her desk top with a firm hand, and then turned to me.

'All you've written so far is flap doodle, tosh, SQUISH!'

I was paralysed. Frightened, too, for she was a stout, ominously redfaced lady who rarely smiled. She must have cultivated this persona because when I met her again, many years later in Sydney, I found her a merry little woman.

'Squish?' I could barely whisper the word.

'You've just let your imagination run off the rails. But there's something there. Oh, don't get a big head about it, it's a very small something.'

I just stood there, the walking dead in Helga's ex-best shoes.

'*I* am going to teach you how to write a good sentence. *I* am going to teach you the power of the active as opposed to the passive, the transitive compared with the intransitive. *I* am going to show you that adjectives must be handled with tongs. Are you listening?'

'Yes, Sister.'

I was dying to remind her that Miss Elsie K. Morton, literary light of the *New Zealand Herald*, thought enough of my stories and poems to publish them, but I didn't have the courage.

After that my name was mud. Other students' essays were marked V.G. or Fair. Mine were always damned with Could Do Much Better. She kept me back after school and pulled my work to pieces, cruelly pruning away high-flying stuff, the words I did not truly understand, the over-plus of romanticism. That stern nun really hammered me. She kept saying, 'You're using a fine, flexible language, which is a tool for communication. What are you trying to communicate here? Well, you haven't done it! Tosh! Twaddle!'

I might have been devastated, but my mother was indignant.

'You're only a child, after all. What does she expect, Shakespeare? The woman's a Hun!'

But although frequently crestfallen, somehow I knew that Sister Serenus was saying something, many things, that I had to know. Otherwise she wouldn't be bothered. She believed that I might be a writer some day, when I stopped writing squish. But I didn't know how to stop. No matter how I tried, the lightning didn't flash, I didn't fall off my horse like St Paul. I was still in the young writer's limbo where I thought all I had to do was to pour out words. In short, I didn't know what writing is all about. Sister couldn't help me; I had to experience it. I might have gone on for ever, squishing earnestly, if a horse hadn't dropped dead in the shafts at our front gate.

Was it late summer? Yes, the blackberries were ripe. Up the gullies and along the ditches drifted the jammy smell of sun-warm berries two days away from rot. On the hills, if a child listened closely, she could hear the gorse seed pods bursting, a fairy fusillade. My mother got out her winter combinations, fine woollen longjohns that every adult wore. They were aired, for modesty's sake, between two suspended sheets. Best of all, my father looked into his bee hives, said, 'You and me, we'd better rob soon.'

So dazzling were the chipped or crushed limestone roads that when I went into the house I could see black maps on the ceiling. In the afternoon, when the earth was hot, the air had that trembling dreamlike movement one sees in mirages. Harry Tawhai, when I asked him what the old people had called it, replied, 'The dancing of summer.'

How the summer danced that afternoon the horse dropped dead! Sister let us children go home a little early. Even Roha's smooth brown skin was moist with sweat as we dawdled over the railway bridge – sometimes a passer-by was just in the right position to have an apple core dropped on his hat – and walked along the railway station platform. Te Kuiti was a typical railway town. It grew up on both sides of the Main Trunk, which linked Auckland and Wellington, the largest cities of the North Island.

We were talking about getting married, or Roha was, as she was interested in it though I was not. She was telling me she was half-promised to a cousin in Rotorua when a cloud of blowflies, droning like a willy willy, swirled around us in a hysterical spiral. There before us was a stream of blood, a wide stream, meandering across the hot asphalt. It was already ropy and sticky, an intense rose red. A butterfly dipped, got its feet caught, and escaped after a struggle.

'That's real live blood!' whispered Roha.

I felt my own blood leaving my head and sinking to my feet; I wobbled where I stood. The stream flowed from the crack under the door of the men's lavatory. What we had found was only a tributary.

Someone had cut his throat in the lavatory. The station-master, when we fetched him, couldn't get the door open, as the body had fallen down against it. The young porter was lavishly sick.

'Oh, Christ,' the stationmaster moaned, 'and the four o'clock due any moment.'

We went home, shocked, I suppose, for we hardly spoke. And there in front of my house was an upturned broken cart, and a brown horse as dead as a doornail. Neighbours stood around. My mother, forgetting her shyness, stood at the gate with the baby in her arms.

'He's been gone two hours,' she said. 'Where can he be?'

All around on the grass were bits of furniture, a little table, an old box, a single bed, dismantled, with the mattress rolled up, forks and spoons spilling out of a carton, things like that.

'Oh, he'll be so upset when he comes back!' said a neighbour.

I didn't want to talk to anyone. What I had seen was so much worse than this. Flash Jack was boiling around, agitated at the sight or smell of the dead horse, growling at people, wetting anything that stood still, so I grabbed his collar and walked him into our backyard. I didn't want to think about the blood.

'Just one more Depression story,' said the reporter from the *Chronicle*.

My mother had seen the horse go down on its knees, tremble and die. The driver was tossed out of the cart, but was only shaken and grazed. She had brought him inside, attended to his injuries and given him a cup of tea.

'He was an educated man,' she said. 'Like a school-teacher, he spoke. I asked him to stay a while and rest, but he said he would go into town and get the police to help move the horse, poor thing.'

The stranger had indeed done that before he went to the malodorous lavatory at the railway and killed himself. It was supposed that he was taking his sticks of furniture somewhere, to a relative or friend, who knew where, and the death of the horse was the last straw. That man was never identified while we were in Te Kuiti. His furniture, sold for a few pounds, helped pay for his funeral. Because of his age, he was treated as a returned soldier and given a good send-off, bugle and all.

Before someone came with a team of draught horses to haul the dead animal away, I went and stroked its warty white nose, observing its worn-down shoes, and the shiny marks of old harness galls. Its beautiful translucent eye, astonished, it seemed, was coated with dirt.

Neither Roha nor I told our parents or anyone else we had seen the blood. We never spoke of it again. For a few days after the tragedy, I kept bursting into tears. I was a messy, noisy weeper, and upset my mother.

'Try to forget it,' she said. 'People get driven to dreadful things during bad times like we have now. Poor, poor man.'

But it was the horse I was crying for. Sister Serenus, who knew the whole story, asked me if I'd written anything about it. All I could show her was: 'The horse worked hard all its life. It asked for nothing. But all it had in the end was an eye full of dust.'

'Rough,' mused Sister. 'Yes, very rough. But still . . .' and then she quoted, 'Dust hath closed Helen's eye.'

'Did you make that up, Sister?'

'No, someone greater than you or me.'

She gave me a little spank. 'On your way. You're not going to be too bad.'

Mera had put a tarpaulin over the dead man's belongings after they were brought into our backyard. Days afterwards, when the furniture had been taken off to be auctioned, and he was putting away the tarpaulin, he found that the old box had been left behind. He was in a quandary what to do with it. No one owned it. The whole business of the stranger was finished.

'I'll just leave it in the shed for a while in case someone claims it,' he said. It was left there, forgotten, for months. Then, when we were leaving that house for another, it was rediscovered.

'Probably there are tools in it. He wouldn't mind if you used them, Mel. I mean, you went to his funeral and all.'

My father levered off the top of the box. I could see he felt uneasy. Was it honest or wasn't it?

Inside was a sewing basket full of reels of Sylko, a red satin apple stuck with needles, a thimble. There was a half-finished baby dress.

'Do you think his wife . . . could she have died having a . . .' began my mother. She glanced hastily at me. 'Ssssh!' she said to herself.

Other odds and ends which I have forgotten, yes. But at the bottom, wrapped in a piece of old blanket, lay six books. Three titles I have forgotten, but the others were *Grimm's Fairytales*, *Banjo Paterson's Poems*, and a little grey-blue book published by Methuen and Co. and called *An Anthology of Modern Verse*. I opened this. On the flyleaf was written: 'My Love always. Christmas 1922. p. 61.'

On page 61 my glance fixed upon these words:

We wake and whisper awhile,
But, the day gone by,
Silence and sleep like fields
Of amaranth lie.

and in a flash knew what poetry is, what writing is, what my life was to be.

· 18 ·

In the years following my mother's illness, things changed. Perhaps my father had been devastated by the possibility of his losing her. Maybe the surgeon had had a private word with him about her frailty. At the time I thought not at all about the apparent improvement in our circumstances. My life was crammed with writing, my responsibility for the impetuous Flash Jack, and a new burden. Sister Serenus had decided that I would win a scholarship.

'If you intend to be a writer, you need to be as well educated as possible,' she pronounced. 'I have, therefore, entered your name for a National Scholarship, and you will win it.'

'Yes, Sister.'

She coached me after school and on Saturday mornings. She went after me like Flash Jack after a rat. I was eleven at the time. My head bulged with information, mostly useless, or entirely without relevance to our life in the southern hemisphere. I knew who Richard Crouchback's brother was, and that Disraeli wore rings on the outside of his gloves. I knew a hundred antonyms and how tides work, including those in the Bay of Biscay. No one could trick me on the All Red Route. It was a wonder I didn't mentally choke. But all this useless knowledge was required by the syllabus.

The country floundered in economic anarchy, though far worse was to come. Export prices were down 40 per cent. New Zealand had always been, romantically, 'the back garden of the Mother Country'. But Britain was in a parlous state and didn't want the butterfat, cheese, honey, frozen lamb and other agricultural comestibles that made up more than 70 per cent of New Zealand's national product. Added to this, powerful British interests had invested heavily in the Argentine, which produced much the same kind of thing. The Argentine began to be called, in the same sentimental manner, 'a faraway British colony', which was excellent P.R. though not for New Zealand, and a lie anyway. Even export of New Zealand's superb hardwoods – no one had thought they were irreplaceable – had almost ceased, and as no one at home could afford to build anything, many mills stood idle.

The Waitomo Council advertised a vacancy for a nightman, and before 5 a.m. there was a queue of fifty men waiting to apply for the humble job of removing cans from the unsewered lavatories.

Yet somehow, in this time of extremity, Mera bought a house. It was a modest white timber house with a green corrugated-iron roof. It had linoleum on the floors, an indoor bathroom and even an indoor laundry. There was an orchard and a paddock, and a wonderful barn where crumbling horse collars hung on wooden pegs, and the cracks between the broad pitsawn floor boards were yellow with chaff.

'And hot water!' marvelled my mother. 'You turn on the tap and out comes hot water!'

On a hook in the barn, wrapped up in a sack, hung my father's khaki uniform, thick wool like cardboard, useless pockets, brass buttons, puttees, the Boy Scout hat. He hated and despised war and warmongers, and I never knew him once to march on Anzac Day. Gradually the uniform became stiffened with dust. I used to unroll it sometimes to show the other kids.

'War was invented by the old bucks to get rid of the young bucks,' Mera said.

He came home very late from Europe, with the last of the New Zealand troops, because he'd been a long time in hospital. He was a champion rifleman and had been asked to volunteer as sniper. He refused. He said the offer was the worst insult of his life.

How did Mera manage to buy the house in Nettie Street? I can only conclude that he took out yet another mortgage, the mortgage which was eventually to send him bankrupt and break his heart. Even though my mother yearned for a home of her own, she argued against the purchase, but his mind was made up. My mother usually had good judgement, but scarcely ever did it prevail.

Still, we loved that house, its snowdrops and greengage plums; the row of flax bushes where the tuis came to sing and suck honey; a certain shrub with large violet blossoms which no one in town could identify. It was sensitive to cold, so my mother made it a remarkable garment, a kind of horticultural cardigan, to protect it from the frost. It was my job to clothe Purple Flower every evening. I didn't find out its name until I went to live in Australia, where I saw whole streets fringed with the ravishing Brazilian, the tibouchina.

I like to think my mother was happy there. My father must still have been getting contract work with the County Council, for all three lorries were constantly on the road. He drove the venerable Republic, Mr Tawhai the newer International, and a sulky, squinting Maori named Ruru the tip truck. Ruru means morepork, and he certainly was one. My mother was always at Mera to replace him with someone more competent.

'Ah, the poor cow,' was the reply. 'You only dislike him because he has one eye pointing west.'

'That's not true,' she said. 'He has a liar's face, that's all.'

· 81 ·

'There you are, exactly what I meant,' said my father complacently. 'Women all over.' Then he softened. 'He has seven kids and a wife with carbuncles. You have to have a heart, girl.'

'You've got too much,' she replied tartly, and she was right.

· 19 ·

I was completely satisfied being myself at that age. It was finely poised between the manipulated, unfree days of babyhood and pre-adolescence, when one is likely to be loaded with disagreeable responsibilities. Long ago I had decided never to be an adult. This was no Peter Pan fancy; I had never heard of *him*. Simply, by and large, I had no high regard for adults. I looked upon them chiefly as curiosities, bound hand and foot by inexplicable rules.

Being adult was plainly a waste of good living time.

Conscientiously my mother warned me that growing up was unavoidable. She even said things like, 'When you have children of your own.' This made me feel faintish, as remarks about umbles had done in earlier life.

I wouldn't listen, flew off, ran up hill and down dale, bounding over the rusty swamp pools where the mud eels lived, scattering drowsy horses and wandering hens, in rapturous enjoyment of my strong lean body that was completely my own and never would be beholden to anyone else.

The times were cruel, but they rolled off me like water off a duck's back. I read my three books and I wrote, scarcely ever stopping either occupation, as I also read and wrote in my head. That year I began to have a cloudy comprehension of other people's writing; perhaps it was of style or conceptual richness. I could not define it, but recognition of some truth as yet unknown to me was there. Whenever I wallowed in adjectives I had an uneasy fancy that the Grimm Brothers (I fancied them whiskery, stout and severe) stood beside me shaking their heads; they did me an immense amount of good, so much so that when I eventually read Hans Christian Andersen, I thought him flowery and on the verge of goofiness.

In spite of this condition of bliss, I was fly enough to put on a grave face when Sister made us say a decade of the Rosary for someone's father, fallen in the quarry and laid up with a broken leg.

'How will they *manage?*' people murmured.

My mother was always ravaged by other people's disasters. She cried over a neighbour's child who went through the murderous winter in a cotton dress. From some sister's unpicked woollen coat, she ran up a little jacket. It was green.

'For your name, you see,' she said to the child Ivy.

The girl put it on and tore off home, mad with pleasure.

Ten minutes later it was thrown over our hedge, without a word. The mother was a widow, struggling to rear three children on a war pension, and living with a vile old devil of a father-in-law who banged the kids about. But she had her pride, brutal and unyielding pride. She wouldn't take charity.

'I believe she'd let those children starve first,' said Mera.

'No, I should have managed it differently,' said my mother sadly.

She knew about charity, and it was bitter knowledge. In her childhood, when her father Karl Johann was on the spree, Grandma pregnant and unable to work, the girls often had to go to neighbours and 'borrow' a little food. Later I was to learn something of that humiliation when the nuns' outworn underclothes came my way. The kindness of the giver has nothing to do with anything. St Vincent de Paul put it well when he told his helpers, 'Don't expect the poor to thank you. It is their right to hate you.'

In terrible circumstances self-respect is the last thing to go, and most people in those times held on to it desperately and often fatally.

My mother rehearsed me in diplomacy.

'Whatever you do you mustn't hurt their pride. You must make them think they're doing *you* a favour.'

This form of devious drama suited me down to the ground.

'Mrs Ryan, Mum says it'd be a kindness if you'd take some of these vegetables off her hands. The cauliflowers are beginning to bolt and we'd never in a month of Sundays get through the carrots . . .' and the poor woman, seeing through my specious innocence as if I were a pane of glass, would say with well-done reluctance, 'Of course we mustn't waste good food. That'd be a black sin.'

Women my mother suspected of greater sophistication were approached another way. She sent pots of her apple jelly, firm as a rock and a wondrous yellow-pink, and myself saying hesitantly, 'Mum's worried about it, she thinks she didn't put in enough sugar, and as you're so expert, Mrs Tomalin, would you try it and give your opinion?'

It certainly wasn't that we had more money than other people; probably there was none at all. But we had the luck to have fruit trees, a big garden and my father's skill with rifle and fishing line. My mother's domestic accomplishments added greatly to our welfare; these were not regarded as exceptional, except for her dressmaking, which was professional. Inability to mend, cook, knit, clean, preserve, nurse the sick in some degree or other was practically unknown amongst those independent people, men as well as women. You looked after yourself, and your family, had a go, tried your hand, made do. It was part of the spirit of freedom and hardihood that had made your parents or grandparents leave Europe for the colonies.

Oh, my mother's way with rabbit! If Mera came home with a brace of young bunnies, I knew the next day would bring my favourite dinner. Before I ran off to school there'd be the command, 'Quick, down the yard with you and get me a handful of shallots, another of parsley, some sage and thyme.'

We didn't know about oregano and coriander, but we did marvellously well with rosemary and mint, and an occasional lavender head or two in the quince jam.

The rabbits were disjointed, lightly floured, placed in a large pie-dish with the shallots and herbs, and covered with milk. The pie-dish was put on the very bottom of the oven, where it gently bubbled all day. An hour or so before dinnertime, thick slices of bacon were laid over the top to frizzle and season the lot. Unpeeled potatoes were baked at the same time, and perhaps a jammy bread pudding made with four duck eggs and yesterday's cream.

My Grandma said the Archbishop of Dublin could wish for no better, Christian or not. This enigmatic statement must surely have referred to the Anglican Archbishop.

· 20 ·

Grandma often came and stayed with us, but she fretted sadly over the welfare of Poor Jack. He worked in a boot factory as a clicker, and every week signed the wages book for a third more than he actually got. This was common practice, but at least it meant that Jack stayed in work all through the Slump. While Grandma was in Te Kuiti, he boarded with one of his sisters, who no doubt treated him as badly as her husband allowed her to get away with. In those days I had no idea why they behaved towards this mild gentle boy so Hunnishly, but of course they were jealous of Grandma's love for him.

Grandma had had another little son, near the top of the family, who stumbled into the open fire on which she had to cook, and so died. His name was John Thomas, after her beloved father back in Ballindrum. When she had this second son, after all those scrapping, highly strung, wicked girls, and when she was in the heel of her forties, it may have seemed that the lost child, for whom she had grieved most bitterly, had come back to her. Jack's name was Karl Johann, after his father, but Jack she called him.

Grandma fussed over him like an old hen, and the girls ground their teeth with rage. They said smart, cruel things to him. It was just as well Grandma was as deaf as a beetle or they'd have caught it hot.

'He's as thin as a Protestant herring,' she protested, as she gave him an extra egg for his tea, and he was.

I don't think my mother and her sisters ever had an

inkling of what Poor Jack meant to Grandma, not even when they had children of their own. Jealousy and envy are strange and enduring blinkers.

I knew my Grandma very well, as even in the days of bare floors and Helga's shoes, sometimes enough money was scraped up to permit my homesick mother to take us children to Auckland to stay with Grandma. I was train-sick all the way, and the baby yowled steadily, but our mother was so overjoyed to be returning home that she bore with us sweetly.

By the time I was nine or ten I was promoted to the responsible job of fetching the refreshments. Was it always the middle of the night? After the murky warmth of the train the cold country air hit one's face like a shovel-ful of hail. People with their eyes still glued half-shut staggered across the platform, breaking miraculously into a sprint when they saw their fellows already six deep at the refreshment counter. Children inevitably found them-selves behind a solid wall of ruddy farmers buying pies. I knew how vexed my mother would be if, her tongue hanging out for a cup of tea, I came back to the train empty-handed.

'Please, please,' I squeaked perfidiously, 'my Mum's feeling fainty and she does so need a cup of tea.'

Eventually someone would rumble, 'Let the little ginger through!' and though I gritted my teeth at the insult, I passed to the front row, smiling gratefully. They were kindly people, and never doubted me for a moment.

The tea came in a Railway cup. The rim was so thick that the drinker felt he had grown a third lip. Tradition said that once a passenger threw a cup out on the line and it derailed the following freight train. With the tea I bore a large wedge of what was known as blowfly cake, light fruit cake composed of fossilised lemon peel and raisins loosely connected by vivid yellow material.

'Made with egg powder,' my mother said censoriously. 'Really!'

Grandma and her son Jack lived in a shabby weatherboard house fronting Eden Terrace, a street probably long vanished.

Thin and spry, she could not have been mistaken for anything but a grandmother. She belonged to a generation which marked some imprecise birthday with a revolutionary change of garb. A grandma's dress uniform was a black dress and coat, little white scarf held with a cameo, comfortable black shoes with a kind of annex for the bunion, and a remarkable hat of jetty silk, cunningly swathed over a brachycephalic skull of unyielding buckram. Individuality was permitted in the hatpin. Grandma's favourite was like a lump of coke tastefully touched up with gold paint.

For both personal and literary reasons Grandma was, and is, special to me. She was not the Grandma of the trilogy centred around *The Harp in the South*. 'Relics of old gentility', as the Irish song has it, hung about her like the lavender water she always used. She was blunt and straightforward, but never vulgar. Though she has been dead for almost forty years, I remember her with warm affection. I have only to close my eyes and see her standing there, the monkey on her hat.

How did a monkey get on a grandma's hat? Though a brief tale, it must wait.

Grandma had no teeth in her mouth because they stayed in their original dentist's box in her bureau drawer. Nothing would make her wear them, not even the extravagant, often tearful performances of her lovely daughters, who wanted to take her out and show her the big shops in Town, or the cathedral, or even Luna Park. She preferred to be gummy and go her own way. This independence of family manipulation impressed me greatly. I only wished I had half as much grit.

Courage was her major characteristic. Before she was eighteen she emigrated to New Zealand, penniless and trained in nothing but farm and housework. She went to the priest and he found her a job scrubbing bare floors in a boarding house for a woman so mean, said Grandma, that she'd boil down a flea for the oil. Like all her daughters to be, she had a fine complexion and what she described as a bucketful of grand auburn hair. Presently she met and married a Scandinavian seaman called Karl Johann Peterson.

He was a well built man with dark hair, aquamarine eyes and good features. He paid off in Auckland and never went to sea again. He worked instead on harbour dredges and various dockside jobs. He was also tall. Grandma maintained he had such long legs that if they'd gone on another inch his tripes would have fallen out.

Aside from my height I owe a great deal to this unknown man – I never saw his face or heard his voice – if only for his genes.

I have never felt so much at home anywhere as I feel in Norway and Sweden, where I saw myself and my children everywhere. He called himself a Scandinavian because officially he was one. Norway and Sweden were a united country in his day. But having looked carefully at the features of both races, I am certain that his was a Norwegian family living and working in Stockholm, up one of the breakneck cobbled lanes of the Gamla Stan. My eldest aunt also told me that he spoke Norwegian as well as Swedish, though I suppose this would not be uncommon even now.

Karl Johann does not appear to have been a good husband. During his marriage with Mary Ann, he retained the nineteen-century seaman's habit of long periods of sobriety, interrupted abruptly by a fighting mad drunken spree. While not excusing this, I must admit that Grandma could not have been an easy woman to live with. If ever there was a tread-on-the-tail-of-me-coat Irishwoman it was she.

However, hers was a hard life. Much of the time she supported their young family by continuing to scrub boarding-houses. Early in life she became deaf, and so retained her seductive accent, and a sumptuous supply of picturesque words and phrases. When I married into the very Irish Niland family, I was able to beat them at their own game any tick of the clock, because of Grandma's vocabulary.

I first loved her because of this; she was full of splendid words, mostly sharp, for she believed a tongue was made for use. But even when I was being given the rounds of the kitchen, I stood there beaming. A fladdy-faced spalpeen, I was called, and a tom todger, and a bold little crab.

She didn't mean anything by this ballyragging. She was generous, affectionate, and full of ironic fun. She didn't mean it any more than she meant seriously the raised hand, edge forward, with which she threatened to give us kids a clout alongside the earhole. My father accidentally got in the way of that gesture once, and he said it was like being hit with half a pound of candles.

It was no use whatsoever being sensitive around Grandma. Friend or foe, she let you have it. She informed one of my uncles that his nose was so long a body could hang her hat on it. When Poor Jack, at the age of twenty-five or so, dared to have a beer after work with his mates, she told him and everyone else that his breath would have lighted a candle at the far side of the room. My favourite saying of hers was that her own grandmother, who looked after the orphan as a child, *had a ghost up every sleeve*. I took this to mean that the old woman had a fund of ghost and fairy stories, which I longed to hear. But so perverse was Grandma that I never had as much as one of them.

Grandma also got names wrong. Her parish church was St Benediction and her favourite film star was Mary Picklefoot. Long after Miss Pickford's prime, Grandma and I went hunting for movie houses that still showed silent films starring her. Talking pictures had deprived the deaf woman of this small pleasure. We walked, of course. I began to know Auckland like the palm of my hand.

She was very devout, in an explosive Old Testament way, and went to church twice a day. However, she was hardheaded and domineering with the saints. I heard her address St Christopher as a poor sort of old son who needed a puck in the eye, as she vindictively dropped his medal down a drain. He has now been abolished, so perhaps her wish came true. It was shortly after this episode that Grandma got the monkey on her hat, but she had a wholesome mind, not given to the guilty search after the cause for the effect. She did not blame St Christopher for the monkey and indeed why should she, when I was there.

There we were, walking around looking for Mary Picklefoot films, Grandma chattering away, and myself displaying interested expressions, for although she could not hear a word she liked to be answered. Suddenly there was this fairy squeak and a light thud, and I observed that Grandma now had a tiny grey monkey on top of her hat, hanging on for dear life to the coke hatpin. I was paralysed and so was the monkey.

For fear or freedom, it had leaped from a high verandah above us, and made this fortunate four-handed landing.

Puzzled, Grandma put up her hand and cautiously felt all round the brim of her hat. The monkey was perched high on the crown. Baffled, Grandma muttered a bit and continued her rapid pigeon-toed march down the street. How was I to tell her? How to convey with non-frightening gestures that she carried a wild beast on her hat?

Passersby gaped at us, bug-eyed, and I, with a child's shameful horror of any association with a spectacle, could have submerged in the ground. So we proceeded until Grandma caught sight of herself reflected in a shop window. What a shriek she gave!

'The devil's on me hat!' was the burden of it.

Poor old lady, she had to be borne into the shop and given a nice hot cup of tea. Fortunately the hurly-burly had alerted the monkey's owner, who rushed down the street and snatched up the little animal which, equally agitated, jumped about in hysterics and sank its teeth in his chin.

I was in disgrace for days.

'Why didn't you knock it off?' chided my mother and the aunts, ignoring what they knew perfectly well – that any grandchild who took a swipe at Grandma's hat was asking for trouble of the worst kind.

Grandma also was of the opinion I should have done something about the violation of her hat, and stated positively that I had the black drop. Perhaps I have, and she was the place where I got it.

Grandma's firmness and independence did all of us children good. Her legpulling and sardonic humour took the mickey out of us when we were silly or obstreperous. Best of all, her handling of her own daughters let us know early in life that our parents were only people.

Years later I went to the tiny village in Ireland where she had been born, Ballindrum, in Derry. With the help of the parish priest I had no trouble finding the white-washed cottage, now roofless, standing in a silvery field of barley. When John McBride, Grandma's father, died, the villagers had pulled off the thatch, in the strange way of Ireland in those days. The cottage had never since been occupied.

So I walked around that little house, seeing the white-washed hearth where Grandma had learned to cook on an open fire, the one bedroom she had shared with her own grandmother, who reared her after poor Elisabeth died in childbirth. Her father, whose worn letters Grandma had re-read every night until she died, had slept in the box bed in the kitchen. They are poignant letters, the kind written by so many parents left behind when their children venture into new countries.

'Ah, my Mary,' says one of them. 'You say you are homesick always for your father and your home. Let not the children suspect. It is for children to be always as happy as a prince.'

When she was dying I looked at that closed up, indifferent face. A severe face, for all Irish faces are severe when the flesh draws close to the bone. I had never been able to ask her all the questions I wanted to ask, because she could not hear me. Because I suffered profoundly with homesickness myself I wanted to ask, 'When does the homesickness stop?' Most of all I wanted to tell her that she, capricious and wilful and ardent, had been a delight to me, that she had opened my ears to words and phrases I might never have heard from anyone else.

While she was still well, I had been able to convey to her that I had married a man not born in Ireland, but still an Irishman to the last gene. She looked at me approvingly.

'Ah, dotie,' she said. 'You've done right. The Irish are the worst in the world, but there's none better.'

· 21 ·

One Sunday Sister Serenus, sailing out of Mass like a brown galleon, hissed at me, 'Come to the Convent before you go home.'

I was panicstriken. Children were summoned to the Convent only when they had done something perfectly vile, like swearing or making a mess in the toilets.

She received me formally in the parlour, which had that odour peculiar to convents, beeswax, flowers, and the whiff of a recently extinguished candle. Sister Serenus jingled in. This small musical sound of large swinging rosary beads attached to the belt was a godsend to us children; no matter what crime we were committing, we always knew when a nun was approaching.

'Sit,' said Sister. I sat.

'You have won a National Scholarship,' she said. 'Naturally.'

I tore home to tell my parents. This meant that I would have three years' free secondary school, with a small living allowance, and an opportunity to sit for a Senior Scholarship at the close of the first. It was a miracle.

A boy at the Public School had also won a scholarship, and when the *King Country Chronicle* published this, making a little Te Kuiti brag of it, they made no mention of me, though in fact my marks had been superior. This was the only time I experienced any anti-Catholic prejudice in that town. We children had a kind of good humoured rivalry, admittedly, often shouting, 'Yah yah, Cattledog!' or

'Proddyhopper!' as the case might be, but that was all. Mera was angrier than I had ever seen him.

'I'll go right down and pull his Orange nose out by the roots!' he said.

But the editor was not an Orangeman as far as I ever learned. The incident was just one of those paltry meannesses one sometimes comes across. Or so Sister Serenus said when she spoke to me privately the next day.

'The world will make it hard for you,' she said, 'because of prejudice of one sort or another. Because, for instance, you are a girl.'

'A *girl?*' I couldn't believe my ears. 'But why?'

'I don't know, and neither do the people who will penalise you because you are a girl. But they will do it.'

'But that's mad!'

'Irrational is a better word.'

I couldn't believe her. I thought she had it wrong. Not wanting my parents to think her foolish in such a belief, I didn't even ask them about it.

That was the last good luck the Park family had for several years.

My father came home shaking with rage and consternation.

'That blasted Morepork drove the tip-truck over a cutting at the Three Mile!'

The lorry was totalled, and as was to be expected, it was under-insured. What money Mera received went to pay the disastrous Ruru's hospital bills.

The same week the Council decided that the Republic's hard tyres, immensely expensive but longwearing, were cutting up the unmetalled roads, and ordered the vehicle to be laid up. Mera was left only with the almost new International. Rangi Tawhai came to him at once.

'You'll want to drive her yourself,' he said. 'And I want no back pay until you are on your feet again.'

But Mera never got back on his feet. Within a month or two the Government had cut rail and roadworks almost to nothing, and ceased funding public works in general. This lamentable decision stalled the national economy and threw countless men out of work. The Waitomo County Council, funded meagrely at the best of times, reduced public work to a trickle. My father took what work he could get, removals, freight-carrying from the railway, sometimes a load of timber from a surviving mill so far from the town he did not come home till nine or ten at night. He could not pay his mechanic's bills, even his petrol account. I can imagine how the Bank harried him. For him there was no light anywhere.

It was my job, when I heard the International's engine far away in the quiet country night, to run out and open the gates so Mera could drive in without stopping. Then I closed the gates and went to greet him.

He did not get out from behind the wheel.

'Come on, Daddy! It's freezing. And Mum's got dinner ready for you.'

'I'm done,' he said.

I thought he was pulling my leg, as he did so often.

'I can't move,' he said.

I ran in and got my mother. But in the end I had to fetch two neighbours to lift that big man out from behind the wheel and carry him into the house.

What ailment had struck my father, so strong and durable? The doctor called it neuritis, a meaningless word. He could not walk at all, and he could clench and unclench his hands only feebly. He was not in pain, except after the doctor's treatments. The things that were done to that helpless man! One remedy I recall was the injection of salt water into his flesh. His legs swelled up like pillows, and his stifled groans could be heard for hours.

Today I believe his illness was psychosomatic. He could

see no way out of his misfortunes; the sea of troubles threatened to drown him, and his body called enough. Here I stay, it decided, in the way we now know bodies can do.

For three months there was no improvement in his health. He was helpless. His strongly muscled footballer's legs began to atrophy, the ruddiness faded from his face. God knows what he must have suffered mentally. His honourable, simple view of life was that of a past generation – work hard, owe no man anything, do whatever kindness is in your power. He believed that manhood and integrity were synonymous.

What did he think about, lying there helpless, while his savings dwindled to nothing, and the bills crowded in? What we all think about in times of crisis, I suppose . . . the careless follies, the bad judgments, the too-great trust of other people. It must have been the most harrowing time of his life.

His mechanic, a rusty-faced Scotsman, visited him.

'Park,' he said, 'you owe me not a bloody penny.'

He brought out a wad of my father's bills, now torn to shreds.

'Missus,' said he to my mother, 'put yon rubbish on the fire.'

My father said, 'Jock, don't do this to me.'

'I'm doing it to you, Park, because you'll no' do it for yersel',' said Jock, as he stumped out.

When my father was an old man, he said one day, 'I've always hoped I'd win the art union, so I could go back to Te Kuiti and pay old Jock. It's been a kind of dream.'

Of course Jock, much my father's elder, would have been dead for years. But still the desire was there, to repay a man who had been magnanimous and kindly to another down on his luck.

Sometimes I inspected the Republic, a solemn task. I

was awed that this mighty machine, the school-shaker, matchless assailant of holy pictures, should now be a beached hulk in a paddock, unusable and unsaleable. Coarse grass grew amongst the wheels; a neglected hedge bent and collapsed on the roof of the cab. The side curtains had grown brittle and cracked, fallen into ruin. Looking in, I saw two furious little eyes looking back. Overcome with delight, I rushed to tell my father.

'Daddy, Daddy, the bantam hen has nested on the driver's seat!'

A curious look came over his face.

'I don't know whether to laugh or cry,' he said. He looked at my mother. 'That sort of ties it up, doesn't it, the whole rotten mess.'

I knew I had put my foot in it somehow; what had seemed quaint and amusing to me was not so to my parents.

'It's a nice nest,' I offered miserably. 'She's pulled the stuffing out of the seat and . . .'

'Go away now,' said my mother.

Nothing more was said, but many times I pondered over that obscure, trifling little scene. My painful incomprehension was that of many children who have not been informed of the full facts. I knew things were bad for my family but I did not know they were critical.

I could not imagine that my father faced the probability that he would not walk again; that not only would he never drive the Republic again, but he would never drive any truck. He was, in fact, already one of that huge anxious mass, the unemployed.

Mr Tawhai continued to drive the International, picking up what work he could for my father, and refusing to take wages.

'What wages do I need when we have a handful of land to grow potatoes and corn, and a creek where the children can spear eels?'

Sacks of firewood appeared mysteriously on our verandah, a bag of flour, a flax kit of freshly caught trout. People
did what they could for each other, even though their own
situation was frightening.

My father was so humiliated that when I sat with him
after school, he wouldn't look me in the face. He blamed
himself for everything. My mother told me later how she
had sometimes tried to reason with him – the Slump, the
calamitous cessation of roadworks, the gormless Ruru. But
he listened to nothing. He had let himself and his family
down and there was an end to it.

'He kept saying,' my mother told me years later, 'My
God, we might even lose the house. What will happen to
the girls?'

Spirit had gone out of Mera somehow. He was never
quite the same man again.

Whether my mother called for help from her elder sister
Wendela or not I never knew, but one day a Ford car pulled
up outside, and there was Wendela and her new husband
Hugo. Her first husband, Helga's father the Norwegian,
had died years before, and Wendela was tired of being a
widow.

I approved greatly of Uncle Hugo, an interesting
Englishman who had spent most of his life in various types
of soldiering. He had even been a Mounted Policeman in
Canada. My Uncle the Mountie dominated my conversation at school for days.

Uncle Hugo was assistant manager and Old Reliability
at a famous merino stud on the Hauraki Gulf, Glen Afra.

'So far away from everything!' my mother commiserated
with her sister.

'Bought her for £39,' Uncle Hugo said of the car,
complacently kicking a mudguard. Fortunately Mera took
to him, as who wouldn't?

He had been classically educated at Harrow and other

prestigious educational establishments before his wandering life began. He had also fought at Gallipoli, where a piece of shrapnel had passed through his cheek, leaving him with a mighty dimple, no deformity, but a quirky, merry physiognomy. He went through all my father's affairs; found out, too late, that he had had no need to pay Ruru's hospital bills, as the latter had been full to the gills with sly grog at the time of the crash; added everything up pro and con, and said, 'Rotten luck, old man. Bankruptcy's the only thing.'

I can imagine how my father fought this final disgrace. But Uncle Hugo persuaded him.

'First however,' he said, 'we'll stack the car to the roof with your personal belongings. Otherwise it'll all go west in the auction.'

My father protested at the dishonesty of this, but Wendela, to whom he felt everlasting gratitude for her goodness during his wife's illness, told him that he needn't know a thing about it, such things were best left to rascals like herself and Hugo. So away went the Ford to Auckland with my mother's sewing machine, my father's tools, china and cutlery, rolled mattresses and no end of useful odds and bobs.

'What do you want to keep?' Auntie Wendela asked me with a wink.

'My school books and Flash Jack.'

So Mera was declared bankrupt. My mother, brave as a lion as always, declared stoutly, 'We'll make out somehow. We're all together. And my sisters will stand by me.'

As the time for our departure drew near, I remember Roha and myself looking at each other in dumb bewilderment. Neither could comprehend what had happened, or why it had happened. The world changed overnight; your own bed was not there to sleep on. Fear had walked into our lives and the children were not told why it had.

'Stop pestering me,' they said, vexed. 'You wouldn't understand.'

Roha's full lower lip was quivering. 'I don't care if you're going away,' she shouted suddenly. 'I don't like you anyway.'

'I don't like you either!'

It was the only way we knew how to cope with a moment that filled the chest with swelling suffocation, and the throat with painful stiffness.

'I've got lots of other friends!'

She jumped backwards, scowling at me, and then ran away. I thought I heard a sound like a dog wailing, but I might have been mistaken.

I never saw or heard from Roha again.

My mother couldn't understand why Roha didn't come around to say goodbye.

'You've been such great friends. You just march straight up to Tawhai's and say goodbye like a civilised child.'

But I didn't. I hid in their hedge for a while and then I came home and lied about it. My mother didn't understand that one thing Roha and I could never say was goodbye.

· 22 ·

Mera travelled to Auckland on a stretcher in the guard's van, and I kept him company. Flash Jack, lost to all consolation in the anguish of trainsickness, was in a grated box nearby.

So we left the King Country, where at least we had lived well off the land, and journeyed to Auckland, where all a destitute family could live on were the relatives.

PART TWO

· 1 ·

That winter's evening Auckland looked what it was – a pinched, bleak little town. Languishing after the first World War, it had run down hill before the unstoppable Depression. Already it had the cringing look of cities I was to see during the second World War, boarded-up shops, peeling paint, gutters full of starling nests.

Bewildered and fatigued we stood on the railway platform, Mera crooked and trembling on his crutches. Aunts and uncles bore down on us shouting welcome. Our little group was also besieged by people selling things, people coatless in that needling wind, sockless even.

A young boy repeatedly shoved a jar of pickled onions at my mother.

'Only a bob, missus! They're corker, honest!'

'Home-knitted socks . . .'

'Fresh young rabbits, caught this morning.'

'Oh, good God, just look, it's still got its ghastly little head on! Go away, you awful man! Cis, Mel, poor dears, you must be exhausted! Go *away*, you pest!'

That was Auntie Theresa, cross as a bagful of cats. Train an hour late, raining all day, a wind whipping along the platform that could nail you to the wall. The rabbit man was lucky he didn't get his shin kicked.

I was deaf and dumb with panic. What were we doing here in this alien, formidable place, half-choked by the stink of hot metal, wet coal, trapped smoke? A murky crimson sky glowered between what seemed to me prodigious buildings; rainclouds streamed above their roofs.

Looking up at Mera for reassurance, I surprised on his face such an expression of disquiet and apprehension as I had never thought to see. My mother put her hand on his dwindled arm.

'It's all right, Mel, stop worrying,' she said gently. 'Everything's going to be all right.'

I saw in her expression that there was something between them which, as a child, I could not yet fathom. It was the mysterious supportive interchange of married lovers. But what child knows about that?

Arms around me, a kiss on the nose, a fragrance of freesias. That was Auntie Wendela, come all the way from distant Glen Afra to lend a hand, talk things over, work out some way to help.

Seen en masse, the aunts didn't look as I remembered them. They had transformed themselves into sinuous skinny creatures with hems flaring around their calves. Their chests had been remodelled, for the brassiere had ousted the camisole and the bodice. Each wore a small headachey hat pulled over her right eye. Rosie had laid the sheepdog to rest and now had a fox coiled about her throat, its murderous tiny face under her left ear.

Recovered a little, I breathed in the smell of Auckland, so different from that of the King Country – a disturbing smell of wet rocks, wharf piles rinded with green mussels, sopping mangrove flats, islets and reefs webbed with salt and guano. Overhead a horde of homegoing gulls spiralled, exploded, yipping like puppies.

Somehow they manhandled my almost helpless father into the back seat of a taxi. The uncles with cars divided our possessions between them. From the taxi boot came a calamitous yoicking that indicated that Flash Jack was still alive and suffering.

'How has he got anything left to be sick *with*?'

The aunts had arranged everything, in the enthusiastic, high-handed manner that characterised their lives. I found myself sharing a closed-in verandah that had been turned into a bedroom for myself and my cousin Stuart, two years younger than I and as hostile as a singed cobra.

'There were men selling dead rabbits on the railway station,' I ventured.

'Oh, shut your face!'

· 2 ·

Was it wise to move to the city? As an adult I'd say no, it was a disastrous decision. I think my father's shame over bankruptcy, and my mother's longing to be with her family were what prompted our precipitous flight. However hard people had done it in the country, it was as nothing to what the city unemployed endured. At least in the country we had been able to eat.

That Depression is rightly called the Great. It was more like war. New Zealand was occupied by a mindless enemy, poverty. People who had never experienced complete and hopeless destitution can hardly comprehend it. You are as bewildered as a foundered horse. Something or someone, you know not who, has made you so, and you cannot understand how or why. You do as you are told. Come here; go there; sign that; no, not there, you fool. Who are you to object, you unit in a long list of statistics?

Almost every country in the world experienced the same economic and social anarchy. I can speak only about Australasia.

So there was New Zealand, population approaching a million and a half. Social welfare for the workless? None. There was something for which men had to register, at the end of 1930. Sustenance, it was aptly called, as it sustained breath in the body but nothing else. However, it was not paid for years. Unemployed women were easily dealt with. They were ignored. Like Maoris, they were not counted in the unemployment statistics. However when a specific tax was levied on the wages of all employed people in order to create an emergency Unemployment Fund, working women were equally taxed. In 1932 a motion by the Labour Opposition that sustenance should be paid to unemployed women was defeated 39 to 23. A motion that employed women should not pay the wages tax was defeated 36 to 24.

'Oh, how do they manage, where can they go?' lamented my mother for those unemployed non-persons – factory, shop and office girls, domestic workers in hospitals and other public institutions which had reduced staff or closed altogether. Where, indeed?

No one saw unemployed women gathering in hangdog groups in city doorways or under the verandahs of abandoned shops as we saw men, six or seven perhaps, speechlessly passing a cigarette from one to another. God knows they were a sad enough sight, aimless, unwanted and beginning to believe it. They had the unmistakable look of the workless. The power of poverty is formidable. You cannot keep yourself clean because you have only the clothes you stand up in. Your teeth rot. Homecut hair looks like the backside of a terrier. You become at last so shabby, so demoralised that you no longer expect to be given a job.

But where were the jobless women? Later the City Missioner told me that after tramping the streets from 6 a.m. looking unsuccessfully for work, they took refuge in churches and the Public Library for hours at a time.

'Out of the cold,' he said. Some of these women stood, breakfastless, in job queues for three hours, waiting for an interview. Often they, and men too, fainted with fatigue and hunger. When he was well again, and repeatedly stood in queues like these, Mera saw many such collapses.

'It's bloomin' awful,' he said. 'By right their families should be looking after them.'

'Maybe they're supporting their families, maybe they're the breadwinner, as my mother was,' said my mother, with unusual sharpness.

But my father had no answer and neither did the Government. Women were not supposed to be breadwinners, therefore they were not. Into my head began to filter some slight comprehension of the Establishment's lethal ability to deny what was in front of its nose.

Everything was topsy turvy. The order of social importance had changed. Doctors, for instance, were no longer on the top of the status tree.

'My back's giving me jip. I'd better go and see the chemist.'

Chemists ruled the health scene. If you became ill you did not consider visiting a doctor because he was likely to ask you for his seven and sixpence first. True, some doctors gave their services free, even surgery. But mostly you went to the chemist and asked for advice.

It was not the fault of chemists that patent medicines became literally the people's opiate. Most of these were only a shilling a bottle, much cheaper than the visit to the doctor and payment for his prescription. Drugs now considered dangerous were lavishly dispensed. Chlorodyne, for instance, a world-favourite remedy for more than a century, contained morphine and chloroform. 'Asthma cigarettes' were pure cannabis, and said so on the label. A certain cough lozenge offered not only cannabis, but morphine, chloroform, and prussic acid. Its characteristic flavour was provided by treacle and liquorice.

Any pill advertised as a miracle remedy for 'women's disorders' described as anaemia, irregularity or nausea, was almost certainly an abortifacient. Women took huge overdoses, and destroyed their kidneys. Pregnancy, in a family already on the verge of starvation, was a calamity.

People died frequently of 'pleurisy', possibly neglected pneumonia, complicated by insufficient food and thin, worn-out clothing in severe winters. And as for the 'dossers', the men who slept out of doors under layers of newspapers, who can tell of what they died?

Hospitals were not free. The folk belief was that if, in an emergency, bleeding badly or in advanced labour, you went to a hospital, they could not by law turn you away. This was probably correct. There were some free outpatient departments, serviced by honoraries, though sometimes an ailing person returned day after day before being seen.

Toothache was the burden of many people who could not afford dental care. Once I had a back molar extracted without anaesthetic. The small cavity could easily have been filled, if my parents had had three and sixpence to spare. People in my position let the tooth rot, or tried to kill the nerve with creosote and other unlikely substances, or they packed the hole with gutta percha and risked septicemia.

I chose to have the tooth pulled. It was crushed by the forceps, and the pain was so atrocious that I lost consciousness and could not be revived for half an hour. The dentist was grey with fright. My father had accompanied me, and as we left to walk the three kilometres home, the dentist recovered sufficiently to plead, 'For God's sake, mister, give me a couple of bob if you can. There's not a penny in the house.'

Splinters of that tooth worked out of my gum for years.

The things that happened to me, through cold, insufficient food and clothing, sheer misery, were commonplace, and nothing to be compared with what was experienced by many other people.

My scholarship would have been operative at several good high schools and I had taken it for granted that I would return to school almost at once. At that time the leaving age was fourteen. But I soon found out things had changed. My education was finished.

'But why, Mum, why?'

'We can't afford it. Uniforms, books. Don't keep on at me about it. It's just the way things are.'

I thought I was going to drop dead. The air filled with black gauze.

'It's not fair!'

'And don't you dare mention it to your father while he's so ill. He's got enough to worry about. And so have I!'

Never in my life had I doubted that I was going to be a writer some day. It had been as if a voice spoke from a burning bush. Now that voice was silent. How could I be a writer if I were uneducated? Because I was a child I was in captivity, helpless before what I saw as wicked injustice.

Why my mother set her face against the utilisation of my scholarship I do not know. At this time of family misfortune the living allowance would have helped. My remaining at home in no way ameliorated the situation; legally I was too young to work, even though I did later look for work.

My mother never did explain herself. She was, I think, half out of her mind with confusion, anger and despair. Whether my father spoke up for me I don't know. Perhaps he was too ill to care.

Months before, I had received my first payment from the Department of Education to purchase the textbooks for the high school syllabus. Now I was in constant terror lest I be forced to sell them. But my mother never mentioned them, not even when she caught me studying. Her ambivalent attitude only added to my anxiety, and I went around in a stupor of apprehension lest something worse should happen.

· 3 ·

So we lived with Grandma and Poor Jack, and then the aunts in turn, big-hearted women that they were. Their husbands must have been patient, or perhaps easily cajoled. They endured Flash Jack's harrying of their cats; his loudly expressed distaste for their kids. The city must have been an awesome experience for this wide-ranging, country-bred dog, but his spirit remained as high as ever. He growled at trams and crossed the road as he wished, contemptuously barking at cars. My sister and I lived in dread that he would be run over, a prospect that harrowed us far more than that of any possible damage to the adults who swirled, quarrelled and rampaged about us. I prayed earnestly for Flash Jack's safety, now to different recipients, as the formless cosmic powers of my King Country life had dissolved like mist. It was, anyway, difficult to remain aloof from Grandma's formidable pantheon of saints. Many of these were possessed of beguiling habits; one crossed Lough Neagh on a curled-up leaf, and another, even better, used to hang his hat on a sunbeam.

I was so homesick I was ill. I was a fish out of water, but unlike that exile I was unable to die. Still, I tried. Though

I had always been so healthy as a trout, now I caught every infection that ravaged the half-starved town. Boils, abcesses, styes, earache, and a painful cough. My mother took me to the chemist. He said it was my age and my health would improve dramatically when you-know-what occurred. They spoke like that, then. I was prescribed a tonic, red, cherry-flavoured stuff called Parrish's Food. But I was poisoned by longing for my own home, a very real syndrome that I saw manifested in elderly Italian migrants to whom I tried to teach English years later in Australia.

Mera didn't like Auckland, either. I knew because, when I sat beside his bed, it was so easy for me to bring the conversation around to things we had both known in the past. I called this escapist game Going Home. Perhaps he did, as well. In our conversation, sometimes, we visited Kawhia, that Maori settlement which the old Republic had so astonished, and where we subsequently had gone for camping holidays.

'Remember the campfires on the beach at night, and the old Maoris talking, talking, and the young fellas edging up to listen!'

Yes, I remembered crouching at the edge of the fire-light, pakeha child respectfully quiet, chewing on an ember-baked potato, hearing the Maori kids whisper, 'What did he say? What does that mean?' because often the elders spoke in what was called 'old Maori' of which even Mera could understand little.

'And when you asked where the Maori people had come from, the chief sprang up, pointed to the west and shouted, "There! There!" '

When Thor Heyerdahl published his theories about the Polynesian's eastern origins, Mera thought he must have a screw loose.

'I don't believe that Hun ever actually *asked* anyone,' he said, bewildered.

In those starry and planetary evenings the wind rising on the sandhills squeaked like bats. Mera couldn't hear it, but we children could. The black sandhills, drifters, tricky and always changing, stood between the town and the west coast surf where the hot springs were. The dunes were miraculously inhabited by froglets so small they fitted in a matchbox, gaudy mites that lived a handspan down in the damp sand.

'And the old *Tainui*, the great canoe that brought the Kawhia tribe across the ocean, a thousand, two thousand years ago, still buried in that tapu grove. That's something to think of.'

What I thought of was being chased out of that sacred grove of ancient manuka by a white-haired fiend with a hatchet. How he could run for an old granddad! But I could run faster.

Thus we reeled, rather than roamed, through small familiar scenes that gave our threadbare uncertain lives a little substance.

In two or three months my father's health began to improve.

'The doctor's a sort of Hun,' said my mother doubtfully. 'But he has kind eyes.'

One of the Uncles had tracked down this man, and paid for the treatment too.

The podgy little doctor, like many others, had read in the German elections of September 1930 a signal so old, so traditional that he had not waited for its consequences.

The National Socialist Party, tolerantly regarded by the external world as a rabble of young firebrands, had won 107 seats instead of their previous fourteen. They had never kept secret their intentions for Germany and its people, so the Jewish doctor quietly left his country. He could scarcely have reached a destination further away from Berlin than Auckland.

'These Socialists,' reported my father wonderingly. 'They say they'll take over the world. Dingbats. As though anyone could, even these Nasties as he calls them.'

This doctor's treatment was simple. He put my father on a diet of milk, nothing else, pints and pints of it a day. And he coaxed Mera to talk. Sitting beside the sick man's bed, then the easy chair, then the bench in the sunny porch, he listened to his troubles.

Possibly he was a psychotherapist; who knows what those early refugee doctors were? My father began to walk. He visibly regained his strength. As soon as he got to his feet, he began to work as best he could. To earn a little money he dug people's gardens, mended their boots. They could not afford the price of leather, so Mera used scrap linoleum. This was hugely superior to the cardboard and thick paper insoles most people had to utilise. We also sometimes went to boot factories, the two or three which hadn't closed down, and for a shilling got half a sugarbag of leather offcuts with which my father patched uppers. Sugarbag days they were, for nearly every man carried one. Small, light, easily boiled, sugarbags were a godsend for 'snagging'.

Snagging was a Depression word for bargain-hunting. But in this specific case one did not snag for economy, but in order to live.

Mera did not mind lining up for leather offcuts, but it almost killed him to be forced to hunt around for cheap food.

'It makes a man wish he had gone west in the war,' he said with uncharacteristic bitterness, and I heard that other returned soldiers often said the same thing.

Such remarks filled me with foreboding. In my experience Mera didn't say things like that. I expected him to look different, gaunt and grey, because of his illness, but I was not old enough to understand why he should *be* different from his ruddy, cheerful, King Country self. Passionately I longed to say the right things to him, to get back on the old best friend footing. But I didn't know what to say. No matter what I thought of, it seemed trifling, inappropriate, so I remained silent.

'You'd better stop sulking around Daddy,' my mother advised me. 'It's not his fault all this has happened. He's got enough to put up with without you adding to it.'

How to explain, when I was inarticulate already? She had forgotten, I suppose, that the most lasting pain in children is not only secret, but dumb.

How strange it was that in those times no one told the children the total truth about anything. Do they now? We guessed, speculated foolishly, eavesdropped and snooped. We were often bewildered and terrified. In random periods of détente, we cousins conferred in whispers, became angry, argued. One boy got it into his head that his parents were about to divorce; they had said this, looked that way, wrote letters to people he had never heard of, such as solicitors. What would become of him? He saw himself abandoned, helpless, in an orphanage. His misery drove him into all kinds of witless delinquencies, born solely of fear.

His parents were baffled. 'What's come over the little devil?' the devoted couple asked each other, as they proceeded with the sale of their house.

So we children blundered along, not knowing where we were going, fobbed off with evasive or facetious remarks, not sure where trouble lay, but feeling in our bones it lay somewhere.

Almost timorously I offered to take over most of the snagging.

'I don't mind,' I lied. 'It's all experience. A writer has to have experience.'

No one laughed at this inflated announcement. Either

they goodheartedly refrained from saying that dreams wouldn't do me any harm, or they were too distraught to pay attention.

'Maybe you'll use it in a book someday,' comforted my mother. But in fact I never have until now, mostly because I never thought twice about it. Snagging was what we did in order to keep alive until times got better. Some people, including my father, felt demeaned by it, but to me it was merely a device with which to lick illness and bad luck, or whatever it was that had put us on the bottom of the ladder.

This excellent philosophy by no means prevented me from feeling self-conscious, conspicuous and obscurely angry as I stood in the queue outside the Weetbix factory, where in due course the godly Sanitarium people sold us each a sugarbag full of fresh crumbs for sixpence. What I was peeved about I do not know, certainly not about the fact that I had to stand there, or 'the times', or anything else that would indicate the dawning of social consciousness. I think my anger was fired by plain discomfort, wet shoes, numbing winds and the metronomic sniffing of the man in front of me.

Many of the same people turned up each morning. We became sick of each other's faces. In a half-vengeful manner I snagged amongst them as well, picking up a cauliflower ear there, a bulldog jaw here. There were many awful false teeth, blue as if with cold, and untended squints, or casts as they were called then. I fancy that if you were born with something crooked, it stayed crooked your entire life. One man had a preposterous nose, pushed entirely sideways. It hadn't ruined his life at all. He was a cocky fellow, who, catching someone gaping, explained genially that the doctor had done it with his spanner when he was born. This man, far from being shy, had the nerve to complain if the famed crepitation of the Weetbix crumbs wasn't up to scratch. I later gave this bentnosed character to D'Arcy Niland, but other snaggers' attributes appeared in due course in my own stories, as did the unforgettable odour of people wearing aged garments from secondhand shops and St Vincent de Paul's repository – wintergreen, mothballs, stale tobacco, and sad personal smells from unknown lives.

Weetbix harvested, we hastened to the Marmite factory. Carrot pulp, that was, a big billycan full for threepence. The bakery was probably glad to get rid of two-day-old loaves for twopence each. The jam factory offered only more carrot pulp, and no matter how often your mother tells you it's good for your eyesight, it palls. Occasionally a batch of burned or mouldy jam was passed out the back door of the factory, but this did not interest our family. Other snaggers had doubts, too.

'You don't never want to eat raspberry,' a toothless lady advised me. 'They make the pips on a machine, out of old boxes, like. Them pips jam up your chubes like nobody's business.'

What a lot we were, down at heel, shabby, perished with cold most of the time, and yet ostentatiously cheerful. This was called *cracking hardy*.

'Can't last for ever!'

'Nah, course it won't. Even the war ended after five years.'

'Long as you're all together, that's what I say.'

'Dunno about that. We got Grandpa and Grandma now, both a bit dippy. The wife whinges a lot.'

· 4 ·

At this time a good thing happened; we got a place to ourselves, three rooms behind an elderly fruitshop in Eden
Terrace. What did my father think of my mother's joy at
moving into this eccentric, rickety dump? I saw the look
on his face, but he said nothing. Did he understand that
her happiness was only because she had so hated being a
burden to her mother and sisters? No matter how loyal
the kinsfolk, how generous in times difficult for them as
well, there is always the afflicting sense of obligation, of
the indecency of simply being there, at their tables, in their
bathrooms, in their lives.

Once again an uncle was involved. His was the fruitshop. In fact, he was an illegal bookmaker, a dashing thing
in the eyes of us children, so that we admired him no end.
Occasionally he was raided, noisy stormings by bulky
gentlemen referred to as The D's. But Uncle Roley had
a friend at Court, a Judas cop who rang him when a raid
was imminent. They had a code. The Judas said 'Beer!'
and Uncle Roley said 'Bottles!' Then the warning was
delivered.

As I grew older, in busy times I sometimes acted as bookmaker's clerk, and answered the phone. Alarmed, the
policeman croaked, 'Who's that?'

'I'm Bottles' niece,' I said.

'Oh, that's all right then,' he said innocently. 'Tell
him . . .'

Our new home had pressed metal ceilings four metres

high, and walls padded with twelve layers of wallpaper. When Mera pulled it off, it was like an archeological dig. In the end we got down into Victorian wallpaper like crimson flannel, embossed with dim golden fleurs-de-lys.

As he could not afford new wallpaper, Mera papered the walls with newspaper and calsomined it white. The effect was fresh and light, and I thought it beautiful.

The coal range was so old and rusted it was unusable; my mother cooked on a gas ring. In every room the roof leaked; once I saw my mother in bed, tranquilly reading, a pie-dish on her chest to catch the plink-plonk from the ceiling.

'It doesn't matter,' she explained. 'Anything, as long as we're by ourselves.'

On the single gas ring this good cook became a culinary genius. Stale bread, soaked in water and rebaked in the big saucepan, became fresh once more. With the addition of a pennyworth of soup bones and a few onions, carrot pulp became delicious soup. Weetbix, versatile and wholesome, turned into meatloaf, with the addition of grated onion, cheese, and a half a pound of mince meat at threepence a pound. Weetbix were also the heart and soul of boiled puddings, with chopped suet, carrot pulp, fruit from the greengrocer, who must have been fed to the back teeth with the repeated cry of every child in the neighbourhood . . . any specks, mister?

Yet, although we had enough – and more than many other families – the food was not nourishing enough. I always felt half-hungry or a little faint. My grandmother summed it up well, 'God knows you feel full, and God knows you feel empty as well.' She knew what she was talking about; as a youth her father John McBride had seen people eating grass in the Great Famine.

In an unacknowledged way I became less unhappy. Perhaps it was just being a child, for compared with my cousins of the same age I was still very much a child. As Ingmar Bergman so perceptively says, 'The prerogative of childhood is to move unhindered between magic and oatmeal porridge.' Though I had mourned that the magic of my early life was gone, I now tried unconsciously to find other magic in the porridge. Probably the landscape spoke to me, as all landscapes do – the mouldering Victorian semi-suburb, the higgledy-piggledy old working-class timber houses; closed, falling-down factories; our own row of shops, each leaning against its neighbour, the ones at the ends in parlous straits. Fantastically steep side streets spilled down from the west side of Eden Terrace, into a rift valley so deep that at sunset wraithlike mist rose from the dying creek in its depths.

I wrote constantly, in my head if not on paper, of which there was little. My ambition was to own a big sixpenny writing pad, and somehow my parents managed to get me one for my birthday. I developed a new style of writing; very tall, skinny letters, so I could get more words to the line, and it says a lot for Miss Elsie K. Morton that she not only read this mediaeval handwriting but continued to publish my stories in her children's page.

My little world, now that I had opened myself to it, was far from dull.

Now that we did not have to live with them, I enjoyed often seeing my aunts. Sometimes they blew in for a fight, not with my mother, who placidly went on with whatever she was doing at the time, but with each other. They were extraordinarily adept at picking up secondary and probably non-existent meanings in commonplace remarks.

What do you mean by that, I'd like to know?

Oh, yes, I'm perfectly familiar with *that* wiggle of your eyebrows, never fear!

Of all the two-faced articles . . .

Flushed faces, flashing eyes, and eventual tears and

hugs – this was the order of things. Then they'd turn to me and say, 'Aren't we awful? Don't you pay any attention, lovey, we're just awful.'

They were still creatures of mystery to me. Their airy obliqueness puzzled and enchanted me, as I suspect it did their menfolk. But even then I recognised echoes of their common personality in myself; there was something edgy and disconcerting about us all.

A couple of years later, when I turned into the usual fourteen-year-old old-fogey, knowing everything and terminally critical of everyone else, I began slowly to recognise their highly coloured faults, their jealousies, self-indulgent dramatics, and loving but fierce tyranny over husbands and children. But when I first lived in the city, what they meant to me was kindness and laughter.

In their eagerness to give us a gladsome experience, two of them hauled Grandma and me to the zoo. Then, as now, I was against the caging of animals, and Grandma declared definitively that she'd get more uproar in Confession. Still, off we went. A grand day was enjoyed by all until Theresa got it into her head that we should crown our pleasure with a ride on Jamuna the elephant.

How anyone got Grandma on an elephant is beyond human comprehension. But they did and we rose into the air about twenty metres, the aunties shrieking with merriment and Grandma and myself blue in the face with funk.

This Jamuna had lived in Auckland almost for ever; she was part of civic history, renowned for her sweet, docile disposition.

So we gently swayed round and about the gravel paths, hello to the lions, and hi there to the emu, and I was almost beginning to enjoy it. Then Rosina became bored with Jamuna's deliberate speed, majestic instancy, and fetched her a corker on the ear with her parasol.

The old lady was deeply affronted. Turning, she proceeded into her bathing pool, where, despite the hysterical shouts of her attendant, she knelt down and prepared to roll.

'Jump! Jump!'

How we soared! Grandma flew, as she put it, like a Holy Soul between two angels, her daughters each seizing an arm. She fell face down in the somewhat murky water. Still, she was splendid, grabbing Theresa by the collar and hoicking her upright, slapping Rosie across the face and curing her hysterics in midflight. After some disagreeable shouting from the zoo staff, we got a taxi and went home. The driver charged double fare for making his cab wet and funny-smelling.

'I enjoyed it more than words can tell,' said Rosina sincerely, though several days later.

Sadly, I missed George Bernard Shaw's visit to Auckland, but I was present at Mr Bosco's Final Fit.

Mrs Bosco ran the haberdashery business three doors down. She was a woman whom Life didn't like. Her husband had a silver plate in his head – his kiss-me-foot from Gallipoli, she called it – and when he wasn't having a fit, he often sat out in the sunshine on the back steps and quietly sobbed for hours on end. As well as Mr Bosco, Mrs Bosco looked after her aged father, who, inexplicably, always walked backwards. He had a fat dog, and if he went into a shop, his custom was to put the dog for safety into the nearest rubbish bin. I often saw concerned passersby clucking about dreadful people who threw away dogs in rubbish bins. Then the old man would come out of the shop, walking backwards, and they would go away quickly.

The haberdashery shop did not provide a living income, and the little woman, prematurely withered, always with bits of cotton in her hair, made corsets for one of the big stores in the city. My father called her a harness-maker, and my mother said, 'Oh, you be quiet, what do you know!' very annoyed.

The shop for which Mrs Bosco did piecework sent her boxes of lolly pink coutil, accompanied by blueprints, and she sewed the bits together on her heavy duty machine, which I often heard roaring away in the middle of the night. The thick coutil upset me a good deal more than Mr Bosco did; it was terrible to think that I might some day have to wear something like that myself.

Mr Bosco, getting worse, began shouting in the night. Once I came into our kitchen to find his wife sitting there, painful tears oozing from her tired eyes, slow as syrup.

'I can't bring myself to put him away, Mrs Park,' she said. 'When he's all right he begs me not to. Oh, God, why do men have to go to war?'

She had looked after him for seventeen years, and the almost senile old father for ten.

'I've had no life, Mrs Park,' she said. 'I don't suppose I should complain about it, but that's the truth. Charlie joined up only six weeks after we married. No, I've had no life. None.'

But a fortnight later Mr Bosco fell down in a fit outside the shop door. Uncle Roley put a rolled-up handkerchief between his teeth; I ran to call Mrs Bosco, and my mother rang the doctor. The poor old father stood by, agitatedly putting his dog in and out of the rubbish bin. When it was all over, people clumsily patted Mrs Bosco's back in the way they have.

'It's all for the best, dear, it really is.'

But I could tell that Mrs Bosco wasn't sure at all.

'Thank God I've still got the Dad,' she said.

· 5 ·

I was grieved that I had missed Bernard Shaw. My mother
saw him by accident when she was returning from Mass.
On that sleepy Sunday morning he was strolling along,
looking at this and that, my mother said. I bombarded her
with twenty, thirty questions. A Famous Writer! How I
longed to see one. I thought GBS would look different from
everyone else, a golden luminosity about him.

'What did he look like, what?'

My mother considered. 'He was a well-scrubbed old
cockalorum,' she said thoughtfully, 'with frightful teeth.'

'How ever did you see his teeth, Mum?'

'It was when he shouted "Shoo!" '

We had now found out about the Public Library, and
sometimes I was permitted to walk to the city to spend
the afternoon there. Because my father was not a ratepayer
I could not join the lending library but the reference
section, old and ill-stocked as it was, was paradise.

For the first time in my life I had access to real books,
classics, poetry, non-fiction. I got drunk on those books,
staggering home in the freezing spring afternoons scarcely
knowing where I was. Away with Thomas Campbell and
other disastrous versifiers of St Joseph's, Te Kuiti! Now
I could read Homer, Emerson, Browning, Francis Bacon,
John Clare and Gerard Manley Hopkins, who surely must
have crept into that dusty impoverished library by mistake.

There is a certain madness in a child such as I was, all
of a sudden bemused by literary genius, dazzled and

blinded. I copied long extracts of prose, learned poems by heart, reciting them as I walked home in a trance of bliss and excitement.

On Library days I often walked from Wellesley Street down to the *New Zealand Herald* office, a humdrum grey pile, but glamorous in my eyes, for there worked Miss Elsie K. Morton, my idol. Not that I thought of her as actually *working*. A gentle word here, a masterly stroke of the pen there, and obediently would appear the children's page which had meant so much to me since the age of eight.

I used to look at the windows and wonder which one concealed this divinity. I would no more have attempted to call upon her than I would upon the grey-eyed Hera. (I had recently discovered Charles Kingsley and *The Heroes*.) It was enough to know that Miss Morton was there.

But Auckland and I still had no connection. The city was where I lived, not where I was. I knew the way to Grandma's house, St Benedict's Church, the Library. These places were a scatter of islands in an unknown sea about which I had no curiosity. Still faithful to the King Country wilderness, and beyond that to my original godparent, the forest, I turned my eyes away from all that was seductive in the town – art nouveau glass, its tulips and curlicues panelling doors and windows; white bungalows built of heart of kauri, incorruptible hardwood, the finest in the world, we were told; steep backyards, almost perpendicular backyards that only a dog or a chicken could traverse without falling, and so were left to hide themselves under honeysuckle, and cascades of blue convolvulus that Grandma called Marygown.

The only building at which I looked, and that with painful envy, was St Benedict's School, which my sister would attend when she turned six. Plain as a box, the building looked across Symonds Street cemetery to old

Partington's Mill, its stationary sails skeletal, fretted by fire. I always took a shortcut through the cemetery, a charming oasis, and a strange one to find almost in the centre of the city. It seemed to have experienced a downpour of snowdrops, so prolific was the growth of wild garlic, which we children called onionflower. Amongst the respectable white gravestones I marched, reciting 'The Hound of Heaven' or 'The Blessed Damozel' in my head, aware of the thousands of untold stories that lay under the moist, flowery earth and wondering whether mine would be untold as well.

In this dreamy state of mind, the tensions in the family, the hushed arguments that my sister and I heard through the bedroom wall, seemed to me to be cheepings in the distance. But my sister, a sensitive child, often wept with distress or foreboding.

So it was with a sickening shock that I heard the words, 'How would you like to go and live with Auntie Win?'

'Go *away*? From *everybody*?'

'Just till things get better.'

I saw through them, yes I did. And I was outraged. Until things got better! That was like the snaggers talking about when their ships came in. I was grievously humiliated to learn that my own family could not afford to keep me. I was to be given away like a parcel, and to people who possibly didn't want me. Like all girls I blamed my mother for this ignominy, as everyone knew that men didn't understand things the way women did.

My mother tried to placate me, unpicked a couple of old auntie dresses, and made them up in different patterns for me. She told me earnestly how much I'd enjoy Glen Afra.

'It's only for a while until we get on our feet again. And you love Auntie Win, you know you do!'

Glen Afra was situated on the Firth of Thames, on the tail end of the Hauraki Gulf. To me it was as distant as the Antarctic. Until the previous year or so it had been inaccessible except by scow and barge. It was remote from the world. I thought vengefully of killing myself – jumping under a tram, chewing through the electric iron cord.

'Don't make a fuss,' said Mera. 'Be a good sport. It's the best thing for you just now. You understand how bad things are. Gee, I'll miss you,' he added dolefully.

In spite of my plans to leave this world in a shower of blue sparks, that made me feel a little better. But it didn't last. I was desolate. So I went around with a tragic face that must have driven everyone crazy, until I caught a glimpse of it in a mirror and stopped.

'Can I take Flash Jack?'

'Not to a sheep station. Not that little gangster of a dog. The Big Noise would have a fit.'

Glen Afra was the property of a Brigadier.

'Bound to be a Hun,' said Mera, whose hatred for war was equalled by his contempt for staff officers. 'Wore out the seat of his pants at H.Q., more than likely.'

In fact the Brigadier had a notable war record. He was a handsome old man who patrolled his property on an Arab gelding, wore riding breeches (Hun pants) and boots which, rumour said, his valet polished with a bone.

'Human bone probably,' I was to hear my Aunt Wendela say.

But the Brigadier had a lordly persona. You would never have guessed he was as mean as catsmeat.

Though never much of a weeper, the prospect of exile to Glen Afra caused me to spend many a night snorting and snuffling into my pillow. My little sister, a sympathetic child, whispered, 'At least you won't have to see *them*, for ages and ages.'

They were my boy cousins. It had been purgatory living with them, and even knowing them. Unfortunately they had almost all reached the psychological no man's land of male adolescence. They had awakened one morning to find they didn't fit their bodies any more and everything that had been good and interesting now was not. Some of them existed permanently in a speechless state of sulk; others were unable to cope with everyday life except by spitting, barking, blurting and fighting. The world was incomprehensible to them and their view of it incomprehensible to everyone else. Being a girl, a near-stranger, and above all the reluctant possessor of a pair of walnut-sized breasts, I was teased ruthlessly.

Given my vocabulary, I could have shut them up with brutal descriptions of their own physical shortcomings, and many such sentences did I rehearse. But I was forbidden to defend myself.

'We owe so much to Auntie and Uncle. Please, *please* don't say anything. Just walk away.'

'There's nowhere to walk to! It's Fraser's house!'

'Yes, that's the point, you see.' My mother was melancholy. 'But surely Fraser isn't too dreadful, that dear little boy?'

'He's the rottenest human being in the whole world.'

'Well, whatever he is, you have to learn to be a good sport.'

'Why do I have to be a good sport? People are always asking me to be a good sport. No one ever asks *them* to be good sports and leave me alone, the pigs.'

My mother sighed. 'Just because.'

At the time I did not connect my mother's maddening reply with Sister Serenus's astute remarks about girls and the world at large.

Nor, for that matter, did I consider that the boys may have intensely disliked my family cluttering up their houses

· 129 ·

and lives, and that the only one of the intruders that they could kick was me.

The young Fraser, a handsome little fellow with courtly manners and eyes like blue stars, had been born old and demonic. Sophisticated to a degree, he understood and could manipulate adults. When they were still a big jabbering enigma to me, he had caught on. He understood their elliptic speech, their meaning looks.

All we children hated him. He was the kind who watched, smiling approvingly, while the rest of us golloped that rare treat, an ice cream. When it was all gone, he would offer us a lick of his, at a penny a swipe.

He also kept a pet beard. It was a tiny dog of fantastic hairiness and unlimited powers of repose. When it walked one discerned not a single canine feature, merely hair. But it never walked. Fraser always carried it. Instead of a security blanket he had this security beard.

Yes, I would be grateful to get away from Fraser. The relief almost balanced my already active homesickness for my family, my dread of Flash Jack's being run over, my inescapable feeling that I was being disposed of. If they could keep Flash Jack, why couldn't they keep me? And the Library! Now that I had found it, that treasure-house, how would I live without it?

How could I write at Glen Afra? They read no news-papers except in fortnightly lumps, when one of the men drove into Clevedon for stores and the mail. So I wouldn't be able to see the *Herald* children's pages or learn about competitions. How could I get stamps to post away stories and poems? In the city we children sometimes followed drunks around until they threw down their bottles. A penny a bottle, a penny a stamp.

'Ah, Christ, lemme alone, willya, kids? Take the flaming bottle!'

We used to marvel that they didn't redeem the bottles

themselves. Surely pennies were as valuable to these drunken men as they were to us? It never occurred to us they were being kindly.

One of our uncles worked for the Civil Service, and although he, like all his colleagues, had received severe cuts in pay, we regarded him as the luckiest of men. Imagine! In work all through the Slump! Never stood down for a single day!

This uncle later caused me a great deal of anguish when, in his middle years, he turned into a Peeping Tom with me as the object. But he did a thoughtful thing that Christmas I was sent south to Glen Afra and, as I thought, intellectual banishment.

He brought from his office a gladstone bag, which businessmen carried instead of brief cases. It was full of Government forms. There were forms for complaints, tenders, evictions, queries about the unconscionable number of pencils certain departments were using.

The backs of these forms were blank.

'I thought,' said Uncle diffidently, 'that you could write stories on them.'

The excitement! Life changed immediately. My heart filled with hope and my head, instantly reacting, with ideas.

My little sister cried, and Flash Jack, with the second sight common to all dogs and most cats, lay down in my suitcase and tried to look as if he were dying. But now I accepted that I wasn't going away for ever; it would only be for a while; I might get back to school sometime, and my father was becoming his old self again. And I had paper to write on.

· 6 ·

'Aren't you lucky there's a road now!'

This road was a potholed, ill-graded clay track, hewn out by gangs of relief workers. At the worst places it was corduroy – rows of small tree trunks hammered down into the mud.

I had a companion on the long journey, an angelic Border collie in pup to an expensive sire. We travelled with two new station workers, the single men's cook and his offsider, in a rare vehicle. It was called a Trojan, and my memory, possibly at fault, is that its axles were somehow driven by chains. Moss and I shared the boot, or, as it was called, the dickey.

Always susceptible to travel-sickness, before an hour had passed I was puking over the side. Ten kilometres on, the moist green countryside, twigged with creeks and branched with rivers, was turning round and round and lost dimension. The trees bent down, became clouds, and walked away by themselves over the swelling or shrinking hills. Moss was asleep, I thought. In fact she was unconscious. No one had thought we were only a few centimetres from the exhaust.

At Glen Afra I managed to fall out of the dickey seat by myself. All I could see in the lamplight was a crowd of wavering booted legs.

'What's the matter? What's up with the kid?'

Almost at once Moss began to miscarry, and as each hairless little blue body appeared, the Brigadier groaned,

'There goes another sixty guineas!'

Auntie Wendela took charge of Moss, and nursed her back to health. Although she produced many champions in her life, she was never again the brilliant worker she had been. The carbon monoxide had affected her brain. Nobody investigated my brain, so I presume it remained normal.

I dare not return to the Hauraki Gulf in case time, progress and 'they' have changed it. It was a place where you could truly see that there once had been a morning of the world, and here things hadn't moved on even to midday.

The light was different there, clear as water, making nothing of distance, like a sword, a sharp sword, laying the sky bare. There was blue in it somewhere, the fainting blue of water sliding over a limestone bed.

The landscape, too, had the profound sensuousness of country never built on by mankind. From the end of the eighteenth century Europe had plundered it for timber, masts, spars, flax for cordage, kauri gum for resin; gold, silver, copper, coal and lesser minerals. Europe had destroyed the peerless kauri forests, left the swamps and river flats savaged as if a mob of pigs had rooted there. But no cities had been built, and so the country was able to reclothe itself, cleanse its streams, and set up new forests.

'You can run wild for a few days,' said Auntie Wendela, holding the lamp high in Helga's little room. 'And then . . .'

'What, Auntie?'

'Uncle Hugo will teach you French and Latin and anything else he can remember. There!' She was as pleased as a child with her news.

My mother had told her of my passionate desire to return to school! This realisation filled me with joy; she understood after all. I had brought all my textbooks, intending to study as much as I could. But I had forgotten my Uncle's exceptional education, and never realised his goodwill. It was a miracle.

Helga muttered querulously. She didn't want me in her small, film-star papered room.

'Keep your head off Joan Crawford!' she snapped. 'Move the blanket away from Gary Cooper!'

She was a good-natured girl but set in her solitary ways. When I knew she was asleep I slid from my bed and crept through the house, which smelled hauntingly of wood-smoke. I longed to see the Gulf, for I had never lived near the sea.

Out there, its voice filled the sky, a vast whisper as the Pacific tide welled luxuriously into the sunken rift valley, past the barbed or bearded islands, the bays and peninsulas, the cockle sands. Darkness, darkness, the Coromandel Range a darker wall to the east, faint blurs of little settlements across the water, their lights so ambiguous that if I blinked they were gone. A cloud blew apart, and instantly a string of reflected moons swam along the breakers and exploded on the beach.

'A flicker of fractured moons,' I thought, and almost choked with pleasure. At last I had made up a line that was *right*.

Back in bed, I said the words over and over to myself, absorbed in that mysterious exaltation which attends creativity, however small. Impossible to explain to the uncreative, but 'when it comes,' as Mozart said 'ah, what bliss!'

'Quit muttering,' complained Helga, 'and if you put your feet on Charles Boyer I'll kill you.'

· 7 ·

Uncle Hugo began my lessons the next week. His Latin was classic, the pronunciation strange to my Catholic ears. His French was Canadian, his English impeccable. He enjoyed these lessons as much as I did. He admitted his brain had been shrivelling into an old potato in remote Glen Afra.

'But there you are!' he said complacently. 'La vie s'arrange!'

Glen Afra must have driven that lively worldly man berserk. I don't believe he would have remained there for a week if it had not been for the Depression. The job, meanly paid as it was, was secure; it provided his family with a house, firewood, meat and milk. Clever all-rounder as he was, he was simply marking time until the economic situation readjusted itself.

It was a diversion for him to be able to pass on some of his education to an absorbent sponge of a child. He was a strict teacher; there was no goofing off with Uncle Hugo.

He did me a world of good in many ways. His family crest was *Contra Mundum*, and I thought I might adopt it for myself. However, as he cautioned me, to be against the world isn't the best thing.

'What you have to be against, and watch out for, are the villains in the world. And, by jove, there are plenty of 'em.'

I promised I would do so, though not at all sure I'd recognise them.

From that time my life changed for the better. My longing for the King Country, Roha and the house in Nettie Street dissolved like a cloud. I never felt it again. Added to Glen Afra's pleasures was the fortnightly mail. I had never received letters before, and they became an anticipatory joy. My father wrote weekly, my mother less. Hers were full of anxieties about me, no swimming in deep water, no getting lost in the bush; his were full of jokes. That year was one of the worst Depression years. Times at home must have been devastatingly bad. My father had obtained two days a week on relief work, busy work most of it, draining swamps, shifting sandhills, slashing blackberries. He earned scarcely enough to pay the rent. In 1931 the registered unemployed were 50,000, a ludicrous figure. The actual number, considering the compulsorily excluded, was more like 180,000.

For many years after the Depression had become merely a bad memory, relics of relief work showed like unidentifiable ruins on the countryside; half-finished tunnels; long grassy hummocks of spoil from swamps where drainage had been abandoned; stone walls around the houses of important people – like those stone walls which marked the passage of the Great Famine in Ireland in the previous century.

The irony was that at this time of desperate hardship, the Government continued to pay off overseas loans instead of investing its money in necessary public works, which would have employed men by the thousand.

'A gang of jellyheads,' said Mera in a letter. 'We ought to line them up and shoot them.'

Who would guess, in peaceful, sedate New Zealand, that such a time was approaching, or close enough anyway?

My solitary cousin Helga moved by day in a constant squall, growl and grumble of animals. They found her irresistible. When she passed, horses leaned over fences and mooned at her; her pet sheep, a monstrous heap of unredeemed wool and mutton, would have slept on her bed had he been allowed. She cared for, fed and groomed three sheep dogs and four breeding Labradors, belonging to the Brigadier but being trained as gun dogs by Uncle Hugo. She had rescued and reared two wildcat kittens whose mother had got her head caught in a salmon tin and died of starvation. These fierce atoms lived in trees near the house and let no one touch them but Helga.

For the first time I lived with enough animals, though I came fifth or sixth with them.

Still, Senta the goat despised everyone at Glen Afra but me.

This creature, black and shiny as a cricket, dominated the four-legged population. Dogs turned craven, horses wheeled sternfirst and got their back legs in position for lashing out. Sheep she reduced to huddled masses; she had a fearsome habit of getting up on her elegant hind legs and *walking* at them. Once I saw her hammering with her front hoofs on the bony head of a huge merino ram which had dared to mildly challenge her.

She ate humans' washing, ravaged their gardens, monstered their children. She also came fishing with me in the dinghy, sitting on her tailbone in the stern with her two back legs sticking up and her front legs planted between them. Hours passed this way, myself fishing and dreaming, and Senta chewing placidly on a lump of dried seaweed and gazing into the depths.

At Glen Afra I was permitted to explore at will, spend whole days in the bush on the ranges, visit the few remaining Maori families in that depopulated countryside. Aunt Wendela's wholesome philosophy about her many child guests was that if you were older than nine and got into trouble, serve you damn well right.

The only place out of bounds, aside from the bunkhouse, and the Brigadier's grand residence and its gardens, was the relief workers' camp. This was now three kilometres down the road, slowly advancing towards Glen Afra. The gang was grading and surfacing the clay track cut through by previous relief workers, and it was common belief that the Brigadier had somehow cozened the bigwigs in the Department of Works into extending the road free through a couple of kilometres of his private property.

It was tit for tat, I think, as certainly he frequently sent fresh meat, potatoes and even the occasional bag of flour to the camp. The camp itself was a miserable row of tents; a portable cookhouse of timber slab, with a chimney made of beaten-out kerosene tins; a latrine of tall teatree bush lashed to uprights. I knew because Senta and I often sat on the hill above the camp and observed, partly because it was forbidden territory and mostly because of curiosity.

There were sometimes blazing fights and scuffles, men threatening each other with pick handles. They were feverish with discontent and resentment of a world which had treated them unjustly.

Auntie Wendela would have killed me if she'd discovered I knew a lot more about the relief workers than other people did.

One afternoon Uncle Hugo came home in a state of excitement.

'You'll never guess!' he said. 'Who's working at the relief camp, I mean. The one and only James Douglas Stark! The famous Starkie!' he added as we gazed without comprehension.

He then went into the cantankerous mode adopted by all human beings whose great news has fallen flat.

'I've told you a thousand times, Win. That extraordinary fellow who *kept doing things* during the war. He was the talk of the Army. Yes, I did tell you. Starkie! At Gallipoli, and in France too. Even in the Imperial Army we heard of him. And at Gallipoli I helped carry him off after he'd been wounded the second time. Amazing blighter, used to go out alone into No Man's Land on what he called hunts . . . with a bowie knife.'

'That's enough, in front of the girls, too,' snapped Auntie Wendela. 'And what's more I have to punch up the bread.'

With that she turned the dough out of its warm basin and began thumping the blazes out of it.

But of course I persuaded Uncle Hugo to enlarge on this fascinating subject.

'Why do you want to know?' he asked, for he too had strong opinions on what should interest girls.

'I want to tell Dad, of course. He might even know about this Mr Stark.'

'Oh, every soldier knows about Starkie! He was a pain in the neck to the Army bigwigs, but just the same he was the sort of hero you come across only once in a lifetime.'

From his abstracted look I could see that this daredevil had profoundly impressed my Uncle Hugo. Starkie was a man who did everything other soldiers were sensibly reluctant to do.

Auntie Win, however, continued punching the dough, muttering things like 'You men! Why make a hero out of *that* kind of fellow? No judgement, that's your trouble,' and so on.

Even at that age I had observed that ladies' heroes and men's heroes were completely different in style. But probably through Mera's useful influence, I had an open mind.

'Would it have entered our heads,' Uncle Hugo queried us in a general fashion, 'to cut some of the capers he's famous for? No, it would not. Can you imagine me jumping into a German machine-gun nest armed with an axe handle? Or stalking and killing a clever devil of a sniper nearly a third of a mile from my home lines? That's the kind of thing Starkie thrived on. And he was an escapee from a French military prison at the time, I might add! But instead of going underground like any man with brains he attached himself to the British Army. Mad as a hatter!'

'It's a wonder he wasn't killed.'

'Wounded thirty-seven times, he was. By Jove, what a wild hawk of a man! Not an outlaw, as some people said at the time, just a queer bird with an uncontrollable hero streak.'

Later that evening Aunt Wendela cautioned me privately.

'No funny stuff, kiddo. I know what a stickybeak you are. No hanging around the relief camp hoping to get a glimpse of that man. The men don't want kids poking about. Anyway, it's probably all tales, what Uncle told us. You know how he is about the Army.'

She made me promise. She had got it into her head that here was a dangerous eccentric, a savage of some kind. After all, Starkie was half Red Indian, so it was said, and as far as my auntie was concerned, he might well have a fancy for scalps.

Interestingly, as far as I know Uncle Hugo never made himself known to Starkie at the relief camp, nor did any other of his admirers amongst the men. Nor did I ever see any of the relief workers on the beach close to Glen Afra land. The Brigadier had probably issued a stern No Fraternising order, and everyone knew he was quite capable of firing on the spot any man who transgressed it.

· 8 ·

I knew Wendela better than the other aunts and loved her best, even before I overheard her magnificent statement that I would always have a home with her. She blew her top frequently and chased Helga and me around the house yelling picturesque imprecations, but, as with Grandma, for me this melodrama merely added to her charm. She also had black Swedish depressions, during which she moped, was snappy with Uncle Hugo, and wept inconsolably. Like my mother in the King Country, she was homesick for her mother and sisters, and could not come to terms with it. She was not happy in the country.

'Sheep and cows, pigs and chooks. I'll go dotty! No, I won't, I'll bake a batch of scones instead.'

That year she turned thirty-nine, but was still at the height of her beauty. Skittish and eccentric, she was also as proud as Lucifer, resentful of any slight.

For this reason, certain social situations at Glen Afra really stuck in her teeth.

The Brigadier and his lady brought out the worst in her. She did not hesitate to put forward arguable reasons for her eloquent dislike. They were English (wrongs of Ireland); foully rich (this was true. Each was wealthy independently, and like so many wealthy people, became more so during the Slump); never recognised her (Good morning, Mrs Umm); patronised everyone on the station; thought they were Lord and Lady Muck; ordered Helga around as if she were a skivvy; and you just wait, my girl, until she sees *you*.

Uncle Hugo, that imperturbable man, understanding the British gentry so much better, and not giving a hoot, always managed to laugh her out of it. But even I could see that Glen Afra was an extraordinary establishment, pure Angela Thirkell, or perhaps extracted bodily from Queen Alexandra's Gift Book. The Brigadier's house dominated a man-made rise, and was referred to as The Big House. The maids wore caps and aprons, bobbed curtseys, and addressed their mistress as Madame. The Brigadier was Brigadier, sir. Alas for the good man's desire for respect in his own little kingdom – out on the hills, or in the smoky privacy of the bunkhouse, these two grand people became Bugalugs and Ma Bugalugs.

A strict military hierarchy prevailed at Glen Afra. Those men in responsible positions were English and ex-Army; all were addressed according to rank. A captain ran the store, a major kept accounts; Uncle Hugo, though the most valuable man about the place, scraped in as Sergeant-Major. Corporals and privates were simply Ted and Doug, even to us kids.

There were also several young men, jackeroos, or, as the Brigadier dignified them, cadets. He imported these porcelain-faced lads direct from Home. Quickly they turned into roast-beef faces, and either remained and became regular fellows or hared back to England aghast. I sometimes wondered what became of them and whether their memories of the Hauraki Gulf at the end of the world seemed like dream or nightmare.

Naturally enough, they all longed to find sweet romance with Helga, the only girl on the station, and a very pretty one as well.

No luck. The sight of a young man bounding up the hillside was enough to send Helga through the back door, to take to the hills with the dogs. How disappointing it was! I was at the age when I wanted to observe someone fall in love, just to find out how it was done.

Helga's disdain of men became legendary. Once or twice I ventured to ask my cousin why, but she only glowered and remained silent. Years later I learned from a chatterbox aunt that when Helga was thirteen she had been jumped by a rashly lustful stationhand who dragged her into the cookhouse, all a-tremble to work his will behind the chopping-block. No harm was done, because in her terror Helga seized a frying pan and nearly beat his brains out. According to the chatterbox aunt he was carted away with his tongue hanging out.

Ignorant of this drama, I was puzzled why Auntie Wendela was so complacent about Helga's abhorrence of mankind. I see now that she was nervous for her daughter, and so closed her mind to the strong possibility of a lonely future for the girl.

'Blow the future, it's the present I'm worried about,' she probably said to herself.

So the yearning for romance, the tender susceptibilities of Helga's heart were directed towards the movies. A world of icons, they dominated her life. Able to visit Auckland only once or twice a year, she spent the entire day sitting in a cinema. For months afterwards she could retell those films scene by scene.

'Oh, that gorgeous Marlene!'

We pronounced it Marleen, of course, as did everyone else. And there were Greeta Garbo and Carolee Lombard. I hadn't seen any of these ladies, and listened spellbound to Helga's detailed recountals, which were, after all, stories. My cousin had stacks of film magazines; they were all she read. She drew new mouths and eyebrows on herself; now I'm Ginger and now I'm Constance, who am I now?

The poor young thing had nothing in her life that other pretty girls had. I didn't either, but I had my Work. I wrote every spare minute, continuing at night by candlelight until Helga turned over and groaned, 'You're the worst nuisance! I never thought I'd say it, but I'll be glad when Fraser comes to stay.'

'WHAT!'

'Next week. And you've got your great hoofs on poor Charles again.'

I felt as sick as a dog. No sooner had I slipped into the ways of Glen Afra, happy with my wanderings and irregular verbs than the blight Fraser appeared on the doorstep. He had had the measles, and Auntie Wendela had offered to give him an extra week's convalescence at the end of the summer holidays.

My anticipatory gloom was not relieved when Uncle Hugo brought home an invitation for me to attend in due course at the Big House.

'What *for*?'

'Just a visit.'

'Do I *have* to?'

'I'd like you to,' said Uncle Hugo firmly.

I was in a panic of social disorder and anticipated boredom. Being the reverse of Anne of Green Gables, I never chirped away merrily to adults, though I would have liked to know how. Most adults were not at all interested in what I thought most important in the world.

'I won't know what to say!'

'Don't worry,' said Helga cynically. 'You're only supposed to listen politely.'

When she first came to Glen Afra, Helga had been a kind of pet for Madame, but her charm soon wore off.

I had already been to the Big House. One of the feudal customs of the Brigadier and Madame was to second anyone about the place to help out when they had house guests.

'Send up your girl this evening, Sar' Major, six sharp!'

Off Helga would go, her cheeks two furious roses, step-daughter of a serf, a million miles from Hollywood and the glamorous life.

'Send Ginger along with her, whatever her name is. Cook could do with another pair of hands for the dishes.'

Niece of a serf, I went, dying to see life as it was lived in the *Tatler*. Madame's *Tatlers*, when finished with, were passed on through her maid to Auntie Wendela, and many a hearty laugh they gave us.

The queen of the kitchen was a massive Aga stove, cream enamelled, smokeless, humming softly like a contented insect. I memorised all its wondrous details so I could tell my mother.

'Hate carroty hair, hate it!' said the cook, glowering. 'Hate it!'

She harried us into an inner pantry where we peeled, chopped, scrubbed and sieved. I was scared of that cook, and had sometimes fled like a bolting rabbit when I met her on my rambles over the hills. Not that Mrs Brigham menaced me, in spite of her detestation of my hair, but because she was doing her usual thing – having a fight with an invisible companion. It must have been distressing for her, for she sometimes jammed her hands over her ears, shouting, 'Leave me alone, leave me alone! You're always at me!' I had a great dread of mentally unstable people, even those who were very nearly all right, as Helga said Mrs Brigham was. But still I kept close to my cousin, hoping that if Cook took a blue fit, Helga would be handy with a frying pan.

Mrs Brigham was a brilliant cook, managing to turn out exquisite dishes while engaging in derisory, protesting or tempestuous dialogue with her phantom. It was said that Madame paid her double wages.

Although I had met Madame for only long enough to say Good Morning, I knew far more than I should about her. The Brigadier's lady was a *belle laide*, a supreme example of the manner in which a woman with a fine complexion, couture clothing, and a boundless belief in her own superiority can fool the onlooking eye. She was a small woman, prone to obesity which she kept in check by twice daily enemas, I presume an oldfashioned form of bulimia. This and many other intimacies of her life we learned from her maid, Horrible Hattie, a conscienceless little devil who provided much hilarity in Aunt Wendela's house. Helga was allowed to hear this actionable gossip because she was seventeen; I because I couldn't, at my tender age, possibly understand.

Horrible Hattie was a tiny Londoner, unregenerate and bold. She looked like a squirrel and had a squirrel's faith that she could pick up a nut or a job anywhere. She had floated around the world on her serving skills; she could cook, dressmake, serve as parlourmaid, and was a gifted hairdresser. Her name was Daphne, but Madame always called her maids Hattie and her cook-housekeepers Mrs Brigham. Neither of the current ladies minded in the least. They knew they were on top. Madame had the greatest trouble, even in Depression times, to get young women to take a position at isolated Glen Afra.

'She can call me Fishface if she likes,' Hattie bragged. 'I get a rise whenever I threaten to leave. One sharp word out of Ma and I'll give notice on the spot, even if we're in the middle of an enema.'

She was going to America next, to marry a millionaire, and I am confident that she did.

There were eight house guests, several distinguished, but I got a peep at none of them.

My cousin and I were kept at it, cleaning saucepans, dishes, polishing silver, until after midnight. The incumbent Mrs Brigham, by now well off the wall, scarcely spoke to us. When we had finished, she took from the kitchen drawer an envelope and a packet, mumbled a bit, and shoved them at us. Helga was given three shillings for her long night's work, and I a book from the master's unread library. *The Life of Bismarck*, it was called. We stumbled home along the pitch-black road, towards a star at the far end, where Uncle Hugo, in his dressing gown, waited with a torch.

Auntie Wendela was fit to be tied, more for my sake than Helga's, to whom this exploitation had happened many times before. She said she couldn't wait until the Revolution came and the Bugalugs were forced to scrub lavatories for a living. But I was happy with my unreadable and richly bound book. When I returned to Auckland I sold it to a secondhand bookseller and bought a textbook instead.

· 9 ·

With nervous dread I awaited my summons from the Big House. The thought of wasting time on a grown-up lady sickened me. There were so many things for me to see and do. For all at once winter had gone. The earth was warm and flowery, the greenstone green of the Gulf streaked and runnelled with hyacinth blue. Far out the great rays leaped, crashing back into the water with the sound of gunshot. Dragonflies vibrated their wings of mica; the bush blowfly wore a carapace of cobalt. The dark forest hung itself with wisps and tatters of white clematis. The children of the stars, the Maoris called these frail blooms. On the wild quince trees around the ruined missionhouse in the next bay the fruit turned from green wood to yellow wood.

When I had done my house duties, and whatever written study Uncle Hugo demanded, Senta and I set off on meandering expeditions. We roamed over the back hills, those long slopes and crinkled gullies where the sheep hid at mustering time. The upland bush differed from that of the King Country; it was not rain forest, and had moreover been cut out long before. The big trees were younger than those I had known, the thickets of flaky-barked manuka taller, the grasses coarse and nibbled. Now and then on mountain tracks I stepped aside to let a Maori rider pass, a huge old man on a furry wall-eyed horse with raggy feet. A dark, bad-looking hound ran alongside, lifting a lip at me.

'Oh, that would be Tuki,' said Auntie Win.

Tuki was what the white people around Glen Afra called the kingly old man Tukumanu te Taniwha, but no Maori would have done so. He was the latest in line of the old Ngati-Maru chieftains, whose tribe and subtribes had been almost wiped out in battle a century and a half before.

The old man, as he passed me, always inclined his head in a courteous gesture. He knew who he was, and was indifferent to what the pakeha called him or thought of him.

Tukumanu was grandson to Horeta te Taniwha, who, as a child, had spoken to Captain Cook during the discoverer's first voyage. After Miss Elsie K. Morton, Captain James Cook was my other idol, and I secretly resolved to visit old Tuki one day and find out what his grandfather thought of the celebrated navigator. At the time it did not occur to me that this might be something to write about; all I dreamed of was fiction, as imaginative as possible.

But when at last I had conquered my diffidence sufficiently to cross Tukumanu's blown-over fence and approach his house, I found it empty. The old man was away on one of his many long rides through the bush and fern, visiting the remnants of his once wealthy tribe. His farmhouse was on a headland, sheltered by unkempt pohutukawas, the pakeha's Christmas tree. The grey weatherboard of the cottage was scoured by salt and sandy winds; the trees looked frail and brittle as though they'd been there a thousand years. Possibly they had, yet they would still lavishly mantle themselves with crimson when December came. They were mature trees when the *Endeavour* rounded Cape Colville and skimmed down the great Firth, to the astonished rapture of nine-year-old Horeta. He and a friend paddled out to the ship when she anchored, shinnied up a rope and stood unafraid upon the deck of this vast, extraordinary canoe.

Three or four years later I found Tukumanu at home, and heard a third-hand but most likely word perfect account of that momentous meeting. Captain Cook's hair was, he said 'like yours' (red) and his eyes 'like mine' (brown). He gave the adventurous young Horeta a nail, which was treasured for many years – a great mystery, metal being unknown to the Maori, and a grand tool.

By that time I had a camera, a Rolleicord, paid off at three shillings weekly, and I photographed the old chief. The photograph shows the broad capacious brow, the strong jaw and robust skull formation of those aristocratic old Maoris. The article was my first breakthrough into Australian, Canadian and African publication, and I was mightily cocked-up about it.

Tukumanu was one of the two unforgettable men I met at Glen Afra. He said many other things; one I remember with admiration was 'There are but two riches on earth, land to grow food and women to grow men.'

· 10 ·

Fraser arrived, wan and delicate, the beard under his arm. His starry eyes were surrounded with glamorous shadows, his voice had become sweet and docile. I had to admire him. He did a great job of sympathy-getting, and he got it.

'You poor little pet, there isn't more than a handful of you left!'

'I'm all right, really I am, Auntieee.'

'Creep!' muttered Helga.

He was put to bed in the living room, cozened and doted upon. All three of us females were at his tearful beck and temperamental call. I was detailed to take the tiny beard out on the grass two or three times a day. The beard's attention to its private needs was worth studying. Slowly it approached a very low clump of grass. Did it lift its leg? Was that what the very slight disturbance of the hair on the left side meant? Then it stood still, meditating.

The family dogs, if they were at home, whether sheep-dogs or gun dogs, were wary of the beard. Was it a dog? But then on the other hand you could never be sure of cats, which came in cruelly deceptive guises. They circled the beard with their crests up and their lips curled.

'Auntieeee, she's letting those big dogs frighten my Brucie!'

All my life this kid had been getting me into trouble. It was he who assured me that if I put the contents of my mother's change purse into his baroque blackboy moneybox, we could get the coins back again. (Are you mad? How could you be such a drip at your age?) It had been he who set fire to our grandmother, and I who got the whacking. (You're older, you're bigger. Well, then you should have watched to see he *didn't* nick Auntie Rose's cigarette lighter. He's only a little fellow, after all.)

Often I had watched with amazement, and possibly envy, as he chatted up Grandma; charming little fellow, pretty as a saint off the wall, he leaned on her knee and asked just the questions she wanted to hear. At this point in her life she could hear faintly, and Fraser's three-year-old treble was pitched perfectly for her failing aural nerves.

Why do angels wear nighties, Gramma? Do they have holes in their nighties for their wings to come out of? Gramma, do angels have teef? Does God give them toothpaste to clean their teef with like Mummy does with me? What does angels eat, Gramma?

No wonder he was her favourite grandchild. But his masterstroke was his sweet plea . . . 'Gramma, will you make me a scaffler, just for my very own?'

Grandma had several habits which got up the family's nose like splinters. If you were particularly bad, she threatened to make a novena for you. I don't know why this is so menacing, but it was and is. Then, when she was not knitting socks for Poor Jack, she made scapulas for the Far East Missions. Long ago, a scapular was an actual garment, a plain strip of woollen material which hung back and front over a monk's habit. I suppose it was to add warmth, a variety of ecclesiastical cardigan. But through the centuries it had diminished to a tiny square felt bag, hung round the neck by a tape and enfolding a seed-sized object, usually cloth, which had come in contact with a saint's bones or even tomb. A picture was often embroidered on the front, the Sacred Heart, or, alarmingly, St Lucy with her eyes on a platter like two blue fried eggs.

The devout often wore two or three scapulas at the same time. Each provided a different psychic service, but the over-riding idea was protection. Once I succoured a pious Maltese lady who had succumbed to an hour-long sermon, and when I discreetly loosened her clothes, I discovered a perfect nest of scapulas, seventeen at least, ranging from raggy ones obscured by dirt and age to the brand new, bought that very week. They didn't help however, as she went off with a stroke.

A scapula is, in fact, an amulet. The desire to wear such a thing, hang it in the car, pin it to one's bra, appears to be inexplicably rooted in the human psyche. Tutankamen wore an ankh; countless young ladies the Fem sign; is there an Italian boy without a cross given to him by his mother? You may purchase amulets at every Buddhist and Shinto shrine in Japan and at every temple in India. Africa and Tibet abound with them.

In view of this universal love of amulets, one should look with new understanding at Queen Elizabeth's apparently irremovable triple strand of pearls.

My Grandma, therefore, as a small devotional work, made scapulas, or as she called them, scafflers. Later, minute shreds of cloth, or specks of horrid yellow bone were inserted by the Sisters or the missionaries or whomever were the final recipients. Those scafflers given to us, her loved or tolerated ones, were different, and very ungrateful we were. As she had nothing holy to put into them, she inserted an Irish horn bead from a broken rosary, which her father had given her when she left Ireland so long before. This rosary was supposed to have been blessed by a hedge priest the English had killed, thus making him a martyr as good as anyone else's martyrs.

I regret to say that Flash Jack ate mine, but who knows, it might have done him a power of good and saved his life that terrible time he challenged a tram.

My Grandma, Mary Ann Patterson or Peterson, aged about eighty-five, and 'cocked up' because she's had her hair cut for the first time.

Grandma Mary Ann McBride, aged seventeen, when she arrived as an emigrant in New Zealand. The little girl is the child she nursemaided on the voyage.

Mera, my father.
Melville Park, aged about
twenty-two.

My mother, Christina Park, as she was
when I left New Zealand. Aged about
forty-four.

'Coppernob'. Ruth Park, aged two or three.

Auntie Theresa, Ruth Park, little sister Jocelyn and Cousin Robert, and the flax bush where the tuis sang.

Auntie Tress (Theresa), aged about eighteen.

Auntie Wendela, aged twenty.

Aunt Rosina, aged twenty.

Auntie Willy, who ran away, aged about eighteen.

St Joseph's Convent, Te Kuiti, with the old church to the left and the staff on the verandah.
Here Mera and Rangi Tawhai dug and planted the garden.

St Joseph's Convent School, Te Kuiti. Opened 1921. This photograph 1924.

St Benedict's Convent, Auckland. Originally the presbytery of the Benedictine Fathers, it was taken over by the Sisters in 1901. This picture, which includes a new wing, was taken in 1918.

St Benedict's College. Josephine Sisters began teaching here in 1921. The building looked exactly the same in my time there.

Sisters of St Joseph on St Benedict's Convent verandah. Sister Bertille, my loved teacher, sitting on extreme left, Sister Laurencia on extreme right. Sister Laurencia first arrived from Australia in 1892.

A. S. (Mick) Ridling, mentor and godfather to all the copyholders at the *Auckland Star*.

D'Arcy Niland, aged nineteen. Taken on the roof of the old Sydney *Sun* office. The first photograph of him I ever saw.

Ruth Park, aged about eighteen. The first photograph seen by D'Arcy Niland.

Jim Edwards (top), the toughest and most influential of the U.W.M. leaders, addressing the crowd in Queen Street, Auckland, 1932. (*New Zealand Herald*)

Relief workers' camp at Pakiri, 1933. (*New Zealand Herald*)

Kaingaroa, the largest man-made forest in the world. (*New Zealand Herald*)

Dinner time at the relief camp, 1933. 'Skilly and spuds.' (*New Zealand Herald*)

Partington's Mill, Auckland.
(*New Zealand Herald*)

Fraser however, laid his scaffler by, and was careful to wear it whenever he visited Grandma. She looked for it, of course.

'My dotie boy! You'll grow into a bishop, please God.'

Those of us who hated Fraser told him that she meant he had the right ears to hold up a mitre.

So there was Fraser, fallen into a soft place yet again at Glen Afra and making the most of it. Helga and I dreaded his full recovery, and the trouble that inevitably would be our lot. So we were awed and grateful when Fate stepped in and took a minatory slap at his treasure, the beard.

On a still hot morning, February 3, an extraordinary phenomenon occurred. The tide went out and didn't come back in. This was not a spectacular event. The sea did not roll up like a scroll, like the sky in Revelations. It quietly withdrew. Fraser, the beard and I were fooling around in the shallows in the dinghy at the time, and I felt this withdrawal abruptly, as though the water had been yanked away from underneath. We bumped and dragged on the stony bottom.

'Crumbs, what's going on?'

The water went east, steadily and inexorably. There was no fuss of waves, no sound except gentle lapping. It went out so far we could no longer see it; there was a ruffling line of steely glitter in the middle of the Gulf, and that was all.

People began to run down to the beach, Captain Toms from the store, a couple of stationhands, Aunt Wendela flapping her hands and calling us back in.

The dinghy was immovable. 'Come on, Fraser,' I said, in consternation, hopping over the side. 'Get out.' I took hold of the beard so that he could.

But he was scared, clinging fast to the side, milkwhite and unable to cope with this unnatural happening.

'Get OUT!' I yelled.

The beard set up a thin howl.

Panicky fish were everywhere, flipping over the wet stones, trying to wiggle under them. Little fingerlings, bright as new tin, flip flop, scutter, gape and gasp.

I saw things I had never seen before – the sharp incline fifty metres off low water mark, and then the seagrass-covered sandy plateau, flat as a plate, lying as far as the eye could see. The seagrass was all combed one way, as though the retreating water had tried to take it with it. It jumped with dying life. The air glittered with leaping fish, red snapper, dogfish, mullet, and clouds of sprats that had taken to the air in their hysteria. Afar, a huge ray lifted first one wing and then the other in a mad shuffle towards the water.

The crowd on the beach increased. Two or three Maori farmers, having seen the phenomenon from their hillside shacks, came drumming down on their shoeless horses, waving flax kits. They were not going to let all that fish go to waste.

'Someone go and fetch the boss!'

'What the hell can he do?'

'You children come back here at once!' shouted Auntie Win.

She told us afterwards she was afraid that the water might come rolling back as quickly as it had receded, or that the newly exposed sand was quicksand. All of which might have been so. But what happened was that the beard slipped out of my arms, and went off at a fast waddle across the seagrass. It had fixed its unseen eye on something waggling around, scooping sand from under a rock, throwing up a long flexible arm in its hurry to find a hiding place.

I had never seen a live squid, but I knew this was one, and I took off after the beard. The little dog, which had never made a stand in its life, was probably curious. But perhaps, like its owner, it had lost its head altogether.

The squid half-deflated a canvas bag of a body, and momentarily disclosed a large black and white eye. Its tentacles quickly pretended to be a bunch of seaweed.

'Wam! Wam! Wam!' shrieked the beard, and a sound as of chattering teeth came from my cousin in the dinghy.

'Go on, get out of there!' I shouted at the dog. My feet were being sucked into the sand to the ankles. But who can guess the length of a squid's arms? It caught both me and the beard in the same melting movement, one arm corkscrewing up my leg like a frond of ivy, and the beard being whipped in a frenzy of sand, water and hair towards the creature's body. I screamed blue murder.

Nobody tells you that to be embraced by a squid hurts. My leg felt that it was burned with acid. Meanwhile the beard was being choked. For the first time I saw its tongue, looking blue.

Panic-stricken, I hammered at the tentacle, jerking away with all my might. But all I did was to lift the squid's body, now flushing yellow and pink, off the ground. It had twitched three more of its arms around the rock, and another about my other ankle.

It was not a big squid, nor was it truly on the attack. A timid animal, all it wanted was to defend itself against me and the beard.

Then there was a rush, and two or three men grabbed me and pulled. Others whacked the squid with rocks. But it was Poa, one of the Maori farmers, who disposed of it, jabbing his stiffened fingers in its eyes. All I knew at the time was that the tentacles slowly relaxed their grip, like perished rubber.

Poa later told us that the best way to kill octopus or squid is to bite them between the eyes, where there is a vital nerve centre.

'But teeth not good enough, pakeha tucker kill teeth,'

he apologised, showing us a few catty-cornered yellow gravestones.

The beard, stiff with fright, was revived, as was its young master, who presently accused me of carelessness and malice in allowing his loved one to approach the squid. He also demanded return to Auckland as soon as possible, and the Brigadier, overcome by those starry eyes full of tears, agreed to send him there in the Packard the very next day. Helga and I could not believe our luck, and next day watched him go with vengeful self-righteousness that was most satisfying.

My leg was curiously marked with forty or fifty circular red indentations where the creature's suckers had rasped off the skin. I carried the scars for months.

The tide stayed out all day. Sometime in the night there was movement without form, as though a great body stretched itself in the darkness, and the sea returned with a sigh and a rattle of stones, not over-full or over-hurried. It was just a normal tide coming in from a long way away.

By then we knew, via the Brigadier's wireless set, that there had been a catastrophic earthquake which destroyed Napier and Hastings, the largest towns on the east coast, flattened hills, diverted rivers, and opened great fissures throughout the countryside.

The most devastating earthquake that had shaken New Zealand since European settlement, it struck on that warm summer morning without any warning. Amazingly, one of my aunts had been in Napier, lost Auntie Willy, the girl off the rose bush, whose whereabouts no one had known for ten years. Poor thing, she was entombed for days, and was a nervous wreck for the rest of her life. Yet before the cathedral fell in on her and other refugees, she had seen terrible things, the ground heaving and undulating like a great flexing rope, the roadway splitting, one half rising two metres, the other sinking, the cars sliding into the crevasse. The hospital where she had been working collapsed like a house of cards, much of it crashing on the nurses' home, where the night shift had just gone to bed. Most of the girls were killed.

Bizarre stories were to come out of Napier, such as the one about the man having his morning bath who, still in the bath, shot down the hotel stairs from the second storey out into the roadway. And the clients having their hair permed in an upstairs salon where the floor simply vanished, leaving the women dangling by their hair from the oldfashioned waving machines, slowly being scalped.

The sea receded and the land was heaved up, so that the inner boat harbour became dry. It is now a suburb.

At Glen Afra we had not felt a shake or a shudder, nor had my common reaction to approaching earthquake, uneasy pressure in the ears, occurred. Yet the sea in the Firth of Thames reacted in the phenomenal manner described. There was great loss of life in Napier and Hastings as well as almost insuperable difficulty in taking aid to the stricken cities, as the railway lines for a hundred kilometres, so they say, both north and south, were twisted like string.

When I think of the earthquake that, in the twinkling of an eye, destroyed Napier, I recall another time in another country when I experienced a tremor not a quarter as severe. Thrown out of my chair, I saw above me a cement wall bulge as though pushed from behind. As it did, its paint lightened in colour, as if the pigment particles were stretched to fading point. At the same time there sounded an earsplitting metallic shriek, as the sheets of roofing iron fought against each other for stability.

There is nothing like an earthquake for showing you what you are – a speck of dust on the hide of an unimaginably powerful living entity that does not care whether you are there or not.

· 11 ·

I knew my rescuer Poa well, and often visited him, when I felt in need of a little Maori tranquillity. In fact, however, Poa did not lead a tranquil life as his enormous angry daughter gave him a hiding every weekend. Riti worked up the coast somewhere, housework in a hotel, but she always rode that long way home for the weekend. She cared for her father, in spite of the wallopings.

Poa lived in a raupo-thatched whare. Pumpkins and kumara grew higgledy-piggledy amongst the unkempt grass, and thin, wormy-looking cows grazed in rough paddocks along the creek. It was terrible to think that this poor farmer was one of the few Maoris left of the populous tribes that had dwelt up and down the rich Coromandel country, well-fed, prosperous, the lucky owners of Tamaki of a Hundred Lovers as this area, right through to Auckland, was called. For once, one could not blame the European invasion for the depopulation of this favoured land. Over it still stalked the mighty phantom of the greatest of the warchiefs, Hongi Hika.

Poa would not speak of Hongi. When I asked him about the near-genocide of his people, his eyes, gauzed over with cataract, dimly glowed, and he grunted, 'Tangia te wai o te waha!' which translates politely as 'Shut your big mouth'.

In the bewitching lands of Coromandel and Tamaki, Hongi Hika was a name not to be mentioned to the Maori people. Because of him Tukumanu te Taniwha and other nobly descended men were chiefs of almost vanished clans.

The Ngapuhi chieftain was the first highly connected Maori, perhaps even the first Polynesian, to use the white man's technology for his own ends. As he was a man of majestic bearing and intelligence, missionaries in 1820 were happy to invite him to England and show him off as a Noble Savage, a concept still much in favour amongst philosophers. Honours and gifts, even from George IV himself, were laid at his feet. The gifts Hongi swiftly sold or exchanged for muskets, the power of which he had greedily observed.

His ambition was not to attack the European settlers but to wipe out his hereditary enemies, the Hauraki tribes. According to the bushido code of the old Maori warrior, he gave due warning to Horeta te Taniwha, the sophistic-ated and much-travelled chief of one of the Thames tribes.

'I shall swallow the eye of your pet crow!' was his promise.

Hongi's campaign was one of triumphant slaughter, nullifying forever the Maori's historic belief that the club, spear, and manly courage were the backbone of battle. The massacre was celebrated by an atrocious cannibal orgy, probably the last in New Zealand. This so disgusted other tribes, hitherto friends to the Ngapuhi, that they turned away from alliance with Hongi.

Up and down the Gulf we heard stories that early settlers couldn't work certain localities before they had harrowed up the human bones.

'Skulls!' said one old farmer to me. 'They stuck up out of the grass like mushrooms.'

This grisly harvest was put through bone-mills and used as fertiliser on the paddocks.

Hongi burned all settlements and razed fortified villages as he travelled. Ten or twelve kilometres from Glen Afra a great Pa, described in detail by Captain Cook in 1769, had been destroyed by fire. I walked there once, but the site had been reconquered by the forest. Nothing was left but old cooking pits and holes where the carved heroes had stood, poking out their tongues.

Hongi Hika cherished the musket and died slowly from a musket ball in his lung. In later years I saw a picture of his death. Painted from life by the colonial artist Augustus Earle, it is dark, fierce, and evocative of a land and people now gone into history. The splendid chief, a brown Apollo, his body scarred by almost ceaseless warfare, lies on a beach, surrounded by kin and tribesmen. The firelight illuminates his aquiline face, darkly tattooed; his thick curly black hair is adorned by the bunch of white feathers worn by Ngapuhi chieftains.

Thus he died, without regret or complaint, merciless warrior, harrier of the Gulf, the descendant of countless men at arms, navigators and discoverers; men who called that unknown time after death Te Rerenga, the voyage.

· 12 ·

I would have been happy spending much of my free time with Poa, but my relationship with Madame had begun. It was always a mystery; I couldn't work out why she wanted to take up my time. Maybe she was lonely, who can tell, for the Brigadier was around and about the property all day, and she could scarcely have been chummy with the maids or her husband's somewhat sinister valet. On the other hand, she may have had some anachronistic idea about being kind to the little cottager. The little cottager, however, broke into a cold sweat at the very thought of visiting her.

'Please be on your best behaviour,' Aunt Wendela pleaded. 'No showing off, no peculiar jokes, no Latin.'

'She always calls me Ginger,' I sulked.

'Well, you *are* ginger, and very nice it is, too.'

I was profoundly hurt that my dear aunt did not realise the indignity of being called by the detestable name which had pursued me throughout life.

'She's got no right. How would she like it if I called her Budgie Nose?'

'Oh, God, don't!' besought my aunt, and then hooted with laughter. 'Hasn't she, though!'

Madame liked to show me the treasures of the Big House, and they were many. She opened the several wardrobes crammed with tiny shoes, marvellous evening dresses, handbags, hats.

'This is Molyneux, see the embroidery? And Paquin, and Worth!'

Horrible Hattie had told me that Madame sometimes spent the entire day trying on these ravishing garments. They were, I suppose, her toys, a substitute for something, just as the 'flicks' were for Helga. Once every two years, I knew from Hattie, the vast wardrobes were cleared, their contents thrown into large weighted boxes. Uncle Hugo then took out the launch into the Channel, the deepest part of the Gulf, and dumped the boxes overboard. This sacrilege occurred just before the Bugalugs sailed for Home where they spent six months re-absorbing civilisation. During this sabbatical Madame viewed the Paris fashion shows and replenished her wardrobe. At this time also Uncle Hugo became acting-manager of Glen Afra, though not on increased salary.

I didn't give a spit about any of it. Dear God, how I suffered. The boredom of a child that age, dressed in her best and listening to a strange lady rabbiting on about Molyneux's embroidery is beyond adult reckoning. I wanted to be anywhere on the station but there. The red snapper were back, tearing ferociously at the mussels on half-tide rocks, their humped backs sparked with crimson, their dagger teeth loudly grinding the shells. I knew that if I could only get out in the dinghy I could catch a boatload for Uncle Hugo's smokehouse. I longed, agonised, to be out in the leaky boat with Senta, hauling them in.

Yet in spite of this painful turmoil, my demeanour must have been bland enough to please Madame. Sometimes as we wandered in the garden she spoke in an abstracted fashion of her childhood. Very queer it was, too, a shade Mary Poppins and a good deal of Henry James. Hers must have been a wealthy family, established in Society. She and her young brother rarely saw their parents except at bed-time when her mother 'looking divine, dressed for dinner . . . emeralds, her own special scent' glided in to say good night. They had a cruel Nanny who nearly poked out her brother's eyes because he wouldn't close them and go to sleep, but he couldn't, because the nursery was always so cold, except in Nanny's little room where the fireplace was.

Madame had 'come out' in the greatest style. (Come out of what? I asked myself.) She was presented to the Prince and Princess of Wales, presiding for the occasion over the Court. Queen Victoria herself was not present because of her perpetual mourning for Prince Albert. Madame stood for four and a half hours, in an unheated room; no food since breakfast because of her tight corset.

'Couldn't you even go to the lavvy?' I marvelled.

'We had chamber pots in a kind of cupboard,' she replied restrainedly.

Oh, those were delirious days, balls, gowns with trains, diplomats, French royalty.

'France is a Republic,' I stated, not having won a scholarship for nothing.

'The *real* people know better,' replied Madame coldly.

Hattie served afternoon tea, flitting around deftly in a starched apron. I didn't dare glance at her in case she secretly poked out her tongue or looked cross-eyed. Once when Madame had told some particularly grand story, Hattie produced a genteel little fart, though her face remained perfectly impassive.

I had no idea that I was supposed to be envious of Madame's privileged life; it seemed to me that her childhood was frightful beyond all imagining. Wicked nanny with her long poking fingers, the mother who never saw her children, never rubbed their congested chests with loving, anxious hands, made harsh with hard work for those same children, no crazy, giggly, generous aunts, no Mera!

No free rough and tumble, hills and river, gallant Flash Jack, Weetbix crumbs and the problem of what to do with them, whack on the legs, kisses and hugs, wild bloody stories, holy stones and trees? Out of my brimming, revelatory life a genuine compassion rose, and impulsively I blurted, 'I think you're real brave!'

She was taken aback. 'What a funny little thing you are! Why am I brave?'

Unable to explain, I muttered, 'I just think you are.'

'Bless you,' she said, giving me a little pat, which unnerved me further. Later I heard through Horrible Hattie that she had been touched by my unexpected sympathy for her life, exiled from all that was civilised.

'I didn't mean that at all,' I protested.

'I should hope not,' said Aunt Wendela severely.

Poor Madame, how little we understood her, and how little she understood anyone. We lived on different levels of reality. Yet she did me a great service.

· 13 ·

Respite from my social duties came at last. The Brigadier developed a raging toothache and had to be driven off to Auckland in a hurry. Madame decided to go, too, to have her hair cut and waved; go to the races; see a few friends. Uncle Hugo was to drive the long sleek Packard. I was interested to observe that this sub-job as chauffeur brought out all that was independent and spikily British in my dear Uncle. No matter how the Brigadier boomed, bounced and commanded, he dug his toes in. He would not wear a chauffeur's uniform or that blighted little cap. He'd wear his dark suit, be neat and soldierly, open and close doors, say Sir, but no matter what, no leggings, no fatuous breeches, no cap.

Auntie Wendela, Helga and I were very proud of him.

Promising to bring Helga back as many film magazines as he could buy, and Auntie and me fresh fruit and sweets, he drove off in the glittering car.

As often as the tide allowed I went fishing, to cure myself of Molyneux and Court presentations. Uncle Hugo's smokehouse was the old brick chimney of an earlier house which had stood on that property. Inside, it was very soon lavishly hung with the silky brown wings of split, half-cured snapper and trevally.

Senta rarely let me go fishing on my own. When she saw me casting off the dinghy she broke into a goatish canter, bleating furiously. Sitting dreamily in the stern, chewing the salty seaweed, she appeared to pass into the regulation fisherman's trance, bemused by sea shimmer and the sweet clucking of water against the boat.

I never conversed with Senta as I did with the dogs; this idiosyncratic, composed creature did not require it. I saw quite well she was inspired by the coldest, purest motives, to terrorise, dominate, stare the world down. I was quite conceited, in fact, that she allowed me into this anarchic world of hers.

Suddenly she emitted a sharp snuffle and scrambled upright. Senta would never relieve herself in the dinghy; neither would she plunge over the side and swim to shore. Blasting all goats, I rowed to the beach.

Her first task accomplished, Senta departed at a brisk trot for the inland. She headed for the relief workers' camp, now parallel with the dinghy, and my blood ran cold. Pulling the boat as far as I could into the shallows, I tossed out the anchor, which was Maori style – a good heavy stone lashed into an old flax kit. If the dinghy dragged, it would not drag far.

The road gangs were working out of sight; I heard the sharp blast of a foreman's warning whistle, and a moment later the boom of an explosion. They had blown away some obstruction and might be engaged for hours clearing off the fallen rock and earth. Could I dart into the camp, drag out Senta before she committed any depredation and be away, with no one the wiser?

Auntie Wendela's warning had not been necessary. I had always felt repugnance at the idea of interfering with other people's belongings or trespassing in their living quarters. Probably I had been impressed by my mother's care in giving the poor King Country tramps a private place to wash and shave. So I entered that camp shaking like a thief, not wanting to be there, hating Senta for forcing me to be there. For I knew what vandalism that damned goat could effect if I let her remain.

All appeared deserted. From the cookhouse chimney coiled the lazy smoke of a banked-down fire. Probably the cook was kipping before starting preparations for the evening meal.

Senta had vanished. I rushed from tent to tent, calling like a fool, because as was to be expected, Senta was the perverse type that hides when called. Some of the tents had their flaps tied down, but most were open, airing in the fine weather. They were orderly and bare, containing camp beds with hessian ticks, thin Army blankets, shabby coats and old trousers hanging on the tentpoles, shaving mugs, portmanteaux where I suppose the men kept things valuable to them.

When I found her, that devil, she was sitting at her ease on someone's pillow. She gazed at me benignly, as though querying why I'd been so long. A few shreds of a sock lay on the bed and the second hung halfway out her mouth like a long striped tongue.

'Shitty goat! Bloody goat!' They were the only bad words I knew but if I'd known others I'd have used them. I seized her around the neck and tried to pull her off the bed, but she was in her usual peculiarly stable position, with hind legs stuck up in the air and front hoofs planted between them, and I couldn't move her. She had already eaten the back out of the tent occupant's shirt, possibly his town shirt, and torn out the pocket of a rain-stained jacket.

'Move! Shitty goat! Move your bloody carcase or I'll kill you stone dead!'

Senta, bored with harassment, dug her chin into her chest and presented two little sharp horns.

'Need a hand there?'

My heart somersaulted. I almost saw the thing bounce across the earth floor and under the bunk. I knew by the man's voice that he was the owner of the ravaged garments;

while soft it still sounded as though any minute its owner would take someone by the throat and squeeze. Senta also interpreted the voice correctly. She bounded off the bed and past him in one movement, the sock still hanging from her mouth. He clunked one hearty kick into her ribs and away she went like a racehorse.

There was no doubt that this was Uncle Hugo's Starkie. He did indeed look like an Amerindian, swarthy face, jetty hair, and eyes of a singular blackness and opaqueness. His cheekbones jutted like polished brown bone. He was the most foreign-looking man I had ever seen and he scared me to death.

'She ran away. The goat,' I gabbled. 'I knew she'd eat something, she always does. I'm really sorry. Your shirt. Your socks.'

'All right. Clear out now.'

'But your clothes, look at the coat . . .'

'Outski.'

He stumbled towards me, I thought he was going to kill me, but instead he fell on the floor, his dark face yellowish, his eyes closed but showing a strip of black glass. I saw then that there was blood on the side of his head; the hair was soaked.

'It's a wonder you didn't faint,' said Helga later. 'I would have fainted. Or run shrieking from the tent.' She was greedy for drama.

'She *did* run shrieking from the tent, you fathead,' said her mother crossly, 'she ran and fetched the cook. Which was a sensible thing to do. And if you don't stop crying I'll give you such a slap!'

'I can't help it,' I blubbered.

'He didn't do anything to you, did he? Didn't hit you with a shovel?'

'Just told me to clear out. And fell down.'

She was exasperated. 'I've told you over and over he

wasn't badly hurt, got hit with a bit of flying rock when they blasted the cutting. That's why the foreman sent him back to camp. *Why* are you bawling?'

'I don't know. Socks.'

'Oh, for goodness sake! I'll just pinch a couple of pairs of Hugo's, and maybe a shirt, and we'll get them down to the camp somehow. Cheer up now!'

But although I had been upset over Senta's mis-behaviour, I think I was weeping from shock.

How was I to describe the mysterious impact of that man's presence? Nothing to do with Senta, or with me, or his damaged clothing or anything else. He was not very tall, handsome, or young. Yet he was the most remarkable person I had ever seen. It took years before I worked out what it was that James Douglas Stark radiated as naturally as light. It was natural power. Here was someone who hurled himself into life with all his being. Nothing frightened him because he saw all things as part of his own life, so that he was in ultimate control. I couldn't imagine him disliking or resenting his life no matter what circum-stance threw in his way.

Undoubtedly this is what the old Polynesians called *mana*. In their time kings and chieftains had mana, or more likely, those with mana became kings.

Starkie did not become a king however; like so many soldiers he was treated with indifference by the country for which he suffered thirty-seven wounds. I don't think he made old bones. But would he have wanted to?

A few people have been fascinated by Starkie. Robin Hyde, the novelist, wrote two books about him. D'Arcy Niland, also a novelist, when he was tired or blocked, would say to me, 'Tell me a story about Starkie.' He used the man's name, and some of the aspects of his unique character to furnish out his protagonist in his last novel, *Dead Men Running*. Through many years his face has stayed in the back of my mind – alien, impersonal, a talismanic face from a brutal history.

· 14 ·

Madame was back only a day or two when she sent for me. We resumed our inexplicable acquaintance, mostly in the garden, now coming towards its prime.

Her garden was magnificent, its myriads of fragile European flowers and shrubs sheltered from rowdy sea winds by high hedges. Madame frequently spoke of the hours she spent gardening, but in fact the work was done by three Teds and Dougs who were under orders to keep out of sight when Madame walked amongst the roses and japonicas. But I knew they sneaked along behind trees and walls and rockeries, snooping. Everyone was ravenous for gossip in Glen Afra.

One morning she asked me idly what I was going to be when I grew up.

'A writer,' I said. I could hardly say those words without a shiver of anticipatory delight.

'Oh, my poor Ginger, what a big ambition!'

I couldn't have agreed more, and was about to confide about the stories and poems I had had published in Miss Elsie K. Morton's page in the *New Zealand Herald* when she said, quite kindly, 'You mustn't set your sights too high, Ginger. You might be disappointed.'

I wanted to tell her that I knew I couldn't be a writer straight off, but was prepared to spend my entire life practising if necessary.

Before I got the words arranged she said, 'There are so many other things a willing girl can do in life. Look at Hattie. Now *there* is a successful young woman. You could do much worse than take Hattie for a model.'

'But I want to be a *writer*,' I said. Misgivings were already swelling in my throat. I was good at faces, and I could read hers. She was winding up to something I wouldn't like.

She shook her head, still kindly, still sensibly. 'But really . . . well, my dear, it isn't appropriate. Not for a girl in your circumstances.'

I had the hot feeling in my chest that meant the beginning of anger, and I panicked. With me anger burst out in all kinds of unpremeditated and unforgivable ways, and I had to think of Uncle Hugo's job being put in jeopardy. Also I could see a corner of one of the Dougs behind the summerhouse; he was pretending to weed the lily bed.

Madame pondered. 'Dear me, how can I explain? There are professional classes, you see, with background, influential friends, University education. And there are others, like Hattie, yes, who do useful, quite important things in their own way.'

'But I want . . .'

'You must realise that we all have our place in life, as you and Helga have yours.'

'Who said?'

'What?'

'Who gave us these places?' I think my trembling voice put her off, for she answered sharply, 'God did, of course, Ginger.'

She had the loud, ringing voice of the self-assured. I saw the shoulders of the kneeling gardener twitch, and for a split second believed that she had indeed obtained her information direct from Heaven.

My ears buzzed. There was a fire in my chest. I wish I could say that I shouted spirited questions; what about Dickens and Shakespeare? Whereabouts in the Bible does God say anything about class because that's what you're talking about, isn't it? Or even 'Merde à vous!' But I didn't think of any of these things. Crazed with offence and a consuming sense of injustice, I croaked, 'and don't you call me Ginger ever, EVER again! You're a rude, ugly woman!' and banged off over the garden wall and into the bush.

Lord, the despairing fury of the young who know they can do nothing whatsoever about it! I choked, I swore, I kicked the trees which had all turned into Madame and her autocratic assumptions. Soon I was bruised, scratched and bleeding, and I had knocked the rubber toecap off my sandshoe, so that I turned to a milder catharsis, harrying the half-wild turkeys that had free range in the bush. Imbecilic birds, they were, each with a teaspoonful of brain, capable of strutting out with eleven chicks in a row behind her, and returning home with one. I knew very well I was kicking them only because they were stupid and couldn't kick back.

At last shame intervened, and I slunk off towards Poa's farm. Most of it was raupo swamp, or great prickly thickets of teatree. How he made a living no one knew. It was rabbit and pumpkin all over again, I supposed.

Suffocated by masochistic misery, I took a shortcut down the creek bed, stumbling amongst parasoling tree-ferns, falling, getting wet, bumping down the stair of mossy stone, barking my knees and making that an excuse to cry. The awful thing was that Madame had been so convincing; perhaps it was her authoritative voice.

I avoided Big Eel Pond, where lived an eel as thick as my leg, a sluggish creature with dead eyes and backward pointing teeth. We kids fished up and down Poa's creek, never thinking that we were hauling out Poa's food, or some of it. He was kind and hospitable to us even on Saturdays after he'd been beaten up by cruel Riti.

The cows were mooching around his shack, longing to be milked, but I could hear Poa snoring inside. I flung myself down beside the creek, my feet in the water, sometimes nibbled by the tiny brown native trout. My rage had seeped away, leaving in its place baffled woe. Madame had no right to be rude; but I had always had the impression she had never been taught any manners.

What if she were right in what she said?

It seemed that I had four great handicaps – I was a poor man's child, I was a girl, it appeared that I might not attain any higher education, and now a relentless hand had shoved me down into the wrong class. All I was fit for was to be a servant to the like of the Bugalugs. During my brief life I had not heard much about class discrimination, but I knew about it. From my Uncle, who had been one of the privileged back Home, I had learned about the rich man in his castle, and the poor man at his gate.

'Confounded rot!' he snorted. 'But it sort of went west with the war.'

I marvelled that he could say such a thing. I think it was bravado, with Glen Afra right there before him making a lie of every word he said. The staff toed the line, even cheeky Hattie. The stationhands were afraid for their jobs if they didn't show great respect for the Brigadier and Madame, the kind of respect not considered manly or even decent amongst stiff-necked New Zealanders. They accepted wages below the norm, because they knew that, should they protest, a hundred unemployed men waited hungrily for their jobs. Even Auntie Wendela had been nervous lest I get up Madame's nose some way. Which now I had done.

Simmering with qualms about that, as well as rage, terror and incoherent fantasies of revenge, I continued to sit, the bush murmuring at my back.

It was not for nothing that many races conducted their religious ceremonies in sacred groves. Amongst trees the mind quietens, the sediment of anxiety and obsessive thought sinks to the depths; you become aware that you are not only breathing-in the Universe – the Universe is also breathing you. In the company of these grave, pacific creatures you sometimes experience a blazing flash of insight, a psychic shock, when argument and emotion disappear and you see things as they are.

These insights come sweetly to many, but I felt as if I had been punched in the chest. I remember coughing and choking, my feet kicking out, sending the little trout scooting for cover. The lightning had struck, and I realised, completely and unarguably, that I didn't need Madame or indeed anyone to approve of my aspirations. I *wanted*, oh, yes, ardently wanted people like my mother and Mera and Miss Elsie K. Morton to approve of my writing, but I didn't need them.

It truly didn't matter what anyone said, because what such a person offered as a judgement was only an opinion. Madame's opinion meant less than other people's, because she wasn't in touch with ordinary rampageous life. She probably hadn't an idea about writing, how the feverish desire to grab an instant, a scene, a person, and somehow transmit a concept of these things to other people could seize anyone, even a little girl, and become a life-dominating obsession.

Not that I wasn't damned mad at her cheek, but that was another thing altogether.

Not without fear, I saw the truth. Madame wasn't going to be the only discourager in my life, but no one could put me down unless I agreed to be put down.

I had no inkling of the thousands of snubs, discourage-ments and critical brutalities that drifted like phantoms in my future, as they do in every writer's life, but I had seen the truth and that was that. Chekhov said, 'If I had listened to the critics I'd have died drunk in the gutter.' Thanks to Madame's insensitivity I was with Chekhov from the beginning.

Though true, my insight was simplistic, a child's revelation of how the world is. I was fifteen or more before I realised that when someone takes it upon himself to categorise you, to define your position, or tell you how you must be, nine times out of ten he is defending his own status. His motivation rises from unconscious fears as well as ego. Madame's useless encapsulated life could not be sustained without servants. A religious or ideo-logical leader's unique office has no validity or indeed any existence if he has no adherents. First he must convince.

Madame did me a great service when unwittingly she demonstrated that for one party to convince, the other must assent.

· 15 ·

Sounds came back to Poa's creek, the bellbird chiming up the gully, the water clunking in the hollow bend, the flax windbreak around the shack scratching its giant leaves one against the other with the sound of starched linen.

'Haere mai,' croaked Poa, wandering out of his whare and giving me a very black banana. He smelt to heaven of methylated spirits, but it did not occur to me that this was why Riti walloped him.

I returned home full of peace and resolution and confessed to Auntie Wendela what I had said to Madame and why.

'You mean you asked her not to call you Ginger?'

'No. I told her.'

'Crikey!'

'And I said she was a rude woman. An *ugly* rude woman.'

Auntie Wendela paled. No doubt the ramifications of my rashness were clear to her – Uncle Hugo on relief work, no roof over their heads, a general descent into the maelstrom. But she did not bow the head easily.

'So she is, the Hun!'

Why I did not tell her that Helga likewise was confined by Divine ordinance to the role of servant to the socially privileged I do not know. Possibly I was developing some tact. Or maybe I simply did not want to wound my dear aunt's feelings.

Fearfully we waited for the Brigadier to have a word with Uncle Hugo. But he never did, so perhaps Madame kept our altercation to herself. But she never spoke to me again, and when I muttered 'Good morning,' she gave me the kind of baleful look reserved for the dog that has wet the carpet.

Many years passed before I thought of Madame as a person, a lonely woman whose feelings I must have hurt or affronted. Did she ever realise what she had done to mine? Probably not, judging from the tales of outrageous insensitivity her servants told of her.

Hattie, who heard the details from the eavesdropping gardener, took revenge on the nobs in her own way. When the boxes of unworn, discarded clothing were packed for dumping in the Gulf, Hattie extracted a dark blue linen Patou dress and a Schiaparelli jacket. She whisked them out of the Big House and into my suitcase to be taken back to Auckland when I returned home. Uncle Hugo never knew. He was an honest man and wouldn't have stood for it.

The dress was as plain as could be. Nothing hung from it or stuck out anywhere. It was as different from the aunts' dresses as could be imagined. But it had five plackets with invisible fasteners. My mother, the clever dressmaker, was to examine them with reverence.

'That's what makes the perfect fit.'

She altered this one and that, infinitesimally, so that the dress fitted me perfectly too. Together we admired the garment's only ornament, six ravishing little buttons of handpainted china. For many years they reappeared on family clothing, and I still have four of them.

The leaf-green jacket was equally plain, every inner seam oversewn with silk thread.

'Look at the set of those sleeves!' she said raptly.

For my mother studying those garments was better than viewing the Mona Lisa. She was a craftswoman and an artist and recognised art when she saw it.

'And to think that Hun was going to drop this in the Gulf!'

'You're going to look like a young woman before you know it,' observed Aunt Wendela, when we secretly tried on the stolen clothes at Glen Afra. This depressed me. I still thought my body already faultlessly constructed for the kind of life I wanted to live.

However, time works its wonders. I was to leave Glen Afra with the shape of a girl and the resentful knowledge that probably I should never sleep on my stomach again. It hurt the bumps on my chest too much.

'You'll get used to it,' said Helga heartlessly. She herself had the long slender body of the Norwegian, which indeed I was destined to develop myself.

'It's not fair!' I yowled, finding I could no longer button the third button of my blouse.

'What *is*?' asked my cousin dryly.

'Ah, just look at that,' doted the assembled aunts when I returned to Auckland. 'She's growing herself a ducky little figure!'

I could have killed them for even noticing. It sounded as if I were engaged in propagating some choice horticultural specimen. My father studiously never looked below my chin. I've often wondered if it is a shock to a man to find that his wild little comrade of a daughter has always had this secret and amazing ability to grow into a woman while he wasn't looking. However, it's not the kind of question one asks one's father.

But there were greater and more exciting things for me to think about, for I had been summoned back from Glen Afra to go to college. I didn't know how this had happened, I didn't know which college. I didn't ask questions at all in case Fate got the pip and took back its benison.

'It's a miracle, a real miracle,' said Auntie Wendela, shedding a few tears which were all the more gratifying because she never cried, not even in her most passionate rages. This abstinence was not in the family tradition. The other sisters could weep at the drop of a hat, and did so, whenever it seemed the most useful thing to do – pretty showers of dewdrops that did not disturb their faces in the least.

We cousins grew up cynical about women who can cry without getting red noses.

So I appreciated Auntie Win's rare tears, and crackled gratefully. The crackle was because she had wrapped me tightly around the diaphragm with stout brown paper, fastening the bandage with safety pins. My protests had been disregarded.

'I read somewhere that it prevents travel sickness

totally,' she said hopefully.

This is untrue. My sufferings on the homeward journey were compounded by the manner in which the brown paper worked itself down into my pants, creating an uncannily noisy bustle.

But such embarrassments were to come. I left Glen Afra in a daze of excitement and joy.

'If you see any movies, write and tell me *all* about them,' ordered Helga. 'Especially if it's Marleen.'

Uncle Hugo, who didn't hug people, briskly shook hands.

'Bonne chance!' he said.

'Oh, stop showing off,' said his wife.

PART THREE

· 1 ·

How sweet to find one has been missed! The kitchen behind the fruit shop boiled with people, aunts with plates of date loaf and snail bun, a beaming uncle, my mother flushed, saying little but delighted to see me, Flash Jack going on like a lunatic.

'Oh, hasn't she grown!'

'She'd be quite tall if she didn't have so much turned up at the end.'

'Trust you to mention her feet, Roley. You're as tactless as a pig in a pie-shop, and so are all your family.'

My sister had become leggy. She wasn't a baby any more but a solemn child with black eyebrows, flaxen hair in a Dutch bob and a tooth missing in front. Bashful with me after so long an absence, she dodged behind our father.

I had been shocked at the first sight of Mera, my dear friend. Gaunt and subdued, his big bones sticking out at elbows and wrists, his hair sparse and grey, he was very different from the ruddy man who had danced me around the kitchen in Nettie Street. He read my dismayed face, gave me a hug and whispered, 'Things will be grand now you're home.'

At this point Flash Jack caused an effective diversion by assaulting Grandma, whom he abhorred. What an uproar, what a screaming and bawling, though in fact he hadn't bitten the old lady, merely seized a piece of her wrinkly lisle stocking and pulled it out in a long peninsula and worried it.

Extraordinarily, Grandma wasn't at all upset, wouldn't have him smacked, or even put outside.

'I like a dog that'd eat the limbs off you,' she commented.

Critically she looked me over, while I shifted about uneasily, anticipating some scorching observation, which in due time, came.

'I hear you've turned into a clarky big lump,' she said.

I was not at all pleased with the big lump, and spiky indeed with the clarky, which I fancied must be an obscure Irish insult of the worst kind. But what she had really said was 'clerky', meaning studious, or scholarly, and she'd meant it as a compliment.

As soon as I had time alone with my father, I told him I had actually seen and exchanged words with the famous Starkie. He couldn't believe it; to him and other returned soldiers Starkie was the personification of the colonial infantryman, intractable, ingenious, contemptuous of authority, brave to the point of foolhardiness.

'Crikey, the tales that used to run around camp about that joker! He was recommended for decorations six times, you know? Including the Victoria Cross.'

'What for? What did he do?'

'It was in France. He went out into No Man's Land and carried back twenty wounded. On his back. Then in an absentminded moment he gave some officer a good one alongside the ear, so they threw him in gaol. Military prison, a cow of a place. So when the VC came through they wouldn't give it to him.'

'But that's unfair! Gee, that's awful.'

'His sentence was remitted, though. Twenty years just for a friendly clout! That was the Army for you. But another time he was recommended for the DCM by the Black Watch . . . I think he got that one all right.' He sighed and shook his head. 'Starkie! And you tell me that's what he's come to – pick and shovel and a flaming goat chewing up his socks.'

'At the going down of the sun and in the morning we will remember them,' I intoned solemnly. Unwisely also, for such cynicism embarrassed him. Still, he saw my point, and knew I understood what he was thinking.

My father was bitter for the likes of James Douglas Stark and also for himself. He was on the call-up list for a relief camp on the unpopulated Central Plateau, the lonely lunar highlands of Kaingaroa. He knew that country; when young he and two brothers had ridden from Waiotapu to Lake Taupo across the trackless tussocky desert, with side expeditions into the desolate pumice plains to the east. It was a region well over 600 metres above sea level.

'There's nothing there, not even birds. It's a place where the volcanoes have been dumping their rubbish for millions of years. And cold! The wind blows straight from the snowy mountains. And they want to plant trees there!'

He didn't know about man-made forests, only native forest. But he had been chosen because of his long experience with timber. My father was given no choice. Both single and married men were refused relief unless they went off to camps in the country to do labouring work. They were paid thirty to thirty-five shillings weekly. Most of this was sent to the family. The men themselves received only 'tobacco money'. The wage was not enough to keep a family, and in Auckland at least there were constant newspaper reports of wives and children being evicted while the breadwinner was in relief camp.

'Pray God they don't send him in the winter,' said my mother. 'If he gets that illness again, he'll be finished. And so will we.'

The relief camps were as cruel a ploy as any Government, through ignorance and desperation, could devise. In localities such as Aka Aka the men worked waist-deep in freezing swamp water; in the high country some of the men who built a mountain road had no boots, only 'Prince Alberts', strips of sacking wound around the feet and legs. Occasionally, the camps provided were lines of small huts made of sheets of corrugated iron. At Kaingaroa the men lived in tents.

'I'm real glad you're going back to school,' said Mera, on my first day. 'You make the most of it, now.'

He had a Scots reverence for education, thought it opened all doors. He changed his mind when, two months later, on the Kaingaroa Plains, he learned that there was a Rhodes Scholar in the next tent.

Yet he went off willingly, my mother told me, even a little excitedly, wearing his number tag, carrying his old Army kitbag with some packed food, and all the warm clothing he had.

'It was a job, you see,' she explained. 'Something regular at last, even though the pay was shocking and the conditions were for slaves. A job with a name. Planting trees. I don't suppose you understand what that does to a man's self-respect, not having regular work, and for so long, too.'

But all that was to come. Presently my sister and I, she frightened and tearful, myself frightened and hopeful, went off to St Benedict's. I felt in my bones that a new life was beginning for me. But in fact it was the rest of my life.

· 2 ·

St Benedict's, unfunded, unheated, elderly and shabby, how much I owe you! It upstaged St Joseph's, Te Kuiti, by having no library at all. The 'Science room' as I recall it, was equipped with a dozen test tubes, and three volcanic Bunsen burners that shot out blue flames and singed our eyebrows.

The Sisters, again of the Order of St Joseph, were a lively and unselfconscious group. I remember one of them pursuing the cranky and inefficient cleaner down a corridor, crying in a piercing voice, 'You dirty old man!' which doubtless awakened misgivings in the bosoms of passersby.

Several of the nuns were what my grandmother called Quality. She did indeed sketch a creaky curtsey to Sisters Bertille or Laurencia if she happened across either in the church. However, while these Sisters may not have been working-class girls originally, their care was for the children of workers. St Benedict's motto, *Laborare Est Orare* – work is prayer – was certainly theirs. They made us work hard and toe the line; for themselves and for us they took self-discipline for granted.

They were true daughters of their remarkable founder, Mother Mary McKillop, whose love for the neglected, illiterate children of outback Australia was so burning hot she could hardly see a disused chickenhouse without wanting to clean and whitewash it and start a school. The first St Benedict's school, established in the 1880s, had been elsewhere in the parish, set up in an empty butcher's shop.

For their labours the Sisters received few, if any fees. I had the illusion I was the only student taught for nothing. Sister Bertille had taken me aside and asked me never, never to tell the other girls our little secret. In after years I discovered that she had told the same tale to almost everyone, so that no girl's pride should be hurt.

I also had the illusion that no one noticed I had nothing but a summer uniform to wear during the long Antarctic winter, so I was humiliated into the ground when I was called to the Convent and given a sizeable parcel.

'Perhaps your dear mother can make use of these.'

The parcel contained substantial black knickers, elastic renewed; vests, white, with tiny holes so exquisitely mended the final effect was of embroidery; black woollen stockings darned almost invisibly.

I believed my mother would go off like a rocket. But I was the one who ranted and wept, never so mortified before or since. Exactly why I cannot recall. I must put down my anguish to the irrational, rawly sensitive feelings of the newly adolescent.

'Nuns' pants!' was my cry. 'Nuns' pants!'

'Hadn't you better remember Ivy's mother?' asked my mother.

We gave several pairs of the pants to Grandma – there were, after all, at least ten Sisters teaching at St Benedict's – and she was enraptured.

'I was eating me heart out for the warm drawers,' she said. 'Didn't I make a novena to St John?'

He was her best-loved saint because of her father and little dead Johnny.

'But I couldn't bring meself to mention what it was for,' she continued. 'St John was a bachelor, you know,' she added confidentially.

While my father was exiled at Kaingaroa Plains, our old

rapport became strengthened. Every night I had nightmares of freezing cold, a board bunk, half-hunger. I often awakened sobbing. My mother thought I was unhappy at college, but the reverse was true. I had no knowledge of what Mera suffered. He told us nothing until he returned home, and then not all of it.

Since those days I have flown two or three times over the Kaingaroa. It is the largest of several vast man-made forests between Rotorua and Taupo, forests that mark the map with seas and estuaries of dark green. The Kaingaroa, indeed, claims to be the world's largest, it covers 142,000 hectares. Who recalls that this national wealth was originally provided by what amounted to forced labour in the 1930s? My father, though he was a bushman hardened to heavy work and privation, was frostbitten on both hands. He said that as the long line of men stumbled across the plain, blinded by wind, the pumice squeaking under their feet, each with his hessian bag filled with infant pines around his waist, he'd often hear the men next to him crying with cold.

All kinds of men were in the camps, professional men, ex-prisoners, who were paroled if they agreed to participate, schoolteachers, salesmen, dockers. They had food rations of the basest sort, porridge, bread, tea, stew, badly cooked. 'Slopped on the tin plate as if we were dogs,' said Mera.

The tents leaked. Mera had to get up three or four times a night to bounce the snow off the fly. His tentmate was a quiet, elderly accountant whose hands couldn't take the work. He was constantly fined for breaking trees as he tried to get them into the frost-webbed ground. This man had lost his work and his home; his family were dispersed, living with relatives. He had nothing at all except his life, which he got rid of one night.

'The blood froze, too,' said Mera.

· 187 ·

· 3 ·

I found myself living intensely on several levels, as adolescents do. At school I had to work like the very devil, for in orthodox education I was two years behind the other students. Still, Sister Bertille was determined that I should get my University Entrance along with everyone else. Most of my study was done by candlelight, because no matter which house we shifted to, the electricity had been cut off, and was never turned on again. There was about me a certain air of the young Chatterton in the garret, wrapped in a blanket, crouched over a candle, frenziedly studying or writing. For now I had discovered from the newspaper room of the Public Library that almost every newspaper in New Zealand had a children's page, and I fired off poems and stories to all of them. Somehow I had been trapped by my adoration of Miss Elsie K. Morton into disregarding even the *Auckland Star*, which had a first-rate children's section and moreover a system of rewards. For each contribution published the young writer received marks and when she had a total of twenty she could *choose a book*! In a short time I had three books of my own to put beside the poetry anthology and *Grimms' Fairy Tales* – Tennyson, Thoreau and *Henry Esmond* (a grave mistake).

My brain was on fire, I came out in spots and my eyes bunged up, but I scarcely noticed. Who understands the phenomena that lie at the heart of the inexplicable creative processes? One writer says 'I just feel cloaked', and another, 'I feel something queer in my ankle bones.' And yet another, 'I just gaze (at some idea, or character, or title or personal name) and *that* occurs.' Which is the best description of all of the force, phraseless, wordless, that drives the writer or artist on – *That*.

Unfortunately this fiery upwelling of creativity has little relation to the value of what is produced. Technique and long practice need to be added; it was my luck that I realised this, though I was at a loss how to work out the next step.

So many autobiographers can tell wounding tales of their school days; I, with none, feel deprived of a literary opportunity. My years at St Benedict's, though always cold, often hungry, hardworked and sometimes anxious were a time of joy, an opening of windows, and my road to love of many kinds.

As Latin was not taught at the college, my Harrow Latin was put aside; however, as most students were in those times, we were given a thorough coaching in roots, prefixes and suffixes. Loving Latin, I revised my small knowledge frequently, finding it of use thoughout life in my study of English, French and later Italian. Amongst literary people I have never met one who, having studied Latin when young, believes it to have been a waste of time.

Uncle Hugo's Canadian French eventually got me through Matriculation with ease. Thank God there was no oral examination at that time, as Kiwi French is scarcely understood even by Nouméans. But in its temperamental way the grammar remains constant, so the blisses of French literature have ever been open to me.

Time passed. I was appointed Head Girl, and had to make tortured little speeches of welcome to visiting missionaries and Bishops. Tittering, bladder-conscious crocodiles were led by me on various cultural outings, and I was entrusted to fetch home the Sisters' substantial coutil corsets on appro from George Court's, a large department store in Karangahape Rd. Thin nuns, up and down like a yard of tap water, wore the same formidable girdings as their more robust colleagues. It was baffling.

'Stout Corset, when with hook and eye,' I used to murmur to myself.

For some time our headmistress was Sister Laurencia, she who had responded so warmly to Father Duck's pleas for a Josephine school at Te Kuiti. She was a fragile, quite aged lady, with a beautiful voice and soft, flowery blue eyes. One phrase from the voice, one glance from the eyes, and you were gone. She lent me books, poetry and belles lettres mostly, and did all she could to improve my style as a writer.

She had taught at St Joseph's Convent School, Glen Innes, in New South Wales, and although D'Arcy Niland had not been in her classes, she knew the dark, out-at-elbows boy and had read his stories.

'I wonder could you two help each other?' she mused. 'You are of an age, I think. It might be interesting for you to be penfriends.'

Somehow I slid out of it, succeeding at last with the excuse of my Tongan girls. The Sisters had fixed me up with them, too. I had three of them at a shilling each per lesson, delicious honeyskinned creatures with large dimpled hands and torrents of curly wood-brown hair. It was my privilege to teach these trainee nurses English and simple arithmetic.

Sister Laurencia quite saw that I owed a Christian duty to these kindly loves from the Islands, and absolved me from corresponding with any despairing would-be writer in Sydney, Australia. In my mind I was outraged. Another whiney boy? At the time I sometimes went to the pictures with my cousin Harvey, guest night, ninepence for him and nothing for me, depth of the Depression prices. My yearning for entertainment was so abject I endured even his deadly narcissism. Everything that he had done, would do, could think, had thought was precious to him, and, as he assumed, to me. His conversations all began with the mysterious words 'I've seen me . . .'

For me, cousin-poisoned, boys were still nowhere. I certainly was not going to be trapped into spending spare time writing to yet another 'I've seen me . . .' Let this D'Arcy Niland, whoever he was, get on with it.

Some years later, Sister Laurencia got her way, and today, when we have a family gathering and I look around at all these young Nilands I think, 'Little you know, you lot, how much you owe to an old nun in New Zealand who loved reading John Ruskin and listening to Haydn.'

In 1978 the girls of the secondary college were transferred to a co-educational school; the primary school was closed in 1982. Perhaps the battered, threadbare old building was demolished. I do not know. Its ghosts remain in my heart. It is one more place where a fence has been built around the cuckoo.

· 4 ·

On another level my life as an active member of a tumultuous family continued. The fear that had stalked both my sister and myself for so long was at last justified; Flash Jack was skittled by a tram. Somehow he crawled home. We found him in an evil cubbyhole in the shop basement. Dark as night, with a pervasive smell of gas and rotten fruit, it was known as the banana room, though years had passed since it had been used for its original purpose of ripening green bananas shipped in from the Pacific Islands. We girls used it for hiding the stray cats we rescued from the streets, and Uncle Roley dashed in there with betting sheets and other incriminating evidence whenever his policeman friend warned him of an imminent raid by The D's.

The banana room has stayed with me throughout life; I have used it in stories many times. I think it haunts me because of the agony of that little dog, his uncomplaining courage. Twice since that time I have sat with injured dogs until the end, and always they asked only what Flash Jack asked, that their paws be held.

Flash Jack had severe injuries; his shoulder was dislocated, his hide was torn in many places, one foot was crushed, and he must have had internal injuries, for his belly began to swell. He was smothered in blood and black grease. It was late on Sunday, the fruit shop was closed. My father was still at Kaingaroa, and my mother away from home, involved in some emergency of Grandma's.

There was no hope of getting a vet. Even if one had been close there was not a penny in the house to pay him. My sister, then about eight, and I set about keeping Flash Jack alive.

In that bad-smelling dark hole, by candlelight, we put him together as best we could. We rearranged the bones in his paw and bound it firmly, holding all together with one of my sister's socks. Twice I tried to slip the dislocated shoulder back into place. It must have caused excruciating pain. Now and then during this process Flash Jack emitted that shrill, birdlike scream of the injured animal, and softly closed his jaws over my hand. But all he wanted was for things to halt for a few moments until he felt capable of enduring more.

The second time I heard the joint click into place. But it was not quite right, and he had a lopsided shoulder and a funny half-hop on his foreleg until he died.

When my mother returned home she thought he should not be moved. She sent my sister to bed and brought down old clothing and a hot water bottle to keep Flash Jack warm. I saw she did not think he would live. His little black face had grown sharper, his breathing was laboured, his tongue pale.

'But his nose is still quite cold, Mum!' I repeated in desperate hope. 'You know what Dad always says!'

The three of us nursed Flash Jack night and day, dribbling water into his mouth, sponging his lips and jaws, keeping his wounds clean. We cut up and soaked meat, feeding him the raw juice with an eye dropper. And always there was someone rubbing his ear, holding his paw. On the tenth day he staggered outside to attend to his private needs, and after that he began to eat a little.

Dogs are tough-minded, stoic animals, and Flash Jack came of a steely breed. This game, loving little villain lived several years longer and died in the countryside which was his natural habitat. He was flash to the last.

· 5 ·

The aunts were not as good managers as my mother, and became panicky more quickly. So they originated optimistic schemes for making a little extra to augment their men's reduced wages. They rushed headlong into sewing buttons on cards at threepence a card. We all sat round the kitchen table gossiping and drinking tea, sewing, sewing, with triumphant cries of 'That's three and ninepence *at least*!' until our ardour and ambition died.

However, this art or craft served me well in later hard times, when I lived in Surry Hills in Sydney. With sizes and colours of buttons ranged in tin lids on the table, I sewed on buttons while working on radio plays for the Australian Broadcasting Commission. Thus dictating dialogue to my collaborator and loved one, who sat nearby, fingers poised at the typewriter, I turned out scripts and button cards simultaneously.

There were days when Grandma was the subject of most conversation. She was important to us all.

Oh, my dear Grandma, she was having a cruel time just then. Although she had many offers of help and downright interference, she tried to work the problem out by herself.

Even when they lived close by, as my mother did at that time, she never visited her daughters. She stated that she'd had enough of them when young and now they could get on with it. Well I understood her point of view, but the aunts could not come to grips with her lack of concern for the thrilling trivia of their lives, the fights with husbands and each other, the taking of umbrage at what the butcher said, the discussions about Ross's truancy, Grant's pimples, and Uncle Kenny's sudden and suspicious desire to buy a number of rather bright new shirts.

When these subjects were broached, Grandma gave her daughters an evil green glance and said, 'To the devil with ye!'

She did, however, as all knew, love them dearly, even if she drove them bats praying for them.

'But what does she pray for?' they murmured to each other, bewildered.

'That you'll die young in your health and beauty and make a pretty corp.'

'Ooh, shut up, you gruesome thing.'

They looked at each other in dismay, as though they

suspected Grandma wasn't beyond it. The pretty corp was a direct quotation from the old lady. When the son of a neighbour drowned in a boating accident, Grandma hustled me and my cousin Harvey to view the departed. He was laid in his coffin in the front room of his home, the grieving relatives grouped around.

Vibrating with nerves I was, but also mad with curiosity to see how an ordinary kind of dead person looked. (I hadn't felt the dead chief at the Pa had been at all ordinary.) While the stricken mother sobbed, and the relatives recited the Litany in hushed voices, we reverently approached the casket, which was heaped with jonquils.

'God be praised,' intoned Grandma, 'doesn't he make a pretty corp!'

Her tone of amazement was such that one instantly realised that she thought the poor lad had been as plain as a pig in life.

Still, it was true, the dead boy was beautiful, marble white under a square of gauze, his dark hair curling. This first sight of death was a transforming experience for me, for I recognised that this was an unoccupied face. Identity had gone, his soul, his personality, whatever it was. The impetuous thing, confronted by a body deprived of air, couldn't wait a moment. Impatiently it had flitted away, disregarding all familiar things.

'A lovely corp!' said my Grandma with a deep sigh, almost as if she were envious.

Harvey uttered a whooping snort of horror or protest and fled.

'Won't I murder you if you do the same thing!' Grandma hissed sideways at me.

Kind words she said to each of the relatives, though these inexplicably provoked outbursts of crying. Then we went home and had tea and scones, Grandma with the cosy air of one who has done a good day's work.

'Now we'll say a decket for his soul.'

She chose one of the Glorious Mysteries, for as she said confidently, 'He's out of the wind and wave now, God bless him.'

Grandma's view of death was never expressed in words. I can but guess at it, but I fancy it was pragmatic and healthy. Death was a part of life and when you died things were better. She believed she would hear again in Heaven, and meet once more her Dadda, her Johnny, and the young mother whose face she had never seen. I thought her ideas good and sensible, and so strongly resisted other people's, especially those promulgated by the fearsome Redemptorist missionaries.

Naturally, I did not think that Grandma, at her advanced age, had any views on Love, and when the storm broke I was profoundly shocked.

Every Saturday morning my mother and I went to Grandma's house. While I cleaned house, my mother did the washing and sorted garments and bedlinen to be taken away to be mended. Grandma reciprocated in her own way; she knitted socks and stockings for everyone. She knitted so fast the four steel needles flickered with light, and while knitting she said aspirations to the Sacred Heart, Our Lady, and St Benediction. Indulgences were attached to these brief prayers and Grandma carefully counted up the days of grace she had thus earned and dispensed them to various souls in Purgatory. It can thus be seen that as far as indulgences were concerned she was not on Martin Luther's side, but neither was she on the Pope's team. She once gave me forty days indulgence as a Christmas present.

On this particular Saturday we found Grandma in tears. Having never previously seen a tear from the old lady, I was aghast. I thought Poor Jack must have been run over, or caught his dumb head in one of the machines at the factory. But no, he had fallen in love. A girl called

Philomena, a Child of Mary, a devout Catholic. Anyone would have thought Grandma would have called down blessings on her and Poor Jack. Not so. She was out of her mind with rage and jealousy.

There wasn't a thing that was good about that poor girl. From the beginning Grandma adopted the stance that Philomena was a man-hungry old maid who had led astray an innocent boy, and you couldn't have changed her mind with a hammer.

'But Jack's twenty-six, Ma,' yelled Rosina, 'and Philomena's twenty-two!'

'Ah, you'd be looking at her a long time before you thought of a chicken!'

Grandma was seventy-three at the time, built of steel and wire. Philomena was a frail, overworked factory girl, timid and peaky. She often worked an eleven-hour day, as the threat of dismissal was held over the girls' heads if they did not work overtime for nothing.

'And look at her father, what kind of a father is that?'

Philomena's father was called Dead Pauley. The story was that he had the habit of falling into a trance and frightening the daylights out of people. Grandma went on as if he were Lazarus. In vain the helpful aunts shouted down her good ear that all was well, if unusual.

'You call that well, do you? And what if it's catching?'

She forebade the girl the house, and ballyragged Jack day and night. Philomena was all that was sly and devious; she knew a good thing when she saw him and would throw his old mother out on the street in one blink of her eye. The simple, gentle Jack had no answers: he did not know what to say to this loving mother who had turned overnight into a raging fiend.

The aunts were very much on Philomena's side.

'He's not much to write home about,' declared Rosie 'even if he is my own brother. You'd be wasting yourself.'

'I could make something of him,' said Philomena sadly. 'Oh, why doesn't she like me?'

Why indeed? Grandma must have seen that Philomena was just the kind of daughter-in-law who would take her on as a Christian duty and look after her devotedly until she went to her heavenly reward. But her jealousy and anticipated deprivation were too much for her; she wanted her son all to herself; she wanted the usurper out of it.

Grandma now often cried. I used to find her slamming back and forth in her rocking chair and mourning 'Me heart's destroyed!' Perhaps all the tears of her long, hard, resolute life had banked up inside her, and Poor Jack's defection, as she saw it, brought them out in a ceaseless gush.

She had plenty to cry about – leaving Ireland and her father for ever; cruel boarding-house keepers whose stairs and kitchens she scrubbed; the handsome Karl Johann turning out to be a drunk; all those children with no space for recovery between them; little Johnny falling into the fire; pretty, silly Willy running away; her beloved father dying alone in Ireland. And now Jack, the centre of her life, leaving her for someone with a father called Dead Pauley.

It was a painful discovery that someone as old as Grandma could still feel so passionately. My concept of her as a little, rascally, rather foreign woman skittering about on the edge of our real family life, changed for the better, and I loved her all the more for it.

As it was, the engagement was called off, Jack left home and took to the bottle and Philomena died unmarried. Grandma was left to live on her Age Pension which had been reduced to fifteen and ninepence. As her rent was ten shillings weekly, staying alive became an impossibility for Grandma. At the same time all civil servants had their wages cut by 30 per cent. The Governor-General, the respected Lord Bledisloe, offered to cut his as well, and after that he managed on £6,750, which would be a splendid sum in modern dollars.

But Grandma and most other aged, invalid or widowed pensioners who had no family to take them in, found themselves abandoned on the ice floe.

During seven months of this year, 1932, the Auckland City Mission provided more than 100,000 free meals and 37,000 free beds.

The City Missioner, the Reverend Jasper Calder, with whom I had a lot to do in future years, commented, 'Fantastic numbers for a country like New Zealand! And we were only one supporting charity. The Salvation Army fed even more, I believe. Mostly old men. Sad thing. Often the family would take Mum in but have no room for Dad, if he'd been a boozer or a walloper. Rough justice. And then there were many, many cases where a respectable lady just couldn't bring herself to be seen eating a charity meal. We'd see Dad sneaking food for her, a sausage in this pocket, a slice of bread in that. The food was donated mostly – manufacturers, bakers. People were good as far as they could afford to be. But those were appalling times.'

So Grandma began her wandering life, six months with this daughter, three with that. They did their best, and the sons-in-law were admirably co-operative. The aunts and my mother made sure that Grandma ate properly, and was dressed warmly and tidily. They washed and cut her hair, which she had always worn parted in the centre and drawn back to a skimpy yellow-streaked bun. What a surprise! It turned out white and shiny as satin, with a little wave in it. Grandma was what she described as 'cocked-up', and went around primping it at the back and drawing people's attention to it. The only catch was that now her majestic black hat slid down over her eyebrows, causing consternation.

But my mother put a false ceiling in the hat, stuffed with tissue paper, and swathed the crown with a scrap of mauve silk she found amongst her dressmaker's bits and pieces. Topped with this, the coke hatpin sticking out at an alluring angle, Grandma declared she wouldn't call the King her uncle.

Was she happy, separated from her beloved Jack? She did not complain. She still went her own way, plunging abruptly across roads into the path of oncoming trams and giving motormen heart attacks. It was not that she didn't see these vehicles; like Flash Jack she treated them with contempt. We young ones dreaded 'taking' Grandma somewhere; we always expected to be killed.

She walked up to St Benedict's at least twice a day, forty miles to the cup of tea, my father said. She did the Stations of the Cross, bawled out the cleaner, an angry lady of Latin derivation and spunky temper, and no doubt communed with her loved dead. Once when we had a famous organist, the Benedictine Dom Moreno, visiting the parish, I caught Grandma with her ear pressed against the back of a church seat. When the brilliant Spaniard was practising she could feel the vibrations of the music through the timber.

She explained in a whisper, 'It's that dawshy little Father who's been around the place lately. It's himself gladiatoring on the harmonium.'

Jack often visited her, sometimes cajoling her pension out of her, to the aunts' fury.

'You'd give that waster your blood, I believe!' cried Theresa.

'I would,' declared Grandma. 'To the devil with ye!'

· 6 ·

There was a growl in the air that grew and grew, the
ominous undertone that rises from people naturally orderly
and patient, who are now fed to the back teeth with hard
times that are not of their doing. It was that snarl of the
populace which must surely recall to every person in
authority the historic fact that sooner or later the faceless
ones rise up and cut your throat.

Mera said, 'You'd better come along to some meetings
with me.'

'Oh, Mel, she doesn't want to get mixed up in that
political stuff, she has enough to do with her study and
everything.'

'She won't find any real life in those bloomin' poetry
books.'

He pronounced poetry in the oldfashioned manner
– poytry – which somehow seemed to make my secession
from real life all the more reprehensible. It was true that
I spent most of my time inside my head, and it was probably
best that I came out.

The meetings of which Mera spoke were those of the
Unemployed Workers' Movement, a loosely strung angry
semi-union of people who had come to the end of their
tether. The two conservative Auckland newspapers called
them Communists, a dirty word then, but probably they
formed what would at present be termed the extreme Left
of the Labour Party.

Politics broke over me like a high surf. In the top

echelons it may have been a matter of economic manoeuvring and theorising, but down amongst the rank and file, where I was, it was all people, hungry, baffled, impotent people. We listened to Labour politicians, particularly a one-armed returned soldier, John A. Lee, a fiery, eloquent, brooding man. And there were demagogues, too, those extraordinary persons who rise like the spurt of a fountain from the inarticulate masses, to agitate, invigorate or convert; how I loved to feel the crowd pulse, tremble, sway in response to these men. It seemed to me it was not what they said that had such power, for often that was factious and repetitive; it was the tune, the vocal style. All the more did I think this a few years later, when we heard, often and terrifyingly, that greatest demagogue of all, Adolf Hitler, who could rouse and excite even when one did not know his language.

Yet these were such orderly meetings! There was heckling, but not the rumbustious heckling expected by us today; we are people reared on violent confrontation between mobs and police or Army. That generation was not. So many of them had left Europe to get away from military and civilian bullying. Poor devils, those who could find the fare often went home again.

It had been a national shock in January 1932, when there was a riot in Dunedin.

'Of all places!' people marvelled.

The Edinburgh of the south, blue granite, cold, Presbyterian, respectable and Tory to a degree, that was Dunedin.

'There's no one as rampageous as a Scotsman when he's got a bee up his kilt,' observed Mera.

Dunedin had had a misery of a Christmas, and even worse, a wretched Hogmanay. Though the season was midsummer, the temperature did not climb above 13° Celsius.

The Otago Hospital Board seems to have been in charge of dispensing food and other necessities to destitute people. A group of unemployed men and women marched to the Board's headquarters and asked for food parcels, even though some of the men were earning a little on relief. The value per family would have been about fifteen shillings. When they were refused, the crowd rushed to a nearby grocery store and kicked in its windows. They were beaten back by police, and no looting occurred. Most of the day the streets boiled with raging people, until the Board announced the distribution of some hundreds of food parcels.

The newspaper editorials of the day were shameful. Obviously management was of the opinion that it was moral to starve but immoral to riot. They hoped, they said, that the Mother Country would never get to hear of it, thus foreshadowing the time when the Government censored outgoing news cables in order to keep from the world the information that New Zealand was halfway down the drain. We were, in our naïveté, to think just that, but of course the censorship was to prevent overseas creditors from panicking and demanding their money back.

'I can't believe it,' said Uncle Roley. 'This can't be New Zealand. Why, it's anarchy!'

Anarchy it was. Not the riot, but the social and economic disarray. Every public service had run down into the ground. Education particularly was brutally deprived; classes enormously increased in size, all warming of classrooms cut out, two of four teacher training colleges closed, hundreds of teachers unemployed. Religious schools, such as those run by the Marist Brothers, extended free education to school leavers, just to keep the boys off the street and out of the hands of the sweatshop owners who eagerly gathered up children under sixteen for work on starvation pay.

In the South Island the Army was on standby in case of public disorder; the Government extended its term for another year; Uncle Roley gravely told us he couldn't afford to give us any more specks; and Auckland erupted in a wonderful riot, the roar of which could be heard three kilometres away.

'It was grand, it was a bloomin' blast!' said my father, who was in the thick of it, coming home with his face streaked with blood and the fire of revolution in his eyes.

'Oh, dear God!' whispered my mother, imagining pogroms. I was beside myself with fury that I hadn't been present, for it had been a splendid event, a Kristallnacht of the far south, with almost every shop window in Queen Street booted in, cars turned over, heads walloped, policemen unhorsed, the Mayor threatening to read the Riot Act, and Auckland's sober citizens either thrilled or aghast and probably often both.

Orgy of Destruction, said the *New Zealand Herald* next morning. *Appalling Scenes. Worst Outbreak in Dominion.*

Like so many riots this had exploded out of a peaceful situation. Down Queen Street, the major banking and commercial centre of the city, a place of large fashionable shops, marched thousands of relief workers, their intention being to gather at the Town Hall. They had threatened a strike, asking a minimum wage of £3 weekly for married men, with ten shillings for each dependent child. They carried banners. Shouting wasn't the thing in those times, and I daresay this column of shabby men was as gloomy and silent as most marches were. At the Town Hall an industrial meeting of Post and Telegraph employees was already in progress. They were protesting the severe cuts in their wages. The relief workers halted to hear the amplified speeches from inside the Town Hall. There was probably pushing and shoving for better positions, and some peremptory reprimands from the police, a few of whom were mounted. This was customary since the Dunedin donnybrook.

Having survived a number of riots, I can confidently say that where there is a large mob and highstrung emotions, there will also be a dingbat.

This dingbat was a young policeman. He heard the word 'violence', he saw a head rise up out of the restive crowd, and he batoned it. Alas, the head belonged to Jim Edwards, the toughest and most influential of the U.W.M.'s demagogues, who had been hoisted on loyal shoulders so that he could shout, 'No violence, boys!' Mera was standing close to him, and he said this was so. Down went Jim, scalp split, spouting blood, and in an instant the crowd became a mob.

They dashed up Grey's Avenue, the Chinese quarter behind the Town Hall, and hauled palings from the fences of petrified laundrymen and market gardeners. With these they laid about them at police, cars, horses, plate-glass windows and display dummies, with the gusto born of years of frustration. No one was killed, but three hundred cracked heads and bloodied noses turned up later at the Public Hospital, and no one knows how many went home to the wife and a yelling match.

For inexperienced looters take all the wrong things. The prestigious stores carried prestigious and often luxury stock. Supermarkets hadn't been invented; Queen Street was no place for food shops. The things that people on relief really needed – blankets, clothing, shoes, staple provisions – simply were not there. That kind of merchandising was done in the suburbs.

Many a handful of gold watches must have rusted away under floor boards or in the lavatory cistern. One of my father's relief mates turned up with seven or eight.

'Here,' he said. 'Take your pick. I don't know how to get rid of them.'

'You don't get rid of them here!' cried my mother wrathfully. 'Throw them in the creek!'

Here we had thieves without fences, people who became very nervous when they realised what they had done. Aunt Theresa, who served in the fruit shop on race days, had some lively conversations with her customers. She had a little dramatic gift, and repeated them for us.

'Did I go to market! A fur coat! Where did he think I was going to wear a fur coat, one of them swanky ones, too, with huge big bobbles for buttons. Oh, couldn't I imagine myself going to the Marmite wearing my fur coat and my old shoes with the heels run over, and the bobbies coming to the house half an hour later! And where did you get that, missus, eh, speak up, missus. I could just hear them. Fur coat, I asked my hub, and me with me chest and no woollen singlet, and the children perished with cold, and the winter not even here yet. I meant it to be a real nice surprise, he says, sheepish. Surprise it is, I says to him, but not nice. Not sensible, hub. Sometimes I think you're out of your tiny, I says, not rude, you know, but sort of sad.'

'And what happened then, dear?'

'Ah, he did a bit of bellowing about gratitude and that, and then he said all right, I'll wear it meself. And when I went out later to see why he hadn't come to bed, there he was on the couch, a great big bundle of rabbit or squirrel or whatever it was, with his bare feet sticking out the end.'

'And whatever have you done with it, Mrs Bates?'

'Oh, we threw it in the presbytery garden last night. Give the Monsignor something to think about.'

At St Ben's the Sisters were in a state of shock and indignation because the looters had surged through a shop that sold religious items.

'Stuffing rosaries and prayerbooks into their pockets as

if they'd been diamond rings!' said one. Ambiguous, I thought.

'Stealing St Joseph, and *brand new!*' said another. Two or three of us girls were seized with coughing fits and had to leave the room, for we already knew about the life-sized, brightly coloured plaster saint who had lurched up Queen Street, amongst the seething, roaring multitude, bowing to left and right as his supporters staggered under the weight. He ended up in a pond in Albert Park, his plaster melted away and his horrid chickenwire innards exposed. Instead of a lily in his hand he now had a banner of the Unemployed Workers' Movement.

'Dreadful, dreadful!' said Sister, and then her human instincts prevailed and she too had a coughing fit.

One of the more despicable aspects of the riots (several followed Auckland's Kristallnacht) was that students were not only impressed to serve as 'special police' but volunteered. University, Grammar, and King's College old boys all became 'specials', and paraded the streets wearing tin hats and white armbands and carrying batons. They were much heckled by crowds, and nicknamed Glaxo babies. (This refers to a baby food of the time that produced alarmingly obese infants.) There were even a few mounted 'specials', and in the second riot in Auckland's Karangahape Road, Mera saw the spectacular downfall of one, tossed from his hysterical horse through a shop window.

'But why did the horse get hysterical?' I asked.

'Someone in the crowd shoved a pencil up its minnie,' my father replied restrainedly.

It must not be thought that the universities and public schools did not protest. Auckland University's student paper said, 'And so the cry is set up by those in power, we must baton those we cannot feed. God save the King and the British Empire.'

It was appropriate, quite in keeping with the New Zealand ethos, that during the dock strikes of 1913 the farmers whose butter was going rancid on the wharves should ride into town, their horses slipping and sliding on the unfamiliar hard pavements, and enter into bloody battle with the wharfies, in order to load that butter on the ships for Great Britain. But when a softhanded student, son of a doctor, solicitor or M.P., borrowed Daddy's hack and set out to bash in the heads of workless men and women, blood appeared in the eye of the most pacific.

The 'specials' were soon withdrawn.

Without exception, authority condemned the riots, even the struggling Labour Opposition. Wilful wanton destruction were the words most commonly used, and of course this was an accurate phrase. Even some rioters agreed, for it is said that parcels of stolen goods were returned to shopkeepers for months afterwards. The churches were admirable; their leaders may well have reproached their adherents for disgraceful behaviour, but they also spoke out boldly and even radically on the economic crisis. They agreed to a bishop that it was the system that was at fault, that the Government's Depression policy had crippled the country. Though I cannot believe that any of these religious leaders were Labour in out-look – Labour was suspected of being crypto-Socialist, almost as alarming as Communist – the solutions they put forward were largely those Labour had been unavailingly advocating for years – control of imports so that New Zealand could begin manufacturing its own home neces-sities; control of the banking system, still in the hands of overseas power; guaranteed minimum price for seasonally affected primary products.

All these and many more progressive changes were achieved after Labour's landslide victory in 1935. In the meantime the riots appeared to have done a great deal of good. They were reported overseas with varying degrees of sympathy or denunciation. It was, I presume, the first time any Imperial back garden had gone up in flames. They also alerted many comfortable Tory types, who were not doing it hard at all, to the realisation that out there people were desperate. The old order was changing, and the rubble might likely fall on their own heads. Jasper Calder said donations to the City Mission increased greatly.

· 7 ·

It was at this time that I lost hope. It is a not infrequent custom of Life to squeeze one into corners, but as long as this is not taken over-seriously by the squeezed it does not matter all that much. But I had taken the situation with adolescent extravagance. Having grown up somewhat, I could see plainly that my education fitted me for nothing in particular; once I might have won a bursary with my good University Entrance pass, but bursaries had been almost done away with. So University wasn't for me.

My mother yearned to make me a nurse or a teacher; these seemed to her dignified, constructive jobs for a woman, and two of the few that could be taken up again 'if anything should go wrong in your marriage'. The idea of either of these professions, for which I was hideously unfitted temperamentally, gave me cold sweats. But what *was* going to happen to me?

Added to that, I had been diagnosed as having pernicious anaemia. My mother took fright at this. From the doctor's grave expression she deduced that it was worse than everyday anaemia. Doctors, in those times, were almost universally non-communicative, riposting anxious questions with 'Don't you bother your head about that. Leave it all to me.' Possibly they believed this arcane silence added to their charisma. But the aunts, ever ready, scooted about and gathered from their friends horrendous tales which stood my poor mother's hair on end. She did not pass on these tales, but now and then I caught her looking at me and sighing, which put my hair on end, too.

No blood tests had been taken; perhaps they were unknown then. The doctor had examined me cursorily, peered at the inside of my eyelids, muttered, 'Good God, they're white!' and put me on a course of medicine that looked like black tar, tasted like old nails and made my teeth compare with a Japanese Court lady's. It was true that I was a skinny, lanky girl, pale as paper, with no energy at all. I fainted at the drop of a hat, and often caused commotions in church. My mature opinion is that I was exhausted, and no wonder, having to do a four-year study course in two years and under pretty austere conditions at that.

However, my current depression did not originate in anaemia or lack of job prospects.

One night I awoke and knew, coldly and without emotion, that my chances of becoming a professional writer were minimal. I admitted that probably my ambitions were unrealistic, a child's romance. The enchanting mirage of an existence devoted to literature shimmered for a moment on the darkness, and blinked out.

'You're still thinking about what that unfeeling woman said!' accused my mother, and I couldn't deny that I was.

'Here,' she said briskly. 'Clean this porridge saucepan. It's burned. That'll take your mind off your troubles.'

She went about her household duties, muttering, 'Hun!' and 'Imagine saying that to a child!'

'Here, leave that thing to soak!' she said at last, seeing me dropping tears into soapy water full of nasty little black bits. 'You can't go on brooding about things like that.'

'But she's right, Mum.'

'How can you be sure?'

'She knows about writing and getting published and everything.'

We were speaking of Miss Elsie K. Morton, literary light of the *New Zealand Herald*, who had written me a harsh and inexplicable letter. I have it in front of me now, and it still baffles me.

'I've loved her ever since I was eight,' I mourned. 'She's a wonderful writer."

'Nonsense!' said my mother. 'An eight year old wouldn't know a wonderful writer if she bit her. You just like her adjectives.'

This was true, and secretly I had known it since I was ten or eleven, when Sister Serenus brutally pointed it out.

'Miss Morton didn't ask to be your idol,' said my mother. 'You can't blame her for turning out to be someone entirely different from what you thought.'

'But why did she have to be so mean?' I blubbered. 'What did I *do*?'

Yes, indeed. Only a few years after that I was editor of a children's page four times larger than Miss Morton's, and never found it necessary to slap any child down. Today, as a children's writer, I receive hundreds of letters from children, and the same applies. What made Miss Elsie K. Morton, a mature and experienced woman, write so unkindly?

I had never had any communication with her at all; I wouldn't have dared hope for such an honour. I did not even know what she looked like; I was simply a young admirer of her articles.

For almost half my life, whenever I got hold of a stamp,

it had been my delight to post off a story or verse to the *Herald* children's page. Sometimes these contributions were published, sometimes tossed out. We were never notified; that was the way it was. The previous week I had sent off a story with my usual covering letter, hoping that Miss Morton would like it. As I had done so many times before, I added that I hoped to be a writer when I was older. No one expects an answer to a covering letter, but now I had one.

My mother, knowing how thrilled I'd be, had met me at the back door, rapturously waving the envelope.

'Open it, open it! Maybe she wants you to go to the *Herald* office so you can meet her.'

'There might be a job there, some day,' added Mera, pleased as Punch. 'Wouldn't that be a grand thing!'

But all Miss Morton had done was to turn my brief, humble note over, and write a few lines on the back. She made it quite clear that she doubted my ability ever to become a successful writer, and expressed resentment that I had the nerve to write to 'a busy editor' at all.

Her tone was, and is, chilling in the extreme.

Miss Morton's words hurt me profoundly in sensitive places, certainly in my estimation of my own abilities. Most of all in my confidence that my life's ambition had some substance. She killed it stone dead for a long time. To think I wasn't even worth a clean sheet of paper!

Forgetting all about my small revelation beside Poa's creek, now several years ago, I submissively assented to her abrasive statement. Step on my neck, lady, I said, just because I admired her so much.

'Put the ugly thing in the fire and forget it,' said my mother with warm sympathy.

'No,' said Mera. 'One day you'll have a desk of your own.'

'No, I won't, Daddy, I'll never have *anything*, I know that now.'

'A desk of your own,' he continued. 'Pin this letter above your desk, and when you feel downhearted or discouraged, or someone else has put the boot in for no reason, you can read it again, and get as mad as a wet hen. Then you'll go back to work and show Miss Morton just what you can do.'

This was commonsense. Often when I felt that the insecure life of a freelance was not worth the sparse rewards, Miss Morton's words did wonders for me.

They even did wonders for D'Arcy Niland, a person unknown to her. Whenever he was stuck in his work, or had had too many rejections, he rushed to wherever I was working, demanding, 'I need a dose of Elsie K. Morton, where is the old chook?'

In spite of Mera's predictions, I did not have a desk of my own for many years, so I had pasted Miss Morton's letter on the bottom of my typewriter. In response to my husband's call for help, I would turn over the typewriter so he could read those inspiring words. Rushing away, he would subside into silence for a moment or two; then I would hear his typewriter go off like a machine gun. Elsie K. Morton had triumphed once more.

Nevertheless, at the time, her words harmed me almost fatally. I rejected the aunts' suggestion that they were prompted by some subjective cause – her canary had the pip, or maybe she had indigestion? In fact, the aunts were showing wise comprehension of human nature and its horrid frailties. Many years afterwards I heard the writer J. B. Priestley remark, 'Whenever I get a prejudiced or obviously spiteful review I say to myself: "Of course the poor fellow has the most atrocious case of piles." *And I don't forget to tell everyone else*, either.'

As I became older, I concluded that she resented my contributions to other children's pages all over the country. Maybe she had a proprietary feeling about youthful writers who'd started with her, even though she had never communicated with them or given them a word of encouragement. Who can tell? But her action helped shape my own attitude to the many children who write to children's editors and writers asking the desolate question, 'How do I *start*?'

A professional writer must be careful indeed when replying to the letters of kids who say they want to write. They don't all mean it, of course. They have no idea what a writing life entails. But every now and then there is some child in whose letter sounds the authentic voice of desperation. He feels it in his ankles; I can tell that at once. Then I (like so many other writers) spend time and thought helping him a little. It can only be a little, because people can't be taught to write if the literary gift is not there. If it is, they can be taught how to write better, as Sister Serenus taught me when I was something of an age with these young people.

Out of the dark skies of depression and ruined confidence came the terrifying possibility that I might, after all, end up as a nurse or a schoolteacher, or even a shopgirl or a factory hand. There was nothing at all the matter with these professions except that I would never be a success at any of them.

'But, lovie, perhaps you'll just get married,' said my dear Auntie Wendela, who was visiting Auckland just then. It must have been before she burned down her house at Glen Afra.

Get married! I shook with terror and dismay.

· 8 ·

For many weeks my sister and I had been aware that all
was not well in our home. At night we heard muffled
conversations between our parents, and often our mother
looked as if she had been weeping. We girls whispered
together, anxious and ignorant.

'Do you remember when Grant thought his Mum and
Dad were going to divorce, and he put the gravel in the
steamroller engine for revenge?'

'Mum and Daddy would never, never . . .'

'How do we *know*?'

Poor little creature, she was only eight, still with her
classic eyebrows and milky hair, pale and fragile. Even to
me the adult world with its complexities and irrationalities
was still largely a mystery, so what was it to her?

Several times I asked my mother if anything were wrong,
but she put me off gently, once saying cryptically, 'I might
still win.'

Still, she packed up Grandma, who had lived with us
for several years, and sent her off to Theresa.

'But why, Mum?' I asked. 'She likes it here, so near
the church and everything. Is it Poor Jack?'

'It might be,' said my mother cautiously.

My mother was obsessive about alcohol; when Poor Jack
visited, smelling like a brewery, he had brisk treatment
from his sister. Once she hunted him out with a broom;
again he had bullied Grandma into giving him her pension.
Grandma, expectedly, was all on Poor Jack's side, crying,

'Bad luck to you, Cissy! Wouldn't you get a hand-and-foot if I was in me youth!'

Was there ever such a sad and universal cry? Nevertheless, Grandma was borne away to Theresa's comfortable home. I helped her pack her few possessions – the picture of her Guardian Angel, which we cousins, when young, believed depicted two little children being shoved over a cliff by a large feathered person; her pension book; her father's letters from Ireland and other worn, illegible documents; and half a pound of broken rosary beads.

'If you were not off to the country I wouldn't have to go and put up with that Roley and his socks,' she accused. The mystery of the socks I put aside.

My consternation was great. Now I not only understood my mother's distress, I had a major case of it myself.

'I thought maybe I could argue him out of it,' she confessed.

My father had been offered a permanent sawyer's job by one of his brothers who was then managing a mill in an isolated Bay of Plenty valley. He thought it wise to take it. Mera was confident that now 'our side' – the Labour Party – was in Government, life would gradually return to normal. Rightly, as it happened, he believed that fulltime work, a free house, and other small benefits, would permit our family to get on its feet again.

'But isn't there some other way?' cried my mother desperately. 'To go into the backblocks again! What about school for your sister? What about work for you? What was all your hard study for if you're to be buried at a lonely sawmill?'

The uncles were on my father's side. The aunts were not. They flocked indignantly about my mother, making gloomy skies gloomier. Tanekaha Valley offered not a thing in the world. Particularly it would be the stony finish for me. I was destined, they predicted sorrowfully, to marry some farm boy with manure on his boots.

'You with your lovely red hair!' they lamented, and I had a stark picture of myself and my lovely red hair trudging off to the cow bails at four in the morning, followed by weedy chilblained children with running noses; snivelling, they were, poor kids, and harried along by a huge stubbly person with manure of every available kind on his gumboots.

'Jesus, Mary and Joseph!' I cried, breaking into a bawling fit.

'No swearing around here!' said my mother. But in fact I was praying.

My father travelled to the Valley before us, to prepare the cottage and see about schooling for my sister. We morosely packed, putting most furniture in storage in aunts' garages and toolsheds. It was a grey, grey time for us all. Once I had been an intemperate child, alight with faith in Life's bounties, now I was a dejected half-woman, with black teeth and white blood and no discernible future.

But Life still loved me. The mysterious power, the Cosmos, the Force, Providence, God Himself, sent me Miss Muriel Innes, a slender, gentle-voiced lady who had chosen me from the children's pages of the *Herald* and the *Auckland Star* to join a little society she was starting for young people who wanted to write. She had a flowery complexion and a D. Litt, and she was, I imagine, an English teacher or university tutor. Blessed Miss Innes! She had the graceful dry wit of a Jane Austen lady; she spoke always in elegant sentences, and she knew an astonishing amount about literature. The assignments she set us were innovative and delightful. Best of all, the people she invited to speak to our eager group of twenty-five or thirty, were young and buoyant, successful young people like for instance, Sheila Quinn, who turned out to be 'Wendy' of the *Auckland Star's* large children's section.

Of course I knew that the pages were run by Peter Pan and Wendy, with artwork by Tinkerbell, but somehow I never thought that these romantic pseudonyms were borne by real live people. To think this was Wendy! I was enchanted by this tiny girl, black hair cut in a Dutch bob, large blue eyes, and glasses that kept slipping down her nose, so that one finger had to creep up and push them back again. Wendy! She spoke earnestly about journalism; the best way to begin a writing career; how to keep a neat scrapbook of all we had published; how to get references from teachers and other people who knew us well.

'That's the way I did it,' she said, 'and many of you can write *heaps better* than I ever could.'

Sheila Quinn was in her own person an exemplar of serendipity. She flew into people's lives and out again and always left them better. We were the sweetest friends always; we shared a home during the lonely war, she god-mothered my son. Some friends shed light on all your ways. Sheila was one of these.

I had to tell Miss Innes that I could attend only two or three meetings before I submerged in Tanekaha Valley and despair. She sympathised kindly, which was a little comfort. But a week or so later, Sheila called on me in our half-empty house, sat on a packing case amid the dust and disorder.

'If I see an opportunity of a position on the *Star*, could I contact you? It might be *absolutely fearsome*, like in the bindery, or office girl . . .'

'I don't care, I don't care,' I cried, enraptured. 'I'll be a cleaner, I'll do anything, as long as I can get a toe in the door!'

'Then if anything turns up, I'll send you a wire,' she promised, and pushing up her glasses once more, off she went with my new Robinson Crusoe address.

· 9 ·

The day before we left for Te Puke, the nearest railway station to Tanekaha Valley, I visited St Benedict's to say goodbye to the Sisters. They had a letter for me, sent care of the Convent.

I looked at the Australian stamp, the distinctive handwriting, and my heart did not miss a beat.

'I expect it's from that boy, the clever one Sister Laurencia speaks about,' said one Sister encouragingly.

On the way home I dropped it unread into a rubbish bin and did not tell my mother about it. Other people's literary struggles were not what I needed.

The train journey to Te Puke lasted for ever. The unheated train, fitted with wooden benches, often had to stop and get up steam before going up an incline. Every time it halted at a wayside station I nipped out and ran along to the guard's van to see Flash Jack. Slumped in his wooden cage, his eyes half shut, he was too trainsick even to look at me.

At the harbour town of Tauranga, a majestic Maori woman heaved herself in, strode to the middle of the carriage and dumped down two covered buckets. A splendid creature with a broad archaic face, she had eyes like a deer and a man's felt hat perched on her great stack of hair. She gave us beaming smiles.

A stealthy shuffle and clack came from the buckets.

'I have pipis here for my family in Te Puke,' she explained.

After a little conversation on the best ways of cooking these shellfish, and the remote location and cruel climate of Tanekaha Valley, she leaned forward, and, lightly as a leaf, touched my pallid cheek and dry lips. 'You are pale. Your blood is thin. Not good for a girl. When you get to the valley, and there is a Maori millhand perhaps, ask him to show you puha, the green plant, and another, korau, with leaves like young cabbage. Eat plenty, not cooked hard, just two-three minutes. You eat every day, and soon you will be strong.'

Then she pulled the hat over her eyes and went to sleep. My mother tried to thank her, but she did not answer. She knew herbal lore, she prescribed, there was an end to it.

When we were settled in the Valley, I took her advice, and every day gathered half a sugarbag full of puha (sow thistle) and korau, the wild turnip. I wonder whether puha in particular is Captain Cook's 'New Zealand cabbage', of which he gathered boatloads to feed to his men to keep the scurvy away. Whatever minerals or vitamins these plants contain, they cured my anaemia; I became energetic and restless, though still without optimism.

The Valley was a vast crack in the earth, coming from somewhere near Lake Rotoehu in the earthquake country, they said, and canting towards the coast. The mill had spent decades slowly moving down the Valley. When the bush was cut out, the owner upped-sticks and moved the buildings, machinery, everything. It was a claustrophobic place; when the east wind blew from the hidden ocean the bush on the steeps seemed to topple towards the mill and the ramshackle cottages. It was not like forest I had seen before, but steps and stairs of trees, the mighty ones, rimu, kahikatea, tawa, tanekaha, in places inaccessible to the bushmen; flight after flight down past buttressed pukatea and iron-hard rata, until near the valley floor nothing grew but lancewood, wineberry and small berried things moth-eaten with frost.

The night we arrived, it was so cold I could feel the fibres of my skin contracting, the body turning itself inward to protect its vital fires. I expected bones and sinews to send forth loud cracking sounds.

My mother had not well survived the long, freezing train journey, nor the slow ride from Te Puke to Tanekaha, jolting over a deplorable road. She was chilled, feverish, and silent. When she entered the shack where we were to live, she walked around, the lamp held high – one little bedroom, a living room with a giant fireplace, a lean-to kitchen with a gnomish stove on splay legs. Mera had done his best to make it habitable. Six wild bush whackers had previously occupied it, so probably the cleaning and fixing had taken weeks. There was no bathroom or wash-house, water came from a tank, and the lavatory was up a muddy track.

Mera had lined the rooms with hessian and sheets of newspaper, which he painted with blue calsomine. It was a particularly freezing blue, so that the entire interior looked like a tidy cave in Antarctica. No wonder my mother burst into tears. She must have thought it the end of the world. Mera was deeply disappointed; he believed he had done a really good job in the few hours per day he had to spare from his work – labour far too heavy for his age. My mother went to bed, sobbing, and after a scratch meal, my sister and I climbed into the bunks in the living room.

'I'll just bank up the fire and you'll be as warm as two bugs in a rug,' said Mera with false heartiness.

'What do you think of it?' whispered my sister, when he had taken the lamp away to the bedroom.

My father had so far calsomined only one wall of the living room, and I grasped at the faint pleasure this promised.

'At least I can read the walls,' I muttered.

Suddenly rain plunged over the hills and fell on the iron roof like a wagonload of bullets. It rushed down the chimney, the fire went out, the room filled with smoke. We lay there paralysed with cold, choking and giggling. With an eerie whuffling sound, an updraught sucked all the smoke from the room and up the chimney once more, and we collapsed with hysterical shrieks. Our father appeared with the lamp and the huffs.

'I don't see anything to laugh at. Mum isn't feeling at all well, you ought to have more sense.'

No use. We laughed till we fell asleep with exhaustion. It was not a good start for Tanekaha Valley life.

My mother, I believe, had a small nervous breakdown. For weeks she stayed in bed, the best place to be in that fearsome cold. For it *was* fearsome, unlike anything else I have ever experienced. Some oddity of topography trapped frigid air in low-lying areas, so that frost fell upon unthawed frost, and in secluded patches built up into mushy, earthstained banks. The water tank had a hand's breadth of ice on its surface; in the mornings I had to break up this floe in order to get a bucketful of water.

But Tanekaha Valley had stars. Because of its depth, its tall, precipitous hills, the stars above it shone so close, so clear that no one could doubt they were suns and planets. Breathtaking they were, and many a night I forgot to breathe, standing out there in the violent cold, gazing upwards, bemused by the fantastic millions of worlds that burned or flowered in space.

My sister and I were not at all sure where we were. From the railway station, the mill truck had snored straight out into deathly darkness. Te Puke, population 900 and all asleep, was a faint blob of murk; in its outer areas I saw constellation after constellation of glow worms in invisible hedges. The clay road to Tanekaha had been a moment-to-moment burrowing into country night, the trees shape-shifting in the headlights; water blinking in the ruts; an owl shadowing past on fur-tipped wings.

I knew we must be near Rotorua; we could smell the dry-throated sulphur breath of geysers and boiling mud whenever the south wind hoisted itself over the rampart of fern hills. The valley area was, in fact, on the edge of that pumice desert, the Central Plateau, where our father had planted so many thousands of pines when he was at Kaingaroa. It was an inexplicably waterless land for New Zealand, which is a child of Aquarius. No springs splashed down rockfaces, no bogs invited wetland birds. The flocks of wild duck came from other places. The mill engine itself ran off water pumped by hydraulic ram from a distant mountain stream, the only one I ever found in that forest.

Eventually my sister and I climbed the wall of hills behind our shack, finding pig tracks in the impassable waist-high bracken that had reclaimed the countryside. The land to the west had once been occupied. Long felled and burned, ploughed and planted for decades, these farms were abandoned during the course of the Depression. Chimney stumps stood amongst ragwort and tutu, which killed cattle, and always the intractable fern, which had been waiting outside the fence all the time. Only a few farms survived, rundown and forlorn in that wilderness.

Towards the coast the forest grew without a break, cloud shadows turning its moss green to bronze green, here and there a patch like fur blown the wrong way, where a skiff of wind had risen out of a humid valley. Beyond it were the ocean and White Island, a solitary volcano, fuming malodorously, clothed in poisoned scrub, always with a pennant of steam or smoke flying from its broken peak.

Whenever the claustrophobic valley became unbear-able, I climbed those almost vertical hills, just to gaze upon the ocean, the volcano, the limitless fields of trees, air and sky.

For those months were often unbearable, even after my mother recovered and tried to be her normal, kind, humorous self. Life is never speedy enough for the young, especially the despairing young. I did read the living-room walls, standing on a chair, hunting for consecutive pages. These came from very old copies of the *New Zealand Observer*, and the text was solid Robin Hyde, whose style became so familiar to me I believe I could even now recognise it anywhere. How I envied her, secure in a job, praised as a poet, with a beautiful future. But in fact, at the time she was overworked, ill-paid as all women journalists were, worried about her child, always in pain from a diseased bone, and planning suicide.

A year or so later, too shy to speak, I was to pass her in a newspaper office, unfortunate Robin, a lame, worn-looking woman, pale and ill-nourished, with lank light brown hair. It must have been just before she left for China, a journey that led to her early death.

This desolate wilderness of which I write, Tanekaha Valley, is probably not at all like that now. Somewhere under the pastures must be the long-rotted sawdust heaps that littered the valley like mullock dumps, garnet red and acid yellow; so the slaughtered trees have gone back to enrich and ripen the soil. Te Puke, they tell me, is prosperous. The Bay of Plenty, so depopulated in my time, grows mandarins, oranges, tamarillos and other subtropical fruit, and is a famous dairy district. Perhaps even then it was not as melancholy as I thought. The darkness within my family overshadowed all – my mother's fragility and homesickness, my father's disappointment.

'I can't do anything right for her,' he confessed to me once, and I, greatly daring, for I knew his modesty and oldfashioned reticence, said, 'You made *me*.'

'So I did!' he said, and slapped his knee and laughed.

Nobody who worked at the Tanekaha Mill has remained in my memory except a dark little man with crooked feet who spent his days making string instruments. He was self-taught.

'First time out of the stable I made a banjo from a biscuit tin!' he bragged.

Though I had never spoken to him, certain aspects of his observable characteristics turned up in my novel *Missus*, as the qualities of the protagonist's brother Jer Darcy, a fantasising crippled man. Such is the writer's subconscious.

After we had lived seven or eight months in the Valley, a telegram arrived. It was several days late; the mill lorry picked it up when the weekly stores were collected. Sheila Quinn advised me that very soon a copyholder's job in the proofreading department would be available. Could I come?

'No, you can't,' said Mera downrightly. The blood rushed down to my feet in the old way, I swayed where I stood.

'Look at that!' said my mother angrily. 'You almost made her pass out!'

But he was adamant. 'A girl's place is with her mother!' he repeated several times. His face was flushed; he had the stubborn look we all knew well. Years later I asked him why he had dug his toes in.

'I didn't like you going away from us. All by yourself in the city.'

'But that wasn't all, was it,' I pressed.

He answered with a look half-shamed and half-defiant. 'No, it was because I know men.'

So protectively he argued, while I thought in anguish, 'If he won't let me go, what will I do? My only chance!'

My mother handled it very well. 'We'll go for a walk,' she said, gently.

Ah, *that* I remember. It was the long dusk of New Zealand. We walked up an old disused corduroy track between the black and silver trunks of middle-aged beeches that had grown up since that part of the bush was cut out, long before. The air was made fragrant by the perfumed arboreal grass that hangs from high boughs like a silk fringe. More bellbirds than I had ever heard before were singing. The New Zealand bellbird, treasured korimako, is a shy moss-green bird, usually invisible, and a dawn singer. Why was such a chorus chiming that twilight? But they were, and so when I think of my manumission, I hear bellbirds.

'Mel, I'll tell you straight. If you don't arrange for the mill lorry to take her to Te Puke railway station tomorrow for the Auckland train, she and I will walk to Te Puke. With her luggage.'

He knew very well she would. I was going to get my chance, no matter what effort it took on her part, even walking twenty kilometres on a terrible road. Defeated, he asked tentatively, 'But where will she live?'

'Rose will be glad to have her.'

'The job mightn't pay much.'

'Never mind. It's the start she needs.'

He was silent, and then he cried, 'But she hasn't the sense of a silvereye!'

This metaphor touched me when I was older; perhaps the skittering, flittering flight of the green linnet, its sudden darts and joyful chitters reminded him of a young girl, too innocent to be afraid of anything, trusting implicitly in her own inborn ability to manage life. In many ways he was right, of course.

PART FOUR

· 1 ·

For two years I worked in the reading room of the *Auckland Star*. The *Star* was, in its great days, a quality newspaper, its journalism solid and lucid, its management capable. Its principles were Tory and Imperialistic, but that scarcely concerned me. What interested me was textual style, and thousands of lessons did I receive from sub-editors' slashings and clarifications of reporters' copy. Proofreading requires great concentration, not only for factual accuracy, but for literals, or misprints, for it is astonishing how the eye will slip a missing letter into a familiar word. The *Auckland Star* had some classic near-misses, which, posted up in page proof form on the newsroom walls, struck terror into the hearts of printers and make-up men. In a bold headline in a two-page sale advertisement, paid for with the blood of the city's most prestigious department store, the omission of the letter R in the word SHIRT could well result in the recall of an edition, so precious are big advertisers.

I enjoyed every moment. My good fortune was to work with a kindhearted funny man, A. S. Ridling, friend of all the world. He brothered all us young copyholders, connived at our romantic affairs, advised us how to keep alive on our appalling pay – I received 19/1d. after tax, paid 15/- board, and endeavoured to squeeze fares, clothing, and toothpaste out of the 4/1d. The male copyholders got more; we girls received what was called three-fifths of their rate, but was more like half. Early on Mr Ridling endeared himself lastingly to me by campaigning loudly at union meetings for equal rates for copyholders.

He was indignantly howled down, such was the almost universal male prejudice against equal pay. It was then, as now, mindless. Few men had even a pseudo-rational reason why the idea was inexpedient. Most had none at all. Later, when I became an active unionist, I kept a list of some of the ritual generalisations I heard.

Women are slow workers. No proof needed.

They ought to be home.

They'll only spend the extra money on lipstick and rubbish.

They have smaller heads, therefore smaller brains.

As the young do, I thought that these attitudes were peculiar to my own time; I hadn't studied social history then. However, soon I came across Elizabeth Barrett Browning's comment:

> Men get opinions as boys learn to spell,
> By reiteration chiefly.

Doubtless Elizabeth also knew that identical reasons were used to oppose any radical who suggested that serfs and slaves should be treated, even in a small way, as human beings.

Mr Ridling's most telling argument, which unfortunately I did not hear, as he would not have spoken so before a girl or woman, was that male copyholders didn't watch their copy with their pom-tiddly-pom-poms, but with their eyes and brains, which were, in his opinion, rarely as attentive as those of girls.

My manic energy and singleminded pursuit of literary goals amused this blessed man. Aiding and abetting the young being already a hobby with him, he turned his ingenious mind to the useful exploitation of his vast circle of friends, many of whom were ex-copyholders who had become successful journalists or businessmen.

'You're going nowhere on 4/1d. spare cash weekly,' he said briskly. 'You need other work.'

Already I was pelting away stories, now adult, to other newspapers and journals, with irregular success and fearful trouble in getting any payment, however minimal, out of them. They apparently believed that the prestige of being published in the *Manawatu Times* or the *West Coast Bugle* was sufficient. These stories appeared under pen names, for *Star* employees were strictly forbidden, under pain of dismissal, to write for 'outside'. This was considered disloyalty. Nevertheless, many of us did. One senior reporter even held down, under an alias, a stringer's job with a Melbourne newspaper.

'That's all very well,' said my friend. 'But you need something regular. Think.'

I thought. The Catholic newspaper had a scissors-and-paste children's page of feeble piety and no following. Could I possibly . . . ?

'I'll go and see the editor.'

'Who's his boss?'

'I guess the Bishop.'

'Go and see him. Always go to the Big Noise.'

It took me a while to psych myself up to interview the formidable Bishop James Liston, but he gave me the job. He also became my kind friend and was so until his death. The extra £1 weekly meant that I quickly paid off a second-hand portable typewriter, a dreadful thing with three banks of shift keys, which was my heart's treasure for years.

My life once again became full of button-sewing, this time of a literary variety, and nearly always on Mr Ridling's initiative. I proofread telephone books, a fearsome job, hour after hour of 6-pt type, and an absolute requirement for perfect accuracy. I also entered into partnership with a freelance industrial photographer, Bill Sparrow; he did the pictures and I wrote the brochures. The pay, for me at least, was very low, but I learned how to write effective selling text. Most useful of all, I studied photography with Bill. To see him thoughtfully go over some huge beast of a machine, sensuously putting a streak of oil here and there to gather highlights, was a revelation. He told me a photographer could do the same with a human face; that subtle highlights played down poor features and made an artistic pleasure out of good ones.

Bill helped me buy my first camera wholesale. It was a Rolleicord with a fine German lens; he also taught me how to use it. Now there opened before me a new avenue of literary work, the illustrated article.

All this happened in my first year at the *Auckland Star*. So much work, however, meant that I had no free time at all. Other copyholders were flirting and going out with bold apprentices; there was a good deal of washroom giggling about boyfriends, movies and new clothes in which I could not participate.

'What are you?' asked the other girls. 'A nun?'

Of course, in those times a writer had to work extraordinarily hard and consistently to make a living at all. Nevertheless, all my life I have been baffled by those writers who not only deliver a stream of books, but lead a strenuous social and amorous life as well. Probably the answer to the riddle is staff, or a devoted wife or husband. Where would George Eliot have been without Mr Lewes, or Tolstoi without Sonja?

However, in spite of my tedious industry, I had my secret eye on a first-year cadet reporter not much older than myself. In my eyes Jan's profession made him glamorous, but he was also an engaging lad with blond hair, long flaxen eyelashes, and a habit of falling upstairs as well as down, so enthusiastically did he gallop everywhere.

When I looked at Jan, I experienced a cloudy feeling

of discontent, as though my life of ceaseless labour were not enough. Once, walking along a corridor and observing him excitably hurrying ahead of me, I was overcome with such a sensation of formless yearning that I had to turn into the fileroom, and calm myself by studying *The Dominion's* small advertisements. Later I came to the conclusion that my mysterious discomfiture was caused by the way his hair curled on the back of his neck.

This year, too, I had another letter from Sister Laurencia's young man in Australia, redirected to the *Star* from St Benedict's Convent. It is a stately and respectful letter, carefully written in the sender's amazing hand-writing, and really got up my nose. The writer seemed to think I was some powerful editorial person, capable of assisting him to sell his stories in New Zealand. He was having a hard time, it is true, for the Depression in Australia lasted until the outbreak of the second World War, but no harder than I had had. I banged off a letter on my three-decker monster, saying that I was but a lowly copyholder with no efficacy or charisma whatsoever, and if *he* offered to sell *my* stories in Australia it might be more to the point. Reading this letter now, it is a marvel that the future father of my children did not take a terminal huff and go off and father someone else's. However, he was choked off for months, much to my relief.

Occasionally a new friend visited the Reading Room. In that ceaseless hurly burly we were not allowed to have visitors, but rules were not made for Eve Langley. A waifish creature with black hair and crooked legs, about which she was sensitive and always hid with trousers, she had taken a fancy to me because of some story of mine she had read. She had not yet written *The Pea Pickers*, the stunning picaresque novel of two bold girls afoot in Gippsland; she wasn't famous yet. But she was famous to me, for well I knew her massive cloudy poems, and an infrequent strange glittering short story. I didn't know she was an Australian, a dazzling autodidact with a head full of classic literature, other languages, and uncontrollable creativity the frustration of which was eventually to drive her mad; I knew nothing. But to me she was a living example of all that was rapturous, exciting, literary. She even lived in Partington's Windmill, or so I understood, a circumstance that enchanted me. If only I could live in a windmill, a stairless turret, where no one else could climb! To know that Eve Langley believed I could write, and would some day write better, made me strong.

· 2 ·

Though I had a letter from my parents every week, I missed them and my sister night and day. Regrettably, I inherited my family's extravagant capacity for homesickness. In Tanekaha Valley things were increasingly hopeful. My father had received notification from the Housing Commission that our family, so long homeless, was near the top of the list for a State house. The Labour Government's housing scheme, which provided roofs for the homeless and continuing work for hitherto unemployed builders and tradesmen connected with building, was one of their greatest successes.

'Just imagine!' wrote my mother blissfully. 'A *new* house! I've never lived in a new house in my life. And we'll be together again.'

I was overjoyed. Though I loved living with my skittery Auntie Rose, and my cousin Stuart, who had turned into a handsome, pleasant young man, I had my secret troubles with the Peeping Tom uncle. He was your ordinary, run-of-the-mill devoted husband and jealous stepfather, a good pedestrian man who looked as though he'd been born with glasses. I fancy he just could not resist the circumstances provided by Fate. The downright torment I suffered with that man! If he wasn't standing on a box outside the bath-room window, or looking through the toilet keyhole or ventilator, he was crouching in the flowerbed outside my bedroom window. My anguish was compounded equally of fury, outrage and perplexity about what I should do.

I had never dreamed that a respectable man of venerable age – he was probably forty-five – could be such a das-tardly sneak. At last, having no one else handy, I took the problem to Mr Ridling.

'Shall I tell Auntie, or write to my mother, or poke a knitting needle through the keyhole into Uncle's eye?'

'Spare me days, girl! It's not as simple as that. This little to-do has complications.'

If I had been older, or less distraught, I would have seen them for myself. If I wrote to my mother she would probably order me home out of what she saw as a potential moral morass. If I spoke to Auntie Rose, she wouldn't believe me ('Take it from me, lass, wives don't want to believe such things'). Or there would be a screaming marital row that would make future life in that household impossible for me.

Even I had had the sense to know from the beginning that a direct confrontation with my tormentor would be fatal. Somehow he would manipulate his wife's opinion of me so that I would be told to go and live elsewhere.

'Tough it out,' my proofreader advised. 'You can't possibly upset your aunt, it wouldn't be fair. This is a temporary thing for you, but it wouldn't be for her, or him either, the knucklehead.'

Following his suggestions, I stuffed the toilet door keyhole with putty, had my bath in the early morning instead of night, thumbtacked a blanket over the bedroom window every evening. I added the refinement of a handful of thumbtacks in the flowerbed where Uncle was wont to lurk. These precautions may have slowed him but did not stop him.

'What do you think?' presently asked Auntie Rose. 'Helga's going to come up from Glen Afra and share with us. You won't mind having her in your bedroom, will you?'

It was time Helga joined the rest of the world. Besides, I thought, anticipating Uncle's ever more eager spying, Helga, so adept with a frying pan or other unorthodox weapon, was bound to catch him at it. I could not wait for his day of retribution.

'It would be fun, Auntie!'

'I'm off to Glen Afra to get her,' continued my aunt. 'I'll be away for two or three days; you'll be all right with Uncle and Stuart, won't you, pet?'

I took fright. Suppose I wasn't all right? Stuart had discovered girls and was almost never at home, so Uncle and I would spend several evenings alone together. The more I pondered possible embarrassing confrontations or worse, the more nervous I became. Could I go and stay with Sheila? No, because I'd have to say why, and I shied away from letting my friend know I had something as shabby as a Peeping Tom in the family. I thought at last of Eve Langley in the windmill. She wouldn't mind taking me in temporarily, and she'd probably think a Peeping Tom nothing but an amusing social phenomenon.

When I told my uncle I was off to spend a few days with a friend, he was disappointingly unperturbed. Perhaps he had dreaded my cooking. Had he known that the old windmill had a farouche reputation, he would certainly have believed it his duty to object. But, becalmed in his Government office, he knew little of the outside world. Which is perhaps why he was a Peeping Tom. Even if I had known the ancient building's ill fame I would simply have thought the whole thing romantically Bohemian.

As I flew joyfully through the drizzle, seeing the mill rearing blackly against the steaming sky, thinking of it as a Tower of Trebizond, or Rapunzel's prison, God knows what other fancy metaphors, it never entered my head that Eve mightn't welcome me, or might even be away. Not for a moment had I dreamed that she was married, had a child, and led a starveling existence across the Harbour. Indeed, she had never lived in the windmill, but in one of the ramshackle buildings that cluttered the Partington estate. Dearly wanting a poet to live in a windmill, I had misunderstood her reference.

The mill wasn't like anything in literature; it resembled nothing so much as a prodigious bottle tree, bulging at the base, tapering to two or three scraggy branches. These were the ruined sails, two, not four, for the mill had been burned before our family came to Auckland. It was mighty, archaic, its architecture belonging to an older world. High on its bony ridge, people said that once it had collected every wind that blew. There was, indeed, a ghostly croak and flutter from the sails, hanging down in splinters and gobbets from the forever-frozen cap. More than a hundred years of colonial history stood there before me, and all in darkness.

Heavy rain began to fall. Baffled, completely at a loss what to do, but above all dead set against trailing home again to a lone evening with my uncle, I saw at last a faint light high in the fortress wall. It shone through one of the irregularly placed apertures or windows. Singlemindedly, I knew it must belong to my friend, working at a poem by candlelight.

Stumbling over streaming cobbles, intermittently illuminated by a blinking advertisement on the roof of a nearby furniture shop, I looked for a way in. There was a tall locked door, and a chained wicket, nothing else. Round and round I went, increasingly bewildered. All around the foot of the mill was confusion and disarray – boxes and stove-in barrels, piles of rotting flour bags, a broken cart with its arms up in the air, and what appeared to be abandoned buildings, sheds, a storehouse, cottages. In one of these a party was going on; there sounded drunken laughter and frequent shrieks. The smell of this deserted place was complicated and overlaid by time – mould, dirt, decayed wood, and fermented grain.

At last I noticed, far above, a spidery catwalk reached by a rickety ladder. In this unorthodox way I entered the mill, uneasy and indecisive, longing to run away home but fearing what I might find there. I found myself in a strange chamber, a machine room full of mysterious gears, with a monstrous shaft going straight up through the ceiling. In the discontinuous light from the street, I looked down on millstones, enormous, prehistoric, powdered palely with husks of wheat.

The mill was dank, cold and Gothic, and my admiration for my friend Eve increased as I climbed tortuously upward. What dedication, what endurance, to live in this place and write, write – would I have the same strength of will and spirit? At last I came to that light I had seen from below, a gaslight like the two or three that had half-illuminated the climb upwards. Its soft, faintly fluttering glow showed me a queer cubby shaped like a serving of pie, the outer boundary being the sweeping curve of the mill's wall. I saw a table littered with ledgers, invoices and dirty plates, a camp bed sticking out from behind a screen, and a woman fastening her suspenders. Her mouth was two straight scratches of scarlet lipstick, open in consternation.

'Where the hell did you come from? I thought I'd locked the door.'

Not enlightening her as to my means of entrance, I asked about Eve.

She'd heard of Eve Langley, yes, she had, but not for years. Eve's young man, called himself an artist, had a studio on top of the old storehouse, next door to the mill, and Eve had lived with him there. Donkey's years ago, really. What had happened to that weird girl?

'Here, I'm just going to have a cup of tea. Sit down and have one. Get off that coat for goodness sake, you're drenched.'

Muriel, her name was. Call me Mew, everyone does. She did a bit of bookkeeping for the miller in exchange for this birds' nest of a room. Once quite a few people dossed down in the mill, and they had great old times, but the old codger was a bit crochety now and took umbrage at all kinds of things.

Mew was skinny and a bit forlorn, getting along in her thirties and not liking it. She had the gaunt jumpy look of a chain-smoking woman, goitrous eyes and a sisterly comprehension of my problem.

'Like that, is he? Gawd, what can you do with them?'

She was about to leave for the party down in the cottage, the rowdy one, but as I got up to go, she objected.

'Not out in that! It's raining cats and dogs. Here, stay the night. I won't be back till breakfast time. Then you can go to work or home or whatever you like. Come on, dear, have some common. You'll drown out there. And you *were* planning on staying over with that Eve.'

I suppose I thought it would be offensive to refuse her kind hospitality. I did peep out after she'd gone, but she'd turned out all the lights as she went, and I feared blundering downstairs looking for the way out. Without undressing I lay on top of Mew's bed and tried to convince myself how pleased I'd be some day to know I'd actually spent a night in the old windmill.

In fact, I wasn't, and never have been since. With a fearful start I awakened to find a stranger in an advanced state of nakedness hauling at my clothes and swearing. Another man stood by, swaying and grinning. With one arm he shook a head-lolling Mew back and forth like a dead duck. Over the shoulder of my attacker I saw her tossed into a corner, where she sat shrieking feebly like a stood-on kitten.

'I forgot about her! I forgot about her!'

There was no time for thought; we rolled off the bed, and as we thumped on the floor I brought my momentarily freed knee up between his legs and simultaneously drove my finger savagely into his eye. This was both luck and instinct. Actually, when I saw that bloodshot eye so close to my face I wanted to do something much more primitive.

It was probably a brief and disorderly brawl, fraught with terror on my part and drunken incapacity on the others'. The first man retched and bellowed, between spasms whining piteously, 'She's knackered me!'

'I'll fix her for you, Len,' promised the other, grabbing me by the hair. We reeled about the room, severely impeded by Mew's attachment to my assailant's leg. She may have been paralytic drunk, but she had a grip like a bulldog.

'Run! Run!' she squawked, as though that were not my main intention in life. He dragged her about the room, raining blows on her and me indiscriminately, until at last I fell backwards through the door to the dark landing. I cannoned down the first flight of stairs, not seeing one and touching few. Len's friend crashed after me. He hit something, a post or baluster, and let out a roar. The next flight I saw dimly in the swift light of a passing car, fled down them in mad terror, gulping for air. But now I had the hang of them, keeping one hand on the circular wall, where the treads were broadest, though God knows they were more like a companionway than stairs. Len's friend fell like a load of bricks. He may well have broken a bone, for he lay there groaning. Now there was no more pursuit; I scurried downwards until I came to the machine room, its darkness made darker by formless metal hulks, its air thick with the smells of meal and mildew.

Once outside, I wandered aimlessly, looking for shelter from the bucketing rain, huddling in the lee of walls, even for a while under the wrecked cart. In my state of shock it did not occur to me to go home. It seemed to be early morning. The street lights were out, there was no sound of traffic. Only the rain sloshed along the cobbles. After a while I found a loose board in the wall of the dormered building Mew had called the storehouse. It was a cavernous, mousy-smelling barn, full of rusty derelict machinery. In the mill's prime years it had been a biscuit factory. Crouching behind one of these machines, I mumbled and moaned to myself like a dog that has been in a fight and is not yet over the fear and frenzy. Hurting almost everywhere, I was most conscious of anger of a ferocious kind. Not only could I have killed Mew's friends, I could have killed my uncle for indirectly causing my pain and horror. Far away, a clock struck four. I decided to leave my refuge as soon as it became light, go to the *Star* and tidy myself up. It was Saturday, but we worked on Saturday, so I would work. This was not stoicism, but an unconscious desire to restore my normal routine as soon as possible.

So I waited, half-drowsing, listening to the rats running races over the floor of the loft above, where Eve's lover and later husband once had his studio and was happy.

As I hurried down back streets towards the *Star* office, keeping my head down against the rain, only one person stopped to gape at me.

'My dear,' cried this woman. 'What has happened? Have you been in an accident?'

'A motorbike knocked me over,' I gabbled. 'Going to the doctor right now.'

When in the *Star*'s washroom I examined my body, I decided I could very well have collided with a motorbike or even a car. I was black, green and yellow almost everywhere. My scalp felt as though it were semi-detached from my skull; I had a thick lip and the beginning of a swollen nose. Bitter hate filled me when I saw my bodily damage; if I had known a murderous spell to put on those two men I would have done so.

I stuck with the motorbike story, except to Jan, the reporter, who happened to be the first person I met as I emerged from the washroom. He was returning from meeting one of the Matson Line's tourist vessels; it was the custom for newsmen to be sent to meet these ships, scan the passenger list, and interview any important people on board before the ship berthed. There was something so sweet about his furrowed golden brows, his fair face flushed with concern, that I wept for the first time. He took me into the fileroom, where I choked out my story and dropped tears on his shirt. He said he understood my horror very well because once, on a late assignment, he had been jumped by two muggers who took all his clothes as well as money.

'Can you imagine?' he asked, scarlet at the memory. 'Starkers! Or pretty near! At eleven at night. I had to lurk until the cop came along on his beat, and he lent me his raincoat . . . it was unforgettably horrible!'

Remembering then that he had copy to deliver, he straightened up, said firmly, 'You need someone to look after you, and I'll do it.'

In fact, it was Mr Ridling who looked after me. Taking one look at my dishevelment, falling without question for the motorbike story, he said, 'You're going home.' Calling a taxi, he eased me into it, for by then I was really in pain, and ordered me to call a doctor or there'd be trouble from him. Though naturally I did not do as he said, I was deeply grateful for his practical aid.

Still, young men are young men, and girls will always think them wonderful. My bizarre experience in the mill was the beginning of a delightful romance with the kind and charming Jan, who had so few years left to live.

· 3 ·

For the war was not far away. All through the decade of our growing-up, the black cloud of Nazi-ism had hung over Europe, and in Europe lay, willy nilly, New Zealand's destiny. To those of us interested in history, Germany's Enabling Act in March 1933, which put the Nazi Party in a position of absolute dictatorship, was the beginning of the end. The news came our way, of course it did – bloody purges, assassinations, occupation of other countries, boldly achieved despite the feeble protests from 'our side', the Allies, victors of the first World War, but devastated by that war and totally unprepared for another.

Yet there was a dreamlike quality about these stories, as though they had happened long ago as well as far away. There was not only a great distance between us and Europe, but a time-span incomprehensible today. The newspapers relied on wire services – cables – for information, and cables were always suspect, sent by those with axes to grind, received by those subject to a newspaper's political direction. Later, when the war had begun, and our troops were in direct jeopardy, I myself saw cables edited in the cable room of the *Star*, negatives deleted, numbers of casualties reduced. There was none of the horrifying immediacy of direct broadcasts from calamitous scenes, or the intimacy of television, however selective.

For me many things happened in the year before war was declared on September 3, 1939, by Great Britain and France, and subsequently by the Pacific nations, including the tiny Kingdom of Tonga.

My friend Sheila resigned and sailed away to Australia to be married, and I took her place as Wendy. This appointment had been decided a year before. My wages were advanced by ten shillings and that was the highest pay I ever had at the *Star* office, about that of a male second-year cadet.

Management did not believe in incentive or reward; if you couldn't live on what you received, go and get a job in a factory.

A somewhat acrimonious correspondence with D'Arcy Niland of Sydney had commenced. Once again he wrote to me, and this time, feeling the need for some shop talk, I answered. Dogmatically, no doubt, I expressed my ideas about writing. These he briskly rubbished, correctly, as it happened, and sent me some of his stories. They knocked me over. They were all excessively gloomy, what he later referred to as of the leper-meets-madman school, but I could see very well that this unknown, scrappy young man had a powerful talent and already great control over his exercise of it. He too had begun his working life with an all-out attempt to be a journalist, believing with the rest of us that journalism is the natural training for a writer. Except in rare instances, this is outstandingly untrue. Still, such was our hopeful belief.

D'Arcy finally achieved an even lowlier position than

I had done, as copyboy with the *Sydney Sun*. In extreme youth he had been encouraged by the writer Ethel Turner, who ran the children's pages. He was, he defiantly confessed, a little Sunbeam. After reading some of his efforts as a Sunbeam, I told him straight *I* would never have encouraged him. But after Ethel Turner, her successor Mary Marlowe was kind to him, allowed him to practise typewriting in her office, and eventually procured for him the job of copyboy. No job could have been more miserable, harassed and ill paid, but he was glad to get it. The Depression lasted years longer in Australia; the countryside was full of workless men tramping from town to town in order to get their food ration tickets, a disgusting, inhumane ploy to keep the unemployed from congregating 'in a dangerous mob'. The city was a seething mass of restless, disaffected men (again women seemed to have been converted into non-persons). Astonishingly, Sydney being known as a refractory, big-mouthed city, there was no Kristallnacht. However, many of the unemployed never had regular pay between leaving school and joining the A.I.F. in 1939.

When D'Arcy Niland turned seventeen, he would automatically have gone on to higher wages, so the *Sun* fired him. Dozens before him had suffered the same economy, amongst them Paul Brickhill the writer and Peter Finch the actor.

'What did you do to live?' I asked.

He took to the bush, working as a shed-hand with his father on shearing contracts. The father was a fine woolclasser, but the bottle had beaten him, and he worked only intermittently. Off-season the boy laboured at potato-digging, prickly-pear cutting, and scrub clearing. All the time he wrote and took notes. His notebooks from that period fill a large box. He sold very few stories, and could not understand how I had already sold to overseas papers, including the *San Francisco Examiner*, which was to become important to me. The trouble was, he refused to write non-fiction, while I was writing *illustrated* non-fiction. My experience with the interview with the Maori chieftain, Tukumanu te Taniwha, had given me confidence.

'I'm a short story writer,' he objected, which was true enough but didn't provide much of an income.

Also he had no more idea of literary markets than a child. He was the boy who sent a modestly risqué story to the Salvation Army's *War Cry*, and had it returned with 'Oh, lad, lad!' sorrowfully pencilled in a margin.

'My head buzzed like a hive,' he said in after years. 'I was so mad with the world, no work, drooby clothes, half-hungry, and a war rolling up. I heard nothing anyone said, nothing.'

He went on like that for years. He thought he was standing by his principles but in fact he was behaving like a knucklehead. He argued with editors and was forbidden entry to offices.

Reading one of these laments one day – he had been thrown raving down the stairs by an editor who justifiably went off his head with exasperation – I went off mine too, and wrote him a stinger. Use your brains, I shouted. Think first whether the story is appropriate for that journal or paper, whether it's timely, whether the style is right. Don't argue with editors; just ask if they can give you some helpful advice. Who's going to like you when you're pig-headed, obnoxious, and apparently think your head is there to grow hair on?

In fact, I wrote like a wife.

There was a sinister silence while he chewed it over. He told me later that he came to the conclusion that it mightn't be a bad idea, having a wife. He was rather young at the time, nineteen or twenty, but the idea nested.

At this time, through the agency of Mr Ridling of the

Reading Room, D'Arcy Niland obtained a steady job as a proofreader's assistant on the *Daily Telegraph* in Sydney. When I told my old friend of the difficulties experienced by this clever boy in finding work, he pondered a moment and said cheerfully, 'No worry. I'll just put the screws on Alf Turnbull.'

Mr Turnbull was the *Telegraph*'s head reader, an ex-copyholder of the puissant Mr Ridling, and succumbed to the screws in quick time. He also became our dear friend when I went to Sydney.

Our correspondence progressed from fights to stimulating discussions on literature, life, and to a lesser degree love, though love in a strictly abstract sense. Virtuous and avuncular, he frowningly counselled me not to allow my friendship with Jan to get out of control.

'Mind your own business, you evil-minded bogtrotter,' I retorted hotly. 'This is a romance, not an affair. I've no room for any of that serious stuff in my plan of life.'

'I know,' he answered placidly.

A romance it was, a skittering butterfly kind of exploratory companionship, the kind of thing no longer trendy, but to me invaluable. How else would I have known that men are as vulnerable, hopeful, and as touchy as women if it had not been for Jan? There was no sense of permanence, no talk of the future. Playfulness was the meaning of every encounter, as it is for most young things. Though I was maturing fast in many ways, I could not have dealt with the great ambiguous welter of emotions that comes with a sexual relationship, nor did I want it. My life was far too crammed already with other pursuits.

It can be seen that the correspondence between myself and the unseen young man in Australia was frank in the extreme. I often felt I was talking to myself; he felt the same way. He had sent me his photograph; he had a face out of *Ireland, her Struggles and Sorrows*, gaunt, glowering and dark. He appeared half-starved, which he probably was. He had an intent hawklike gaze. Indeed, if ever a young man was agin the Establishment, he was, and cared not who knew it.

Once I showed this photograph to Eve Langley who, like the wind, still blew in and out of my office.

'That's a good face, lad,' she said to me. It was her custom to call everyone lad. 'Do you know what it's saying?'

'No, what?'

'It says "Take me or leave me." I like that.'

D'Arcy Niland never asked about my work, for he had the unselfconscious, almost innocent, self-centredness of a young man. But this didn't bother me; I had learned a great deal from my cousins. It can be seen that he was a knobbly, one-eyed, contumacious character who would appeal to few girls. Yet there was something there that hit me in the heart – a kind of Stone Age honesty, abrasive courage, and a durability that equalled my own. Above all, he was funny. I started laughing then, and I remember that in the ambulance that carried him to his death twenty-eight years later, the ambulance officers were chuckling all the way.

· 4 ·

It was probably just as well that I was extraordinarily young for my age, for I took to being Wendy with ardour and imagination. It was a varied, enormous job, but like my predecessor, Sheila Quinn, I frolicked through it. The work was an education and a revelation, superb training for one who hoped to become in maturity a writer for children. If we worked far more than the forty-hour week outlined by the new labour laws, we scarcely noticed.

The department had been structured by Sheila and Mike Abbott (Peter Pan), a lively bachelor no great shakes as a journalist but a remarkable organiser. The routine was so excellent that at first all I had to do was to follow on, like a tram on rails.

'I am the happiest girl in the whole world,' I wrote to my mother. 'I now feel I can do anything.'

The *Star*'s children's supplement was not one page only, like Miss Elsie K. Morton's historic kingdom. It comprised four pages of text carefully designed to arouse utmost interest in the children, who in those days had no television to entertain them; children's radio programmes were brief, sparse and sloppy. Two of our pages were devoted to older readers; this text was superb, cajoled by Peter Pan from experts in fields stimulating to older kids, and intended to supplement the secondary school syllabus. We had a weekly article by James Cowan, the country's premier historian. Mr Cowan was famous for fantastically awful handwriting. While in the reading room I had sometimes seen a compositor's attempt to set it up turn out to be about a quite different subject. From this experience I could read his writing, if not with ease, at least with probable accuracy. So when his articles came in I typed them before sending them downstairs to the lino room. James Cowan was crippled with arthritis, and wrote on his chest, peering over his own chin. For this priceless material (for he was a renowned Maori scholar as well as historian) the *Star* paid him fifteen shillings. He provided the illustration free.

In the kids' supplement there were also two pages of colour cartoons, Prince Valiant, the Katzenjammers, many loved old characters now vanished down the corridors of time. In the two pages dedicated to the younger children we ran puzzles, stories, competitions which brought in thousands of entries, and of course their own contributions. The latter taught me what children like to read; often it resembles in no way what adults think they enjoy.

In addition our small staff handled the two children's pages in the *Farmer's Weekly*, as well as conducting an immense winter campaign for knitted quilt squares. The kind mothers and grandmothers of our children sewed these into wool-lined quilts and afghans for old people's homes and needy infants' refuges such as that run by the Sisters of Compassion. How many exceptional people I met through this charity drive; into how many mean and meagre lives I was led gently by the hand, until my way of thinking and even my way of writing became maturer.

My mother made many beautiful baby garments for the newborn castaways cared for by the Sisters of Compassion, for as she said, 'No baby deserves to be greeted with poverty.' I remember these Sisters with love, their exquisite courtesy, the spidery French handwriting of their Superior. Despite this Order's unlikely origin in New Zealand, its foundress was a Frenchwoman, Mother Mary Aubert, who as a nursing student had trained beside Florence Nightingale. The Order was created in the nineteenth century to nurse and care 'for those in straitened circumstances' but in Auckland most of my dealings were with the Sisters' foundling home.

The Salvation Army, St Vincent de Paul, several smaller welfare groups – our children helped them all. Their selfless officers impressed me deeply. For some reason now forgotten, I resolved that if ever I were truly down and out I'd go to the Salvation Army. Fortunately it never came to that, but I remain a supporter of the Sallies.

Amongst this large number of mostly anonymous workers for down-at-heel mankind, my most remarkable acquaintance was the Rev. Jasper Calder, who for a quarter of a century was head of the Anglican City Mission in Auckland. An ebullient character (as a curate he had scandalised his prim world by winning a buckjumping contest), he often offended the political and ecclesiastical Establishment. Nothing tickled him more than getting up the noses of the self-righteous. I thought he would have got on like a house afire with Jesus and the tougher of the Apostles. For a while my dealings with him were abrupt and brief; he called me 'Windy' and continued unabashed until I addressed him as Mr Cauldron. Not witty, but sufficient. I suppose he had never heard of Barrie's *Peter Pan and Wendy*; it was not his style. After that I had a barking invitation to accompany him occasionally on his rounds. A hasty, often impatient man, he had a rough tongue and could tell a skiver a mile away.

Though the Depression had been over for several years, some families had never recovered.

'And never will,' said Mr Calder. 'Sometimes the breadwinner has cleared out, or the mother has died, or the kids got into trouble and are in reform school or gaol. The burden is too great. The spirit goes out of people, and they just sit there and take what comes.'

He also had cases of utmost barbarity. As in larger cities, Auckland had its ratholes and streets of ratholes, people sleeping on sacks nailed on two parallel boards raised on bricks or boxes; children bedded down on heaps of news-papers. Incest was rife; one cadaverous woman told me her husband had violated each of her six daughters from the age of eight.

'The little ones cry a lot when it happens,' she added without change of expression. In a rage I demanded why she hadn't laid charges.

'But how could we live, Miss? Don't you say anything to anyone, Miss!'

How indeed could they live? The mother couldn't work; she was always pregnant, often ill, and indeed fundamentally incapable of holding any job at all. She appeared tubercular, as did several of the girls.

Reports of abuse had been submitted by neighbours and Health Department inspectors, but not only the wife but the daughters denied that anything untowards had taken place.

'They all know what will happen to the younger kids if Dad is shoved behind bars,' said Jasper Calder. 'They'd be put in Homes. The older girls couldn't bear that.'

When we left that house I vomited in the gutter. Mr Calder watched me cynically.

'You're indulging your indignation,' he said. 'That's no part of love for your neighbour.'

He told me the man was a hard worker, fed the family, kept a roof over their heads, did not drink. He considered exploitation of his daughters was a right.

'He doesn't have anything in life, either,' said Mr Calder. 'Don't observe from your viewpoint, observe from his. I know, none of it's right or moral or anything but contemptible, but if you're going to learn about life you have to stand off and not judge. Just do what you can.'

He said some things about underprivileged people that armed me against the time when I too lived in a rathole in Sydney, amongst people much like those I saw when making the rounds with Jasper Calder.

'When Jesus said "the poor are always with you", He meant just that. There is a section of every population that falls through the cracks to the bottom. They aren't bad, they aren't especially dumb, though usually they're ill-educated, and not prepared for life by training in any skill or trade. They just cannot cope with life as others can. They stagger along from day to day, hour to hour, hoping that today will be better than last night. You see a kid

· 252 ·

suffering agonies from a mouthful of rotten stumps, and scrape a bit of extra money out of the funds. Give it to the mother. Does she take the kid to the dentist? No, she buys him a bike.'

'But maybe the boy really longed for a bike,' I protested.

'Of course he did. But it's left around, not taken care of, and in a week it's stolen and there's the kid with no bike and a mouthful of rotten teeth. If they won the Art Union they'd piddle the lot away in a year. In fact I've seen that done.' He laughed.

'What you have to remember, and me too, for God alone knows how hard it used to be for me, is that you have to take that in your stride, as the Lord did. Accept that the poor are always with us, and many of them are like that family we just saw. But the Lord loved them, He didn't think it was a waste of time and effort helping them, and He didn't judge them.'

Jasper Calder was compassionate, as well as worldly and often ironic. He said that what he didn't know about human nature could be written on a cigarette paper. And that no one knew just how successful a human life was, when taken from God's point of view.

Very often I pondered Mr Calder's words. I did not believe that anyone could know human nature as well as he thought he did. As I looked at the faces of my fellow-workers, I felt it an incontrovertible fact that I did not truly know any of them. All I knew were aspects, habits, mannerisms. I felt then that there were no ordinary people; all were individual, extraordinary. I feel it now. This lifetime intuition has been the basis of my system of creating fictional characters.

But I daresay I would, like so many novelists, never have created real characters at all, if people like Jasper Calder hadn't knocked some of the idealism and roman-ticism out of me. It is very difficult to look at your fellows (and yourself, too, by the same token) with total directness. Traditional thinking, concepts and prejudices rise like a mist between us and the object of our observation; it is the way of human life.

· 5 ·

I tried to look at my friend Eve Langley directly and without traditional blinkers of rose or any other colour. Yet Eve showed me always the same aspect, gentle, playful, funny and dazzling. She could not help being dazzling – it was the way her mind was made. Later I learned that to other friends she admitted the facts of her plundered unloved life. To me, never. Perhaps she thought me too young or too naïve.

I see her this moment, that lost woman – eyes of pure half-colour, tousled black hair falling over her brow . . . 'I like foliage. I must have something to hide behind.' Her child's feet in homemade monk's sandals. A face as neat as a cat's; features cleanly delineated. Indeed, she had the elegance of a small animal, a gloss and compactness, all, alas, to be destroyed by the frightful treatment she received in the Mental Hospital, continuous sedation, ECTs and near-lethal insulin comas. She became bizarrely fat, out of shape, grotesque in appearance.

When she comes into my office, always unpredictably, and I am in the midst of writing copy for which the printers down below are howling, I put it aside and listen. I'm afraid that so much intellectual glitter may not come my way again. Years later I find out that everyone who knew Eve uses the same metaphors, 'she made the room warm, kindled other people's hearts'. Douglas Stewart said she had 'a kind of inner radiance, an intensity of fire . . .' Tinkerbell, industriously working away, thinks, 'Somehow I can see my drawing board more clearly.'

No, I rarely speak to Eve; I listen. Doors open in my mind, winds crash through. Sitting on the edge of my desk, quoting Keats, Montaigne, Epictetus, the Greek playwrights, she casts treasure carelessly around me, uncaring whether I pick it up or not. Like a bird singing, she sings for herself.

Eve's *The Pea Pickers* shared the Bulletin's S. H. Prior Prize; It became a cult book amongst the young. Indeed it is a deliciously wry, poetic precursor of hippie literature, which would come with Jack Kerouac and others twenty-five years later.

'I've spent all my prizemoney,' she says, carefree. Firstly she bought a wheelchair for an old Maori woman crippled by arthritis. With joyous whoops she tells Tink and me how she took delivery of the chair at the ferry, sat in it and thundered off down the hills. She also built her artist husband a little studio amongst the scrub that surrounds their North Shore shack. She speaks of Hilary with constant tenderness. Myself, I don't care for him, big bearded bubba with what he fools himself is a way with women.

'And what did you get for yourself?'

'A little stove, a *corker* little stove with bandy legs. Now I won't have to cook on the open fire any more.'

I am taken aback. I know Eve's family is poor, even very poor, but I had imagined a Biblical poverty, bare, clean, and full of airy love. How marvellous it must be, I had thought, two creative people, living together, working together, their little child playing peacefully outside in the sunshine. Would such luck ever come my way?

But in fact, Eve's poverty was of a different kind. She and Hilary were 'the poor who are always with you', feckless, copeless, always at odds with circumstances. For years Hilary had stranded Eve and the child in isolated shanties here and there; for a long time he did not support them at all, and Eve scraped along on ten shillings a week, probably Child Endowment for Bisi, the baby. Hilary continued to live comfortably in the city with his doting mother and admiring friends. Visiting Eve occasionally, he brought a bottle of wine instead of food. Poor bubba, probably he married expecting another mother, and instead he got this extraordinary little creature, with all the magic gifts, lack of commonsense and inability to comprehend the realities of human life of a strayed fairy.

Eve's nervous solitary life, her failure, as she saw it, to make her baby happy, a constant state of half-hunger, and her pervasive anxiety about her husband's long, ambiguous absences – these things may have sowed the seeds of her eventual breakdown. Her mind quaked with the wretched foreboding of an animal in a trap. Not an uncommon situation for human beings. But Eve could not come to terms with it.

She never allowed me to guess her true situation, and I should like to know why. The knowledge would have underwritten Jasper Calder's brutal lessons. In my life experience, love had always strengthened. I might have learned that it can also weaken, enslave, drain away talent and ambition. Even murder.

· 6 ·

At last things had become normal for my family. A new house was made available on a lately developed estate near Mt Albert; my father was immediately offered a job on the local Council, which he held until he retired. Oh, my mother's face as she walked through that house, its pastel walls unmarked by other people's fingers, its modern and virgin stove, its hot water service!

'No ghosts!' she exulted. She had lived in so many sad old houses where people had wept and been sick and despairing, that this was marvellous to her. My mother lived in that bright tidy house for over forty years, and I think she knew there a contentment that had hitherto been absent from her life. The fruit trees my father planted are barren and mossy now; hedges have gone and fences have come; the roses have faded away. But I can still see her, wearing her big straw hat to protect her fair northern skin, feeding the cats, picking up a fallen child, weeding the radishes. She is that house's ghost, I think.

Just before we moved into the Mt Albert house, a curious thing happened. Arriving from Tanekaha Valley, my parents spent a few days with Aunt Rosina while our furniture was taken out of storage. Auntie Rose had a houseful, for Helga was already in residence, and her mother Wendela had come from Glen Afra to visit her. All in all, it was just as well Stuart had joined the regular Army and lived in camp.

As was our custom, we were all drinking tea and

gossiping and laughing when an authoritative hand smote the front door. Two solemn constables brought the news that K. J. Patterson or Peterson had been found deceased, and Auntie Rose's address was in his wallet.

'Who on earth is K. J. Patterson?' wondered Helga, the first one to get to the door.

Auntie Rosie went off like a siren. Highly strung by nature, she could put on as pretty a fit of hysterics as I've ever seen.

'We don't know him,' declared Helga above the vociferation. 'Go away, you have the wrong address.'

'It's Pa, it's Pa!' said my mother to me. She was pale and shaken, but not so shaken that she could not haul off and give the trumpet-tongued aunt a smack across the chops. Yells diminished into sobs, and Helga led Rose away to splash cold water on her face.

'However could Pa get Rose's address?' wailed my mother. 'We were so careful!'

'From the electoral roll, perhaps,' said Uncle crossly.

The word Pa meant nothing to me. I didn't know Grandma's family had called their father Pa; they were so close-lipped about him. All I knew (and I had double-checked with the cousins as well) was that one day when the girls were all in their late teens and early twenties they had kidnapped Grandma, and borne her and Poor Jack and the furniture away from their house, so that when Karl Johann came home he found nothing but his bed and one saucepan. I had never liked the bit about the bed and the one saucepan; it seemed to me mean in the extreme. It is true we were told he had hit Grandma, got drunk, and only worked when he was sober, but I always had sympathy for him. He was, after all, an exile, never speaking English well, condemned to a lifetime of heavy labour and, I should imagine, plenty of uproar from Grandma.

My father, who waited quietly until the noise died

down, spoke to the policemen. It was he and the Peeping Tom who arranged the funeral and attended to all details. I don't think Grandma was told until everything was over. It was Mera, too, who told me what Karl Johann's life had been since he was left alone with the bed and the saucepan.

I saw him once, not his face, but his tall, flat, European back. I was with my mother; we had been shopping in Karangahape Road, and I did not even notice that an elderly man had passed us. My mother grabbed my arm, painfully.

'Don't look round, don't look round!' she hissed. 'That's your grandfather!'

Naturally I looked at once, dragging away from her, in half a mind to run after him and – what? He probably did not know I existed. But still I knew about him, and I wanted to know him better. But my mother held me tightly.

'Don't you dare!'

Thus thwarted, I stared with all my eyes at the receding figure. He was thin, very upright, wearing a black suit so well brushed, so well-pressed, it seemed elegant. Under a black hat his thick white hair appeared foreignly cut, straight across the back of the neck in a style unknown to me. So he walked onwards, this upright man, carrying a stick but not leaning upon it, a mysterious unknown man as close to me in blood ties as my Grandma, or that dear Hellfire Jack Park I remembered as a three year old. In character and temperament I was far closer to him than either of these.

What could have been his crimes? There was never the slightest whisper amongst his daughters, or even from Poor Jack, who was likely to blurt out anything, that he had physically or sexually abused them. My mother's paranoid attitude towards alcohol in any form seems to indicate that his drunken sprees were in some way more spectacular or more disagreeable than were ever described to us children. But the other aunts did not have this attitude towards alcohol; in fact they enjoyed the occasional drink themselves. My mother had a scar on her forehead 'where he threw a cup at me'. Wendela, when applied to for more details, said, 'Well, she was standing there giving him cheek. No wonder.' She also remarked, 'He wasn't a bad fellow at all.'

So, there it is; perhaps I am seeking to excuse a grandfather whom my mother described as 'a bad, bad man'.

After he was abandoned with his bed and the saucepan, he lived in seamen's boarding houses until he retired. Then he lived in a little shack, called in New Zealand a bach (from bachelor), at the end of a garden belonging to some first-rate people. Or so Mera, who went to see them, called them. He looked after the garden, and did repairs about the place, in lieu of rent. He cooked for himself, and like all old sailors, washed and cared for his clothes, mended his shoes and darned socks.

'He even sewed buttons on for the kids,' said his landlady. 'Wonderful to the children, he was. He could make those little ships in a bottle, and every one of our kids had one sooner or later. Never swore, clean and tidy, always polite. A real saint, old Mr Patterson.'

'Didn't drink at all?' asked Mera.

The lady was shocked. 'Oh, no, must have been a blueribboner. Never touched a drop. Went to church every Sunday. We'll miss him as if he was our own, I can tell you.'

Only these kind people and my father attended Karl Johann's funeral. Perhaps Mera had a feeling of solidarity with another hard-labouring man who had had to put up with the mettlesome, unpredictable Patterson girls.

I don't know where my grandfather is buried but when in Stockholm I said a prayer for him in the quaint church where he and his sisters were christened. He remains one of those enigmatic people about whom one may only speculate. Everything profoundly secret within my psyche tells me I was lucky to have him for a grandfather.

· 7 ·

The world whispered and groaned not only with war but with rumours of war. Guiltily my mother began to gather things that had vanished from the market in 1914 – elastic, safety pins, toilet paper, needles, sewing cotton.

'We didn't get elastic back for years,' she said. 'Don't you remember having buttons on your pants when you first went to school?'

In between times she laughed nervously, saying, 'Aren't I a silly article? Of course it won't happen, not to us, anyway.'

Those aunts with boys of conscription age began to look thin and jumpy, and took to smoking heavily and yapping at each other.

'You're so damned smug, Theresa,' accused one. 'Just because Harvey has funny eyes.'

'Funny eyes! Funny eyes! His eyesight isn't the best and I hope to God it keeps him at home, but funny eyes he has not got. He has gorgeous eyes.'

'But he can't see through them.'

'Ah, shut up, both of you!' said my mother, and such was her powerful personality, they did. But later she told me she was thankful my sister and I were girls.

'Don't kid yourself,' said Mera sadly. 'If it comes, this will be a civilian war. Look at Czechoslovakia.'

It was spring in New Zealand, tender blue days full of

sunshowers and rainbows. The first buds appeared on Mera's fruit trees, the apple and early plum. It was just twenty years since he had come home from the first World War, the war to end all wars, but in reality a war which carried within itself all the seeds of the second.

'Crikey, girl, they wouldn't do it again, would they?'

He, like most old soldiers, was heartsick.

'Why us? Why should our men die in Europe? Our old people left Europe just to get away from this kind of lunacy.'

The apprentices in the newsroom at the *Star* felt much the same way. These boys did not have the patriotic upsurge towards Great Britain that many of their fathers undoubtedly had had; they did not fall for propaganda any more.

'Damned if I'm going,' exploded the apprentice who made up my children's pages on the stone. 'Bugger Little Belgium!'

By late August, with the German-Russian non-aggression pact, we knew we were for it. Britain's ally, Poland, upon whom extreme demands had been made by Chancellor Hitler, was now pinched between enemies west and east. On September 1, 1939 Germany invaded Poland, and after so many years of blind procrastination and indecision, France and Britain declared war on Germany. In Europe the date was September 3; in the sunrise countries of the Pacific a little later.

'It must be a bad dream,' my mother said. Most people felt this way, I think, as we took the first steps into a period of extreme unreality. The future had vanished down a crack, and everyone knew it. People began to look different, nervous, as though they had been walking along a corridor and a door had closed, quietly.

We knew we had entered upon a journey of which the end could not be known, except that it would involve deprivation and grief. It was anxiety that wore people away, the longing for news, the terror when one saw a telegraph boy in case he bore that fatal telegram. All the rest – food rationing, shortages of power, services and commodities – these did not matter. They were regarded as a challenge more than otherwise.

'We're lucky, yes, we are really,' the aunts said to one another. 'But still there's always Japan.'

From September 1940, when Japan entered into a Three Power pact with Germany and Italy, we knew that if we were to have any immediate enemy, it would be Japan, the land-hungry.

Jan said, 'I'm joining the Air Force.'

He was blushing and uneasy, fearful that I would cause a great tearful fuss. He was not good at scenes, being young, innocent, and susceptible to the reactions of those he cared for.

'But why?' I asked.

He hesitated. 'I think, really, it's for me.'

I did not understand, no, and he could not explain why most young men must pit themselves against danger. Until Harry Tawhai crossed my path again, I did not understand. But then I saw that small reasons will not do as an answer to this huge question; the formless, elemental reasons lie in the nature of man.

But one thing I did see in Jan's eyes. He had already turned away from his life at home, his young enthusiasms and confident ambitions, and was concentrated only upon the future, whatever it might hold.

Men began to enlist, even three or four of the youths who had been such vociferous pacifists. My good apprentice joined up, to be one of the first killed. Another *Star* youngster, sent across to the *New Zealand Herald* with a tray of borrowed type, delivered his leaden load with his printer's apron on top of it, and vanished for five years.

· 263 ·

Returning unharmed from overseas, now aged twenty-two, he took up his old job. My cousin Stuart sent his mother a much-censored letter. Rosina had not been told he had already left the country on active service, and the letter reduced her to a shocked, weeping bundle of anticipatory dread.

'Oh, Cissy, just look,' she sobbed. 'Dear Mum, we are in HOLE we are HOLE the HOLE and expect to be here for HUGE HOLE Don't worry, Mum. Lots of love and kisses from Stuart.'

It was the first missive resembling lace that our family had received. But a stickybeak will find a way, and through various contacts at the *Star* office, I eventually discovered that Stuart was part of a small group of infantrymen who, even before the declaration of war, had been sent as guards to Fanning Island, the equatorial cable station.

Stuart, who had a fine time boxing and fishing, was duly evacuated when it became obvious to all that Japan was about to leap into the war. He reached Honolulu at the time of the Pearl Harbor attack and survived it, returned to New Zealand as a sergeant-instructor and within a year was shot dead in a freakish accident. He was always a boy for cramming a great deal into his life, and at twenty-two had enjoyed most of it. As a little boy he had lived with us for years when Rosina was between marriages, and I loved him dearly.

But that sadness was to come, a blow that almost destroyed frivolous Rose. In late 1939 she was still frisking happily because of an unexpected family event.

Sharp on the declaration of war, Uncle Hugo and Aunt Wendela appeared, Glen Afra apparently behind them for ever. Their house had burned down. The aunts flocked around with clothing, accommodation, money, commiseration, but the demeanour of the two castaways puzzled all. Uncle Hugo maintained a frightful case of the sulks, and Wendela, totally out of character, bore a demure, chastened expression. Majestic silence reigned between them.

Rumours ran riot.

'I bet, I bet a thousand pounds Win burned down the house herself!'

'You awful article, Rose, what a thing to say!'

'But then,' said Theresa judiciously, 'we all know Win, don't we?'

'Ah, that Winnie,' remarked Grandma, maybe hearing and maybe not. 'She was always the injanious one.'

The aunts rapidly worked out an entire scenario. It had the dash of simplicity and a certain ring of possibility. We did indeed all know Wendela's impulsive and intrepid character. She missed Helga, she fretted about the girl being alone in the wicked city. She was homesick for her own family, everyone knew. Added to that, there was a newsflash from Uncle Roley. Hugo had told him that he'd been offered a permanent post as Army instructor, but he'd been a little slow in making up his mind. The fire was an unfortunate accident, that was all.

'No, no,' said an aunt, awed, 'She lit a match under the seat of his trousers.'

'Always Win's way. No patience.'

'That's why he's looking like a wet week.'

'You can always get to the bottom of things if you really try.'

Overcome with admiration, the aunts pestered and teased Wendela. They wanted to know all the details, the thrilling indecision, the resolution, everything. All of them had contrived some fairly dreadful events in their lives, but not one had thought of urging on a lagging husband with a flaming torch.

'Come on, Win, don't be mean!'

'Please, Win. I won't tell Roley, I won't tell a soul!'

'Not much you won't,' answered Win briefly.

'Come off it, Auntie,' I said, when we were private. 'That fire was an accident, wasn't it?'

'What makes you think so, smarty?'

'The dogs.'

'Blast it!'

The fire had blazed up in broad daylight. When a stationhand working on the beach observed it, he had run up the hill to try to save what he could from the already doomed cottage. What he found was Auntie Win struggling to free the dogs, the two sheep dogs and four stud Labradors, tied up at the rear of the house. In their fright they had tangled their chains almost inextricably.

'You would never have set a fire while the dogs were tied up,' I said smugly. '*I* know.'

'You won't tell, lovie?'

'Of course not. But why?'

'It's given me such prestige. Especially with Hugo. Now he'll never know just what I'm capable of, and it gives him the jimjams. Good for him and good for me, too.'

Wendela had achieved a unique place in the family hierarchy. As for Uncle Hugo, he joined the Army, became a very successful instructor, was duly decorated, and was a happy man until he retired. The Army was the place for him.

'Best thing Win ever did, burning down our house,' he said to me when he was an old man. 'I thought it was an accident at the time, but once I'd chewed it over – well, let bygones be bygones, things turned out really well. But I wouldn't tell *her* that.'

· 8 ·

That year, 1940, was the year the German Army made its dazzling, almost contemptuous sweep across Europe; neutral countries were occupied, nations toppled. Inconceivably, on May 17 the Germans drove into France, and on June 17 that brilliant country, famed for military valour and expertise, asked for an armistice. But before that Peter Pan, our able administrator, said offhandedly, 'I'll be off in a month or so. You'd better take your holidays now while you have a chance.'

'Right,' I replied, 'I'll go to Sydney and visit Sheila.'

I was amazed. Where had those words come from? War or no war, I had no plans for Sydney. My ambitions lay elsewhere, in San Francisco, where by design I had established a cobwebby kind of beachhead by selling numbers of illustrated articles on New Zealand and the Pacific islands to the *Examiner*. The *Examiner* people had written me enchanting letters, saying warmly that if ever I was up their way – this I planned to be, some day, when the war permitted.

For already we had adjusted to the extraordinary distortion of linear time. There was a past, we knew, for we had belonged to it. There was a present, but no guaranteed future. Those who have not lived through a long, critical war cannot comprehend the helplessness of a civilian. You have no rights, no significance and no respect. The faceless ones determine your life, every aspect of your life, and your single prayer is that they remain the faceless ones on your side and not the other.

'You'd better go while America is still neutral,' advised Peter Pan.

A second-class fare on the luxury Matson tourist liner, the *Mariposa*, cost £12.10. Plying between San Francisco and Sydney, with halts at Honolulu and Melbourne, this splendid vessel snored across the Tasman Sea, all lights blazing, whilst past us slipped dark wraiths of Australian or British shipping. We knew they were there only because we could see their outlines against the stars. It was curiously perturbing when, from our radiant island, one looked out over the black water and suddenly perceived a huge silent bulk, or the shadow of a mast tilting across the Galaxy. Did anyone suspect that German mines had already been laid around New Zealand's coasts? I do not think so, for the *Niagara*, on which I returned to Auckland, sank the following June, after hitting a mine in deep water. She carried a fantastic cargo of gold ingots destined for America and safety, and was to be the subject of one of the most gripping salvage stories ever read.

Even second class on the *Mariposa* was a dream of luxury for me; outside of the movies I had never seen anything like it. I could have done without the amorous elderly steward who probably specialised in unaccompanied girl passengers. This did not occur to me; I merely thought he was a shade senile.

'I just admiah to dath your ray-ud hay-er,' he asserted repetitively. 'It fiahs me up.' His hand lay carelessly on my knee.

His accent was winning, but for some reason it changed when I told him I needed to be alone. All the same, I added courteously, he was a dear old grandpop. Shit, he said. Not shee-yut at all.

I intended to spend the three-day voyage working out my life-plan, as far as one could do it in time of war. Not since my wanderings in the Tanekaha bush had I taken a breathing space to assess my career possibilities; just scratching out a living had absorbed all my time and energy. Now it seemed to me that in a lifetime of hard work I had achieved practically nothing. This was not because of lack of industry, enterprise or talent but circumstances over which it appeared I would never have control.

It was disillusioning to accept at last that if I were ever to make a living writing in New Zealand, it would be a miracle. As much as I loved my country, if I wished to become a professional, I would eventually have to leave.

For a long time now I had felt myself to be a solitary bird on a bough, precariously perched, but not in jeopardy, provided I remained where I was. Strangely, I thought of Elsie K. Morton, and all her years at the *Herald*, decades, I had heard. Had Miss Morton talent when young, and been forced to put it on a shelf because she was not given a chance? I felt a cold wind, not yet threatening, merely a frisking of stirred air. Still, it was cold. Not even Jan comprehended how I felt about writing. He listened patiently to my literary ambitions, but I could see his interest was marginal.

He was not alone. After spending a year writing a children's book, squeezing in an hour or two of creativity here and there amongst my multiple jobs, I had submitted it to Whitcombe and Tombs, at that time the only serious publishing house in the country. They offered me £5 for world copyright, and were haughty indeed when I declined. It behoved me, they said, to remember I was a beginner. I then posted the typescript to England, where it did not arrive, the ship being sunk off the Irish coast. The third copy was left in a train by an acquaintance of literary repute, who had offered to assess its value. After this I took Fate's hint and cupboarded it until a later date when I rewrote the story and sold it.

Gloomily I thought that perhaps in writing a book I had been over-ambitious. While in Sydney, I resolved, I would check Australian publishing houses as well as the newspapers. I had several letters of introduction from Mr Ridling and other *Star* friends. One of the latter had informed me that in Australian journalism men and women received equal pay for equal work. Part of me couldn't believe this wondrous thing, and another part gained new hope. Suppose San Francisco didn't eventuate? At least this other door, this golden door, might open to me.

For that is how I first saw Australia. Up very early, walking wet decks, the sun rising behind me, I saw in the peachbloom sky to the west a long low golden line, straight as a ruler. Such a long line, extending such a distance!

'Can that be land?' I asked a deck hand.

'That's Australia, ma'am.'

What I saw were endless sandstone cliffs reflecting the sunrise. A chill ran over my skin, my ears buzzed as they had once done when I was about to experience certainty about something as yet unknown. The sea fled south, its malachite green changing to beaming blue; the sky was sumptuous with a sun hotter than I had ever known.

This was my first glimpse of Australia Felix, the ancient, indifferent, nonpareil continent that was to become the love of my life.

· 9 ·

'Oh, please won't you ask him here for dinner?' pleaded
Sheila. 'It would be so much nicer to meet your friend
amongst people you know.'

As a married woman she felt maternally responsible for
me. I was her protégé who followed closely in her
footsteps, but was now an excited and possibly addlepated
tourist set loose in big bad Sydney.

But no, I felt strongly that I should see D'Arcy Niland
in his specific environment, not one that was essentially
still my own. Off I went on the Manly ferry to meet him
on Circular Quay. A steam ferry; a harbour coruscating
in evening sunshine; an extraordinary amount of water
traffic skimming about like bugs, and all around, it seemed,
the city, which had overflowed irrepressibly in every
direction. The Bridge sent out its long, solemn roar; the
city huffed and puffed and whistled. I had the impression
of exuberant larrikin vitality.

Forgetting I had to meet D'Arcy Niland at the turnstiles,
I ran out to the street which, though noisy with trams,
cars, and a surprising number of horse-drawn vehicles, was
not a street at all but a noble square or quay, paved with
worn setts of stone or wood, and enclosed by grave,
flatfaced buildings that scorned any ornament but a sunset
flush.

Sydney was different then, a glamorous rats' nest of
lanes, stairs and jump-ups, full of mysterious nooks whose
purpose had been lost, and thready crannies that went

nowhere. It had not yet been made civilised and common-place. Steep streets rising south from the Quay were lined with ramshackle, three-storey townhouses where the gentry had once lived. Now they were warrens for students, artists and fly-by-nights. The skyline was stubby, pierced by steeples. The tallest building was the *Sun* office, twelve levels. But to me it was as impressive as the Tower of Babel.

Circular Quay itself, not yet recovered from the Depression, was raffish, unpainted, even squalid, scarcely changed from the days when the European wool clippers had docked there. My Park grandfather would have easily recognised it. Yet it smelled deliciously. The warm air carried odours of frangipani, roast peanuts, hamburgers. Vendors of flowers squatted in corners; I scarcely recognised the flowers, boronia, bottlebrush, and orchids dappled like serpents.

A stout old woman marched past; she bore sandwich boards inscribed: Shakespeare Recitations, One Shilling. Hamlet, 1/6d.

Out of this swirling crowd came my correspondent. I knew him at once. He knew me. Staring cautiously at each other, we shook hands.

'I'm short, aren't I?'

'What?'

'I said I'm short. Bloody short.'

I now perceived he was speaking of himself, with a scowl that seemed more aggrieved than anything else. Was he crazy?

He did not appear crazy, being a well set up young man with black curly hair, fine slate-blue eyes, and a broken nose.

'You're taller than I am, and I think I'm tall.'

'No. I'm bloody short.'

'Suit yourself.'

With that we burst into simultaneous laughter and walked off across the crowded Quay.

· 10 ·

By the time I returned to the *Star* Jan had gone. In the
streets we saw very few young men in the soft grey-blue
of the New Zealand Air Force; they were quickly sent off
to Canada or Scotland for advanced training. In one of
those countries, before very long, Jan died in an air crash.

As the months went on I continued obsessed with the
wastage of his unrealised life, so that I could not sleep, and
inscribed the pages of my journal over and over with the
one word. Waste! Waste! The air was full of refracted
grief. In mourning for one we did not withdraw from the
dispersed, inconsolable grief of almost the entire world.

At the time I was writing for our older readers a
historical review of those wars in which our country had
participated; the photographs upset me greatly, so that I
could scarcely think of anything else. Day after day I
studied those pictures of men long dead, the Maori Wars,
the Boer War, the first World War, and in the exquisite
definition of the old wet plate photographs I began to
imagine that I saw familiar faces. For the young men I
knew, ruddy-faced, light-haired, would, in time, be the
subjects of identical pictures, fading in newspaper files,
thrown in drawers, hidden in albums with brittle cracked
covers. Their hair would begin to look oldfashioned in cut,
their eyes glazed with fatigue, their uniforms muddy, their
faces foxmarked or disfigured with long smears of halation.
Who's he, some descendant would ask. Don't know, but
he died young.

And I thought it is not time that like an ever-rolling stream bears all our sons away, but war. History is men moving through old brown landscapes that with the men have vanished; men who do not know where they are going, hardly conceiving why, men who cannot tell us of the forgotten agonies, the forgotten exaltations.

· 11 ·

'There's a monumental Maori sergeant waiting in your office,' said one of the girls from the *Women's Weekly*, the office of which shared our floor. 'What have you *done*?'

As soon as I saw Harry Tawhai all the old feelings of foreboding returned, filling the room, deafening me. Tears came into my eyes.

'Hey, what's this? Do I remind you too much of Te Kuiti and you and Roha always in trouble?'

'Were we really? I don't remember. Oh, Harry, how did you discover where I worked?'

'Went to the Convent. Nuns always know everything about their old pupils.'

'Rosary wireless.'

He laughed. It was hard for a moment to see how I had recognised in this huge, splendid man the boy I had known well and yet scarcely known at all, glancing sideways out of my humble childishness and my always uneasy feelings. But he still had the same face, the same half-shy smile, though overlaid with a sober and somehow remote adulthood.

The white tag of embarkation showed on his forage cap.

'Your final leave, Harry?'

'Yes, they say we're going to Egypt.'

I saw again the rocky hillside, the crooked trees with leaves blowing silver.

'Not Egypt.'

'We'll see.'

We sat and talked desultorily, pausing every now and then to smile at each other. I didn't feel shy and small with him any more, Roha's big brother, the big boy in Std I, awesome to a child just starting school. He was magnificent, a fit descendant of those old Polynesians Captain Cook had said were the finest specimens of manhood he had ever seen. Like Tukumanu te Taniwha he had a broad capacious body, now alas, suffocating in the thick, unbecoming, over-pocketed uniform the New Zealand forces were cursed with. A classic, Stone Age body, built for majestic nakedness.

'Tell your Dad that my father managed to buy the International. It started him off on his carrying business. Yes, he does very well.'

'And the old Republic?'

'Ended up on the tip. Someone salvaged the engine. Don't tell Mera that, though.'

Roha was married, two children, living in Rotorua. But she had chest trouble, possibly the ever-threatening tuberculosis that haunted the Maori people. I did not ask further.

Harry rose to his feet. He had to catch the train south for Te Kuiti, where he would spend his last week with his family.

'Funny little thing you were. Often scared. Scared now, aren't you?'

Aware there was no point in prevarication, I nodded.

'Me?'

'Yes.'

He sighed. 'Always knew, didn't we? Remember your Maori, do you?'

'A good deal.'

'There's a saying, my people have a saying – *he toa taua, ma te taua.*'

'A warrior goes to battle, a warrior may die in battle,' I translated hesitantly.

'Yes, but you have to say it with a grin and a shrug. Who the hell cares, so what, all of those meanings.'

I understood. 'And the rest of that saying?' For I knew most Maori proverbs had a balance or a paradox.

'Oh, it's *he toa piki pari ma te pari.* That's for you, he who climbs a cliff may die on the cliff, so what?'

He saluted and went. The Maori Battalion, the 28th, sailed in early May 1940, somewhere meeting with an Australian contingent. On the sea when France fell, they were diverted to Great Britain. But their days of glory and death came in Greece, where so many Anzac soldiers died in a bungled, unsupported campaign. Harry Tawhai died at Thermopylae. He was mentioned in despatches for the unusual feat of silencing a German machine gun nest by driving out the occupants with stones. I remembered his uncannily accurate stone-throwing as a boy, and endeavoured not to lament him. Harry Tawhai had life and death by the tail. A warrior dies in battle, so what?

· 12 ·

All this year D'Arcy Niland kept writing, writing. He said, 'I don't want answers. If you're sad, be sad. That's the way of it and we can't gainsay it. But I won't write about the war. There will be years after the war; there always are. When we're together I wouldn't want to look back and see that we'd even talked about such blasphemy.'

'What the devil do you mean, when we're together? Probably I'll never see you again. I hardly know you.'

But I felt I knew him very well. His cool, thoughtful letters, sometimes very long, sometimes only a few lines, came from all over New South Wales, the far west, the Queensland border towns, anywhere sheep could be run. Because of his rural work during the Depression he had been manpowered – ordered from the *Daily Telegraph* reading room into an essential occupation, the wool industry. Sometimes his letters bore dribbles of candle-grease; often the smell of kerosene from a leaky lamp. The postmarks, Narrandera, Deniliquin, Goondiwindi, fired my imagination in all the wrong ways. I imagined him a minute, lonely figure, plodding across vast golden country-side under a sublime sky.

'Sublime sky be damned. It's been raining four days, buckets of the stuff. The pens are full of hungry sheep. The grazier won't let them out for feed because the men refuse to shear wet sheep.'

He drew a picture of idle, cranky shearers, not earning money, playing cards, quarrelling, rubbing each other's backs with wintergreen oil, picking prickly-pear spines out of their hands with straightened safety pins.

'There's an old fellow here, sleeps in his hat. Whiskers like a bust cushion. They throw him out into the mud, he says Praise the Lord, gets up and comes back. God's soldier. Repent and be saved. The blokes call him Elijah the Prophet.'

This steadfast old man stayed at the back of his mind for years, emerging at last as the noble figure of Resurrection Jim in *Call Me When the Cross Turns Over.*

'Keep my letters,' he directed. 'I want to use them as notes for stories. Also I intend to write a novel after we're married.'

'The nerve of you!'

Still, I did, and they formed part of the dense, tough material from which he effortlessly drew his literary work in later years.

Most of his letters were intensely bookish. His ardent desire being to write fine short stories, he had studied and analysed most of the great European and American writers; he did not care for the Australian short story, declaring it to be not a short story at all but a vignette or tale. He pined for his own library of more than three thousand books, gathered mostly from second-hand shops and the bookstalls at Paddy's Market in Sydney.

'Life is bountiful, when you can get *Moby Dick* for a penny.'

Eve Langley educated me, and so did D'Arcy Niland. Eve had literature mostly in her head; this other Australian introduced me to writers of whom I had never heard. He was not a book collector but a literature collector. True, he used his collection as a bribe.

'Surely three thousand books are a considerable dowry? These, too, can be yours, as long as I go with them.'

'But I'm not in love with you. How can I be?'

'In love, in love, what kind of schoolgirl talk is that? I don't want you or any girl to be in love with me. But I would like you to love me when you know me better. Now, regarding Guy de Maupassant. It is my opinion that *Boule de Suif* may well be his supreme . . . '

His letters, eighty or more of them, were the most solid thing in my life during the bitter year of 1941, the year of the Greek and Crete campaigns, when the New Zealand and Australian forces sustained crushing losses. Several of the *Star* boys were left behind on the beaches, along with the thousands for whom there was no room on the evacuation ships. Some were prisoners for years.

I wrote to many of my friends who suffered this fate. They all spoke in affection of the dauntless Greeks.

'We marched forty miles over rough hill country. I was dead almost, dying on my feet with hunger and exhaustion. Saw a haystack of sorts and crawled into it. When I woke up there was an old Greek woman, all in black, washing my feet. She patted lard into them. Hard hands she had, like wood. Then she put clean socks on me. She was as poor as the crows, everything looted, but she gave me an onion and a piece of honeycomb. How can you ever forget such a person?'

Occupying troops shot Greek and Cretan peasants who harboured retreating Allied soldiers, and this old woman must have known that. But she was greater than the knowledge.

Now that we know more about it, we recognise that the Greek Campaign was as criminal a military error as Gallipoli. How ironic that it should be endured by troops from the same nations.

That was the most wretched year of my life. Other bad years came later, but I was maturer and more able to withstand their anguish. There seemed no hope anywhere; all the news was devastating. We lost spirit, dreaded looking at newspapers, found it impossible to see an end to this fearful conflict. Like other people, I did a great deal of purposeless crying.

<h1 style="text-align:center">· 13 ·</h1>

The work load was very heavy, for I was now alone in my fourth-floor office. That year our pages for older children disappeared because of ever-growing paper shortages. Created by the enthusiasm and foresight of Sheila Quinn and Mike Abbott, *Enzed Junior* had been a stimulus to young writers, a conveyor of entertainment and current information, and a showplace for their literary and artistic work. I've never seen any other paper for children quite like it. It was my privilege to carry it on during its most difficult years and sadly see its demise. With its disappearance, management removed Tinkerbell, put her into the Cable Room as a clerk, and more or less said to me, 'Get on with it.' I continued alone as editor of the children's pages, steadily diminishing in size, until they were dispensed with altogether. The small advertisement pages continued in vast numbers, but there you are, children don't bring in the money.

Sometimes, not often now, Eve Langley drifted in. Even when she was pregnant, as then she was, the word drifted was apposite. She had a curiously lightfooted, diffident gait like a half-shy animal. She did not look well; her only clothes were the same old pants, with a man's shirt over them, the rough sandals as small as a child's. But she, and all she wore, were always scrubbed to a point of noticeable cleanliness. So were the two children accompanying her. They were small things, perhaps four and three, the boy Langley robust and chuckly, the little Bisi pale and watchful as though she had already learned she lived in an ambiguous, unreliable world. The children had the unmistakable look of kids from a background of destitution – outgrown clothing, always too light for the severe winter, shrunken cardigans and socks. Once I sewed on a couple of buttons where Bisi's little dress was gaping. Eve did not even notice.

She sat on the edge of my desk and chatted on scintillatingly. In later years D'Arcy Niland described Eve's talk (and by then it was schizophrenic) as a waterfall of sequins. One's mind flew after one glittering fragment while ten others flashed past.

By then, from other friends, I knew something of the barebones penury in which she and the children lived. Yet, even if she had not loved Hilary passionately, what could she have done? Her mother and sister were able to help only a little. There was no community aid for a wife with a living husband. He was supposed to support her, therefore he did; this was the official belief. My Grandma had staggered along for years under the same burden. Life for both of these women would have been easier as widows.

Added to her neediness, she was bedevilled by the climate. It is always easier to be poor in a hot country than in a cold, frequently wet one. Also, climate, when you live in a comfortable house, may well remain external and even incidental. When you live in a shack, climate comes inside.

Still Eve said never a word to me, in letter or in person, of the miseries of her life, her terror of childbirth, her frequent ills, and above all, probably, the fearful dilemma of the creative woman torn between the needs of husband and children, and her own devouring inner fire. But I recognised it.

'What had happened to her?' I asked my mother. My mother halted the busy buzz of the old Singer on which she was making welcoming clothes for Eve's new baby.

'She got married,' she said succinctly.

I went away, thinking of that day when, so unexpectedly, my mother had wept in anguish, saying to me, 'You're a poor man's child.'

And I thought, 'Oh, Bisi, what will happen to you?'

· 14 ·

After the unbearable debacle of the Greek campaign, we heard, by this means and that, that the Australasian armies were training in the African desert.

'Oh, Lord, does that mean Rommel?' exclaimed my father. We had already heard of the dash and strategic brilliance of the German general.

Seeing me despondent, my friend Mr Ridling said optimistically, 'But surely Roosevelt won't stay neutral much longer. How can he?'

General opinion was that the United States were just sitting there, a big fat wealthy country, waiting until the war was won by other people, when it would send in its trade commissions and exploit the markets. But this was incorrect. In that year alone, the Lend-Lease Act was passed, an inconceivably significant event; the President proclaimed an unlimited state of national emergency; the Atlantic Charter (signatories the US and Great Britain) was formulated; the US Army was empowered to keep men in service eighteen months longer than the current term, and a huge revenue measure for defence expenditures for more than three and a half billion dollars became law. After the Axis invaded the Russian frontier, vast credit was also issued to the Soviet Union.

My mother was not an admirer of President Roosevelt. 'Top hats and grand overcoats and all.'

'Cigars long enough to poke out a blocked drain,' added Grandma, visiting with Rosina. Her hearing improved at disconcerting moments; I had often wondered whether the whole thing were not some recherché form of Irish mischief.

My father, on the other hand, was not misled. 'He has a mighty clever face,' he said. 'And don't think the States aren't on to the Japanese either, prowling around the Pacific looking innocent.'

'The handles come off them Japanese cups,' remarked Grandma sternly. Mera went off and weeded the garden, muttering.

As a neutral country, the United States appealed to me beyond measure.

I wrote to the *San Francisco Examiner*, inquiring whether there was any possibility of a job in the future, any kind of a job. To my amazement they said yes, only a gofer, but enough freelance assignments available to keep me from being hungry. I didn't know what a gofer was, but I was fully prepared to be a capable one. This good news – though it also frightened me to death – came in late June, just as the German armies attacked Russia on a 3000 kilometre front. Hitler's speech was a master-piece of crowd-rousing, though surely the average German plainly saw that his country was not stabbed in the back, and encircled, as the Fuehrer claimed. Mera was jubilant.

'This will be the end of them. What defeated Napoleon was the climate and the country itself. If Germany doesn't make this a swift victory, it's all up with them. The winter will wring their necks.'

Queer things happened in our faraway country once Russia was attacked. The supporters of the Communist Party, prohibited, denigrated – damned Bolshies, that's all they are! – crept out from underground and even appeared in parades, carrying unostentatious banners.

The bear that walked like a man, that had come horridly out of its decades of silence to chew up half of Poland while the Axis chewed up the other half, which had invaded Finland in 1939 and grabbed that country's most valuable territories, was now our gallant ally, and indeed proved gallant beyond all praise.

'Come off it!' said Uncle Hugo when I expressed my doubts of such an ally. 'All nations are greedy opportunists. All that matters is whether they're on your side. Russia will keep a good part of the Nazi army busy, that's all that matters to us.'

During this time I endeavoured to get a passport for the US, a work visa, a health certificate. Always in wartime documentation becomes paramount, papers in all directions, and small tyrannical bureaucrats determined to make the transaction as slow and difficult as possible. Because America was still neutral there was nothing against my travelling. People were still going there for holidays, though after the sinking of the *Niagara* they had to consider the risk of mines or submarines.

Still, it took endless months to get my papers. Meanwhile I told my mother of my plans. She wept a little, but said, 'Yes, you're at the age to take flight. And I know how unsettled and unhappy you've felt lately.'

I was disconcerted; I believed I was brilliant at keeping my feelings to myself.

She asked me not to tell my father for a while; it would upset him so much. I did not know, of course, that she suspected in him the heart condition that was to hit him hard a year or so later.

'And we won't tell my sisters. Too much chatter. It's beginning to weary me somehow.'

Aware that this year was probably the last for the children's department, I resolved that we would go out in a blaze of glory. Because our winter comforts campaign was an institution, by the time the poplars turned yellow parcels of knitted squares, warm garments, blankets were already being delivered to the office.

'Oh, God, how can I manage?' I confessed my doubt to the banished Tinkerbell. 'But I do want to show this damned *Star* management that I can cope, no matter what they do.'

'There's always me,' said good Tink. 'I still feel myself part of the department, even if I do spend my days down amongst the casualties and disasters. And suppose we work Saturdays?'

'And ask some of the kids' mothers and grannies if they'll come along? Morning tea and hard labour?'

Blessed women! All shabby, for though we had adequate clothing coupons, when you have children the kids get the new clothes. They unravelled old jumpers (for new wool was now scarce), wound it wet around cardboard to get the kinks out and knitted it up again into squares for knee-rugs, shawls and afghans.

'Elderly people get forgotten when there's a war on,' they said, which is universally true. They brought baby clothing for the Sisters of Compassion; their children had concerts and art shows to raise money. I think we had a larger cash fund that tragic year than ever before.

So with huge labour and ingenuity we made that final historic campaign a ripper. By the time it was concluded I was completely knocked-out; we took the winning club and their mothers to a funny film showing then, with a tea party afterwards, and I recall sitting in that shrieking audience with my mouth full of jellybeans and tears of exhaustion sliding down my face. Also, my final document for San Francisco had arrived, and I was consumed with terror. Now I would have to take this hazardous step, which looked more hazardous by the minute. If America entered the war I would not be able to return home, perhaps for many years. Wartime travel for civilians would be totally restricted. But the very fact that I was so afraid made me resolve that I could not back out now.

'I've made up my mind,' I wrote to D'Arcy Niland, 'I'm going to San Francisco on December 10th.'

A week or so later I had a cable. 'No, you aren't.'

· 15 ·

He told me in later years that he was certain something would happen to prevent me from going to America.

'Somehow it was not in the pattern. I couldn't see the pattern but I knew it was there.'

What prevented me was the Japanese assault on Pearl Harbor on December 7th. All travel was cancelled immediately. My mentor, Jasper Calder, who had been on vacation in the States, was unable to get home. However, being Jasper Calder, he shipped as a seaman on a Sydney-bound vessel and in this roundabout way, duly reached Auckland and reported for work.

My mother was a believer in things working out for the best; she said that she objected strongly to the concept but her experience had proved it beyond argument. When

I told her of D'Arcy Niland's cable she smiled: 'He has gumption, that boy. But the Irish are queer people, they hear bells ringing sometimes. I'm only half-Irish myself, but . . .'

'But what?'

She laughed. 'Oh, I don't know. It's just that I feel you will still go away.'

'So do I,' I confessed. 'But I was terribly scared about San Francisco. Leaving the family and everyone I know; I didn't know how I could face it when it came to the point.'

'Yes, I know that panic,' she replied sombrely. 'I expect everyone feels it when faced with a great leap into the dark. But it can be overcome. I *want* you to move on, if that's what you feel in your heart you should do. Because I didn't, you see. I missed my run. Too frightened, too poor, too many family ties. You mustn't do the same thing.'

'You never told me – what do you mean?'

My mother was such a pretty woman. A faint blush crept over her face. But she shook her head. 'It doesn't matter. Long ago, too long ago.'

She gave me no further information. 'No, that's my affair, not yours.'

She was a very private person. I have always felt deprived of something there. Well did I know her immense courage and generosity, but as a woman who loved her, I would have liked to listen to her doubts, forebodings and hesitancies as well.

For by then I was a woman, or a kind of woman. My eyes looked outward now, into the world. In many things I felt myself capable, and capable of achieving other skills. I was no longer the little girl who had leaned upon Mera, learned from him, thought all men were like him. Looking back at the curly, guileless, confiding creature I had been I marvelled how I had escaped disaster. But there had been honesty of purpose there, too, and a certain hardheaded commonsense.

These latter things were what I had recognised in D'Arcy Niland, as he had recognised them in me. There had never been anyone with whom I had been so completely myself; he knew even my inner self, a person frequently anxious, insecure and depressed. Did I know him equally well? I was confident I did; his letters not only appeared artless, they were so. Probably on paper he revealed far more of himself than he would have done face to face.

I knew this young man well, yet I had no idea what to do with him.

Surprisingly, it was my father who suggested that I should try to obtain work in Australia.

'I keep feeling that the war will go on and on, and you'll be stuck at the *Star* with no opportunity and be thirty years old before you know it.'

No doubt I received this with a blanched face. He was angry when I told him of my latest interview with management. Predictably I was informed that the entire Children's Department was being wiped out, and I would be transferred to the newsroom. This was better than I expected, but the smile faded when the Chief Reporter stated he would do almost anything to prevent a woman coming on his staff, but that he supposed he'd have to make the best of it. As I would henceforth be regarded as a first-year cadet, I would have to take a cut in wages.

My years of hard work and responsibility, including many hours per week of unpaid overtime; hundreds of interviews, articles and stories for *Enzed Junior* (for the *Star* never purchased outside work, aside from James Cowan's miserably paid weekly article); public relations work with children, teachers, young writers' groups, charitable organisations, all on my own time, not to mention the production of a superlative children's section which undoubtedly raised the paper's circulation – all were ignored.

At one stage of the discussion – for I did not go down without a battle – the editor, a person chiefly notable for handwriting that made linotype operators cry, said to me benignly, 'You must understand we really don't *want* to encourage young women to think they can be journalists. If they must, they should aim at the social pages.'

'But Mr Clarke, as more and more men go into the Forces, you'll just have to face it, won't you?'

'That, I believe, is our affair.'

'But,' said the Chief Reporter kindly, 'we shall allow a little extra for your time in the Reading Room, so you will be paid the male rate. We don't have to do that, of course.'

'Oh yes, you do,' I replied bitterly. 'Because there's not a word in the award that says first-year female cadets are to be paid only three-fifths of the male rate. So far there have been no female cadets.'

'I strongly advise you against *that* tone of voice,' said Mr Clarke austerely, and to show the interview was concluded he turned to a book review he was writing about Old Paris, which the distracted compositor set up as Old Pans throughout.

When I told Mr Ridling he hit the roof. 'Spare me days! The lousy bastards!'

'Huns everywhere,' said my father.

Robin Hyde in her time described the *Auckland Star* as a slumbrous elephant that, spying a spark of talent in any member of its staff, rolled on it and put it out.

However, I had productive and instructive years there in Shortland Street, and made some lasting friendships. The *Star* was my first step towards professional journalism. By observing a senior man, Ken Green, I learned the tricks of good interviewing. From a sub-editor, R. A. Kenner,

I learned how to present facts in the most effective psychological order. The *Auckland Star* was a class news-paper in its day, and I am grateful that was my day too.

Doubtless before its demise in 1991 the newspaper dropped its discriminatory attitude towards women journalists. I hope so. But remember I was the first in a newsroom. That's my blood you see on the floor.

· 16 ·

Despite their private feelings, my parents were unfailingly supportive. They had more faith in me than I did.

'Go now,' they urged, 'while you're still full of fight.'

Doubtlessly they were extremely anxious about the war, for the Japanese were progressing southwards in an electrifying over-run of unprepared territory. Manila, January 1942; Dutch East Indies, later that month; Singapore, February; Burma, March. It was obvious that New Guinea, only a step from Australia, was next.

'Weren't you worried about me in an occupied Aus-tralia?' I asked years later.

'That's when my hair went grey,' replied my mother. 'But you had to go. We knew it.'

Only as an adult – I think I achieved this somewhere in my middle thirties – did I truly realise what my parents had done for me by their attitude to what many less perceptive people would have considered a harebrained plan. I cannot praise them too much. Others differed. Grandma never saw me without raising her eyes in prayer to heaven and tossing a few drops of somewhat dank holy water on my head. The aunts cried, Uncle Hugo said, 'By Jove, girl, not in wartime! Think it over, think it over.'

I cried a lot myself, for I was still frightened. Deadly scared sometimes, for I, too, could see in which direction the Pacific war was moving. If it had not been for my frustrating new job, I might have wavered.

That first week of my five in the newsroom, realising that I was not only going to be paid a non-living wage, but was to be employed on rubbish, as any new little sixteen-year-old boy cadet might be, I fired off airmail letters to Sydney. Each contained a cutting of an article I considered good – my interview with the Maori King Koroki; it was a genuine achievement, for he was an extremely diffident young man who shunned publicity. It had been published in a Canadian magazine; I thought this might carry some added weight. I also set about readjusting my foreign travel papers for Australia. This threw the relevant authorities into a dither, as I now proposed to travel between two belligerents, even if they were allied. However, all was made well in the end.

Presently I had a job on both the *Sun* and the *Mirror*, possibly because the Australian newspapers were losing their male journalists at an even quicker rate than the New Zealanders. Not knowing better, I accepted the position on the *Mirror*, a newer paper and therefore, I thought, probably livelier. I didn't know it was a tabloid of a gaudy nature. When, in Sydney, I eventually did see a copy I did not even go along for the interview. But by then I had other plans anyway.

From the moment of my decision, letters had pelted back and forth across the Tasman.

'Now we can get married. I've put in for a transfer to some essential industry in Sydney.'

'Don't be so smart. Who said we were getting married?'

'Well, if you think you're going to live with me without

getting married you can think again. I have my reputation to think of.'

'Just shut up about getting married, will you?'

What was I going to do with this fellow? Certainly I would be pleased to have him working in Sydney. Sheila now lived elsewhere, and until I became used to my new job and that big city, it would be good to have a friend. My mother, too, was relieved that he would be there.

'He has a good Catholic family behind him,' she said. 'They'll stand by you.'

Recalling how his mother had looked at me, rather like Grandma putting the curse of the Killaloe itch on Philomena, I was none too sure. But still, who knew? I had rather liked his father, a sharp little Irish drunk with an addition to long words. If they were not in the dictionary, he boldly made them up himself. I admired that.

'I've been transferred to the Railway. Shall I look for a flat now or when you arrive?'

'I don't want to get married. I don't *want* to get married.'

At first I couldn't tell him that I was afraid I would be eaten up like Eve Langley. Marriage was a mysterious thing to me. Obviously it contained within itself a certain suspension of accepted rules; husbands and wives treated each other differently from the manner in which they treated the rest of the world. How else explain Hilary, or Eve's suicidal devotion? Once Eve wrote: 'I heard myself crying terrible words. "I know you don't love me. But some day you will know what it is to love," and then my head went down in that familiar fashion of women crying, a swan's way.'

Later, through my friend Sheila, who had returned to Sydney while her husband was overseas on active service, I learned that in August 1942 Hilary had committed Eve to the Auckland Psychiatric Hospital. It was very easy to do. He disposed of the three children to foster parents and eventually orphanages, and had almost no contact with any member of his family until the children were adults. Thus, for whatever reasons Hilary Clarke believed were appropriate, Eve fell by the wayside. She was treated like a person with no rights over herself, her children, her brain; her genius was dissipated in formless showers of sparks, her life eccentric and mostly solitary, her death dreadful.

'I like a good laugh, Ruth; hang it all, tragedy has stalked me so often that I like to think that at the end it will find me only a joke.'

When I wrote my last letter to D'Arcy Niland explaining why I was so wary of marriage, I knew none of these things. But I had recognised that marriage had destroyed or would destroy my friend Eve. What I got back was a cable: 'Don't be a ginger bonehead.'

How impossible to describe why such a cable was so reassuring. But it was. Thereafter I took for my banner those words Harry Tawhai had brought to mind: *He toa piki pari ma te pari.* He who climbs a cliff may die on the cliff, so what?

Always a risk-taker by nature, now I became one by intent.

· 17 ·

The flight by flying-boat took seven to eight hours. The enormous craft – it carried nineteen passengers – left Auckland in the spring and bumped down in Rose Bay, Sydney, in the summer. As I stepped on to the landing stage, the sun seized me with metal hands.

What I wrote in my journal that night are the words of a girl long gone. I think she has gone.

There he was, leaning casually over the barrier,
looking older and taller than when I'd seen him last.
He grinned and shook clenched fists in the air, like a
victorious boxer. The officials released me and I was
let loose through the turnstile into Australia.
"Hello," I said. We stared at each other. Then
suddenly those drowsy blue eyes opened wide into a
blaze of laughter and intelligence and happiness, and
we laughed out loud at one another, and I knew that
everything, all the sadness and the pain of leaving my
home and country, was worth it.
"It's turned out nice again," he said.

We lived together for twenty-five years less five weeks. We had many fiery disagreements but no quarrels, a great deal of shared and companionable literary work, and much love and constancy. Most of all I like to remember the laughter.